ACROSS CANADA
BY STORY

A Coast-to-Coast Literary Adventure

by Douglas Gibson

with illustrations by Anthony Jenkins

ECW Press

FOR ALICE MUNRO
AND EVERY CANADIAN AUTHOR.

TABLE OF CONTENTS

CHAPTER 1

THE STORY BEGINS

The Fur Trade and the Book Trade . . . Becoming a Real, Live Author . . . Thunder Bay and the National Cottage . . . Ralph Connor, Scribe of Glengarry . . . Around Winnipeg with Gordon Sinclair . . . The Unique Gabrielle Roy . . . Margaret Laurence's Careful Ending . . . Vienna and Winnipeg's George Swinton . . . The Superhuman Don Starkell

It all began in Thunder Bay. That was where the strange idea of doing a stage show based on my book, *Stories About Storytellers*, first came to me. Now, after a tour involving all ten provinces and more than 90 separate shows, seen by thousands of polite people (no jeers, no tossed tomatoes!), it seems like an obvious idea. It wasn't obvious at the time.

Here's how it happened. The volunteers who ran the Sleeping Giant Literary Festival in Thunder Bay invited me to come there in the summer of 2010, more than a year before *Stories About Storytellers* was published. They asked me, as a former editor, to teach a couple of classes: one about writing, and one about working with an editor. At first, I was mildly interested, but as soon as I learned that the classes would be given in Old Fort William, a historic fur-trade site, I was desperately keen to go.

A confession about one of my wild enthusiasms: I'm fascinated by the history of Canada's fur trade, and by people like William McGillivray (1764–1825), the fierce Scot who gave his name to Fort William. His fort, I knew, was literally at the heart of the North West Company's fur trade empire, which flowed right across the country. This was the central point where the Grand Rendezvous took place each summer, where the Montreal voyageurs who had paddled west from cold dawn to dusk in canoes full of trade goods like blankets, kettles, and guns met their fur-trading comrades from the North and the West, who had raced to get their smaller canoes (the fifteen-foot *canots du nord*), jammed with bales of fur, east in time to make the great exchange. More than 2,000 of these tough characters would converge on the fort for a few short, hectic days to, in Charles Gordon's words, "trade and plot, and perhaps have a drink or two." Then they dunked their heads, loaded their canoes up to the tumblehome, and headed back. Whether they were paddling east or west, every man in every canoe was in a deadly race against the early freeze-up that could kill him.

I had heard that Old Fort William was a marvellous reconstruction of those days, specifically of around 1816, and that it was complete with surprising details like the six acres of potato fields that were needed to keep the year-round fort staff alive through the winter. In fact, I had heard it described as one of Canada's greatest tourist sites, underappreciated because so few people went to Thunder Bay. *Now I was going to Thunder Bay!*

So I was happily agreeing to give the two lectures when the festival organizer Dorothy Colby said from the Thunder Bay end of the line, "Oh, one other thing: besides your two classes, you'll be one of the authors reading from their books on Friday night."

I was taken aback. "But I'm not an author yet, and I don't have a book," I stammered.

"Ah," she said kindly, "but we hear that you're writing a book. So you can read from it as a work-in-progress — and we're sure you'll enjoy reading in a lineup with people like Miriam Toews and Richard Scrimger and David Carpenter and Terry Fallis."

This just made things worse. *No, no, I really didn't belong with authors like that, this wasn't right.* But she was adamant, and I, very reluctantly, agreed to be part of the "authors' reading."

The Friday evening reading was held at the grand old Prince Arthur Hotel in Thunder Bay. It's one of the traditional "railway hotels," very near the old station on the Lake Superior waterfront. (Jane Urquhart, a Northern Ontario girl from Little Longlac, mentions the hotel in her 1997 novel, *The Underpainter*. In a dramatic late chapter, the central character looks from the hotel window at the dazzling snow-covered lake and he dreams he'll see his lover walking to him against a backdrop of the Sleeping Giant: "the huge man made of rock slumbered now on a smooth white sheet, not on the textured dark bed of glimmering water I remembered from my summer arrivals.") In real life, the hotel played a major part in Canadian history. Before the days of airports, national groups liked meeting in central railway towns like Thunder Bay or Winnipeg. So it was here, in 1921, that a group drawn from across Canada formally adopted the wild idea that the red poppy — seriously, a red poppy! — should become the nation-wide symbol of Remembrance Day. For more than ninety years that idea has held up pretty well.

Our own Prince Arthur Hotel event was a revelation. It changed my life.

The reading setup was in accordance with the usual tradition: one author after another trudges onstage to stand behind a podium, modestly introduces the reading, then reads from his or her book for twenty minutes, takes a bow, and shuffles off to make way for the next reader.

You've probably seen readings like this, and you probably know that some authors read aloud better than others. But the static format — and the unchanging setting — is terrible, and might as well have been designed to bore the audience, giving them nothing much to look at, no spectacle, and no drama — just a series of readers barricaded behind a lectern.

I was so nervous about my undeserved role among these experienced and well-known authors — *real* authors — that I prepared my twenty-minute reading with great care. I chose to read from my chapter about W.O. Mitchell. I knew that the early material there was very funny, and the later stuff very sad.

It worked wonders with the Thunder Bay crowd. They laughed till they cried at the early W.O. stories, then they mopped away real tears, with some sobs audible, when I told of W.O.'s joking bravely on his deathbed. (In the audience, my wife Jane's cousin Paul Inksetter whispered that he felt sorry for whoever had to follow that particular powerful ending.)

It was very gratifying. But it was something more. It made me think, in a quieter moment: "Wow, they seem to really like these behind-the-scenes stories about working with famous authors!" That seemed to bode well for my book.

But I also thought, "My goodness, there I was, stuck behind a podium, remote from the audience, who were given nothing apart from me to look at during my static reading . . . *yet they seemed to like it.* Now, if I could change things around, find a way to get out from behind the podium and roam around the whole stage, to break down the barrier between me and the audience, and turn it into a real stage show by giving them something interesting to look at — well, we might have something unique: a new kind of 'author event' that brings it all back to its origins, storytelling."

To cut (ahem) a long story short, I came home from Thunder

Bay and, drawing on the skills I had developed writing sketches for the theatre back in my student days, wrote a one-man play based on my book.

I was encouraged from the start by "my lovely and talented assistant" (i.e., my wife, Jane) and by my friend Terry Fallis, who had been there in Thunder Bay cheering me on, and who was able to help me with the electronic side. Because I knew this was not going to be in any way "a reading." I was going to wander around the stage telling stories. And I would make it visually exciting by basing the stories on the authors who appeared onscreen behind me, in the form of the brilliant caricatures by Anthony Jenkins that punctuate the book. To add even more variety I would build in unexpected bursts of music, and an intriguing new kind of show began to take shape as I inserted scenes that were slightly more dramatic than a man sitting at a desk, editing. Boxing against Ernest Hemingway or imitating a polar bear gutting a sled dog was a little more exciting, everyone agreed.

While, offstage, the book was being printed, I worked with a skilful director, Molly Thom, to sand down some of the play's rougher edges, and I received good advice from theatre friends like Albert Schultz and R.H. Thomson. With Robert Thomson's help I got in touch with Mike Spence at the Arts and Letters Club in Toronto, and we staged a public run-through. It ran too long, but left me feeling able to start a Western tour that had been kindly set up for me by my publisher. We'd see how far this tour went. To our modest surprise it went everywhere. Starting in October 2011, the Grand Tour allowed me to see the country — not for the first time, but from a different viewpoint, as an author. And not only as a storyteller, but also as a collector of tales: stories from that ten-province, coast-to-coast tour form the spine of this book.

Before I left Thunder Bay in 2010, I was pleased to be able to wander around and renew my acquaintance with it ("There's the Hoito, the famous Finnish restaurant!"). As I recount in *Stories About Storytellers*, when I first came to Canada, sailing into Victoria in September of 1967, I crossed the country by Greyhound bus. Only someone who has left the Pacific Coast and crossed half a continent of mountains and prairie and rocks and trees and more trees can appreciate the true drama of finally reaching the Great Lakes. When I spotted Lake Superior, and looked down on the giant grain ships filling up at the Port Arthur and Fort William terminals, it was a hugely important moment, worthy of thunderbolts from the sky. These ships, I realized, flattening my face against the bus window, were able to sail all the way east through the Great Lakes and the St. Lawrence Seaway to the Atlantic Ocean, and then to ports around the world. This, right here, was where the Canadian West really ended.

(In 1967, there were still two cities, Port Arthur and Fort William. In 1970, voters were offered a choice in naming the new single city: Thunder Bay, Lakehead or The Lakehead. In the words of Charles Gordon, "Thunder Bay came up the middle and won.")

Now, in this later visit, as a fur trade enthusiast I got my local friend, the folksinger Bill Houston, to show me the location of the real, historic Fort William, now hidden among train tracks. Then he joined me in renting a canoe at the new Old Fort, so we could paddle up the Kaministiquia River in the silent wake of ghostly voyageurs.

I've quoted Charles Gordon once or twice already. Get ready for more, because I believe he's one of the country's finest writers. And a not-too-bad jazz trumpeter, too. You may remember him as a witty columnist for *Maclean's*, or as a writer for the *Ottawa Citizen*. (When a *Citizen* reader on holiday met his hero by chance in Manitoba, to Charles's delight he exclaimed, "Glory Hallelujah!")

Charles has written books that include *The Governor General's Bunny Hop* (1985), a satire on life in his hometown, Ottawa, and also *The Grim Pig* (2001), a comic novel about the newspaper world he knows so well. He also produced Canada's answer to the wave of boastful and triumphant self-improvement books flooding in from the USA, promising "excellence," with his own brilliantly titled 1993 book, *How to Be Not Too Bad: A Sort-of Guide to Superior Behaviour*.

All of them reveal Charles Gordon as a man with a finely under-stated style that is a joy to read and a dry sense of humour so Canadian that it deserves to occupy our seat at the United Nations.

In the summer of 1996 he and his wife, Nancy (known in the book, to her slight irritation, as "The Business Manager"), set out in the family car to drive across Canada and back. The result is a won-derful book, *The Canada Trip*, which shows what typical travellers are likely to find as they enjoy the journey. (Jane, my very own Business Manager, and I consulted the book whenever our own tour involved driving.) This is not an earnest "Whither Canada?" book as much as a "Whither the moose?" book, or even a "Whither the washroom?" book, and we're all grateful for it.

You may know Charles as the author of the classic book *At the Cottage: A Fearless Look at Canada's Summer Obsession*, which came out in 1989 and proceeded to sell like campfire marshmallows for the next twenty years or so. Better still, you may know the follow-up that showed his greedy publisher (guilty as charged) knew a profitable classic when he saw one, publishing *Still at the Cottage* in 2006. Many sober citizens have fallen out of hammocks laughing at his affectionate portrait of life at "The Cottage, or The Cabin, The Shack, The Lake, The Beach, or Camp" or wherever Canadians choose to spend their summers.

The books are studded with phrases that will bring memories of summer sweeping back. "Is there something wrong with the map, Daddy?" "Does anybody know what made these droppings on the path?" "That rock wasn't there last year." "Do you think we should go ahead with the picnic?" Or even, at The Cottage Wedding, the mosquito-tinged words "I Do (slap!)."

Charles is famous for his *At the Cottage* chapter on "Sex at the Cottage; The Beast with Two Backs and Three Spider Bites." He warns us that despite all of the healthy outdoor cottage activity that sets the blood flowing,

> There is the question of the bed. It squeaks, and the short leg bumps. And the walls are thin and don't go all the way up to the ceiling. And there are people around, at close quarters, so sex at the cottage tends to be a rather muffled activity. Groans and cries are stifled, in the interests of decency and good taste. But there is no stopping the short leg from bumping. That is why sex at the cottage sounds like the approach of a short-of-breath person with a wooden leg.

Halfway between Nancy's home town of Thunder Bay and the traditional Gordon family roost at Winnipeg lies the Gordon family cottage. After all of Charley's affectionate descriptions of the place, so many Canadians know it as "their" cottage, too, that a movement has been started — by me, right now — to have it designated "The National Cottage."

Charles Gordon/Ralph Connor (1860–1937)

The cottage was built on a Lake of the Woods island near Kenora by Charley's grandfather, another Charles Gordon. The elder Charles was known to millions of readers by his pen name, Ralph Connor. This Winnipeg Presbyterian Church minister was, in the words of *The Canadian Encyclopedia*, "the most successful Canadian novelist in the early 20th century." His early bestsellers were based on his adventures preaching in the early days near Canmore, Alberta. *The Sky Pilot* (1899) and *The Prospector* (1904) are described as "fast-paced sentimental melodramas, with stereotyped characters dramatizing the conflict between good and evil in frontier settings presided over by exemplary churchmen."

Readers around the world loved them, and they sold in the millions. So did his historical novels set in Ontario, *The Man from Glengarry* (1901) and *Glengarry School Days* (1902). The Gordon family roots run deep in Glengarry County. An earlier Gordon, the Reverend Daniel, was famous for his role in a dispute over a shared pioneer church there. He kicked in the church door locked against him, in order to preach The Word of a tough Presbyterian God from the pulpit.

Books by Ralph Connor were shipped on the railway "by the carload," as publishers liked to boast in those days, and he became very rich. With his royalties he built both the cottage on the island, "Birkencraig," and the huge three-story family home at 54 Westgate in Winnipeg, now marked by a government plaque (so we have a precedent for the National Cottage plan!). *The Canada Trip* summarizes what followed:

> After the money went, in bad investments while he was overseas in the First World War, the house and the island were all he had, and after he died the house was sold for back taxes. The University Women's Club bought it in 1945 and maintains it beautifully, renting out two apartments upstairs, and using the rest of the house for luncheons and cultural events, renting it out for receptions and meetings. . . . At the last reception, a year ago, I walked into the office and announced that I was a Gordon and we would like to have our house back now. This was treated as a joke.

Stories About Storytellers begins in Winnipeg, where I spoke on Mavis Gallant's behalf at the Governor General's Award ceremony there, and found myself jousting with a separatist winner from Quebec. So it was appropriate to start my stage show tour there, too. It was booked by Paul McNally, the quietly effective co-owner (with his wife, Holly) of the McNally Robinson western chain of bookshops. I must stress here that he is no relation of Ben McNally, the excellent Toronto bookstore owner. (I look forward to reading a PhD thesis investigating the genetic oddity that explains why a significant portion of Canadian independent bookstores are now owned by bright middle-aged men named McNally.) Paul kindly took a chance on me, inviting me to give a show at his Prairie Ink store on Grant Avenue.

He had no idea how many people would be interested in turning up. Neither had I. But I was very grateful that the way had been helpfully prepared in the *Winnipeg Free Press* a few days earlier by the astoundingly perceptive and gifted Book Page editor, Morley Walker. How else can I describe a man who began his review of my book by calling me a "Scottish immigrant and Toronto publisher extraordinaire" who "has a greater appreciation of regional Canada than 99 percent of us born here." Clearly, the man's a genius!

This was backed up later in the paper by the remarkable Gordon Sinclair Jr. Gordon (another case where "no relation" is appropriate) is an almost unique survivor from the days when columnists could write about whatever the hell they wanted to. I knew this big, cheery, green-eyed, smiling charmer very well because I had coaxed an important book out of him, finally, entitled *Cowboys and Indians: The Shooting of J.J. Harper* (1999), about a tragic incident in which an aboriginal leader was shot and killed by Winnipeg police on the street.

The "finally" is significant here, because in his kindly column alerting Winnipeg to my forthcoming show, as an honest man he refers to his link to Gibson the Impatient Publisher. He admits that as one of the writers who has "heard the crack and felt the slash of his deadline whip" he had been pleased to hear that I had had trouble with my own book.

As soon as we hit town, Gordon took Jane and me for a literary and historic tour. He took us across the river to the lovingly preserved St. Boniface home of Gabrielle Roy. Now, Gabrielle Roy was described by my distinguished publishing predecessor Jack McClelland as "the greatest writer in the country" in his correspondence with her, excerpted in *Imagining Canadian Literature: The Selected Letters of Jack McClelland*. His faith in her was so great that in 1976, when Canada seemed under threat from Quebec separatism, he urged her to support the new translation of *The Tin Flute* by Alan Brown, because he hoped her novel might help the national situation. "I mention *The Tin Flute* specifically," McClelland wrote, "because it remains the fact that you are unique in being the only Canadian writer who has totally bridged the gap between the two cultures. You are the only writer who is critically accepted and widely read in both our two languages. There simply is no one else."

This was not a minority opinion. The original French novel, *Bonheur d'occasion* (1945) won many prizes, including the Prix Femina in France, while *The Tin Flute* won many more, including Gabrielle Roy's first Governor General's Award. When Jack McClelland organized a historic Calgary Conference in 1978, where scholars were asked to rank Canada's greatest novels (a promotional coup for Jack), *The Tin Flute* placed second, behind an embarrassed Margaret Laurence, with *The Stone Angel*. Gabrielle Roy, who spent her later years in Quebec City, charmingly resisting Jack's pleas to promote her books more, went on to be elected to the Royal Society of Canada, its first woman member.

I remember Gabrielle in person as a very striking woman whose aquiline face was lined with what I can only describe as wise, mature, beauty. I was aware that when *The Tin Flute* came out in English in 1947, the *Globe and Mail* reviewer hailed it as "the Great Canadian Novel." Later, after producing other fine books, she in turn inspired one of the greatest of Canada's literary biographies, by François Ricard, which I was proud to publish in Patricia Claxton's translation in 1999.

That biography recounts an extraordinary family story. Gabrielle was the youngest in a family of eight children. Over time, her matchless success and fame provoked some jealousy among her sisters, most notably with Adele, who also had hopes as a writer, and who complained primly that her own lack of success was because "her books were not in the fashion of the day (and) not to the liking of young people hungry for erotic sensations." As François Ricard wrote, "What could Adele do about such a situation except harbour her ill temper and wait for the moment of revenge?"

Gabrielle Roy (1909–1983)

That moment came when Adele was eighty-six years old. A Quebec literary figure named Gérard Bessette (far from blameless in this matter) approached her asking if she happened to have "anything unpublished" about her famous sister. The floodgates opened, with a manuscript denouncing, in Ricard's description, "Gabrielle's selfishness and unscrupulous ambition," and so on, and so on. Gabrielle learned of her elderly sister's forthcoming bitter book and tried very hard to stop it from being published. Ricard was himself an important figure in the Quebec publishing world, and records: "From August to October she telephoned me two or three times a week, in tears, each time fluctuating between despair and rage, a towering rage whose target was less Adele herself — 'a poor thing who's very sick really' — and more Adele's publisher, 'one of those vultures who deliberately exploit sensational themes.'"

The pressure on Gabrielle built up. In the fall of 1979, just three weeks before her sister's book was to be published, she suffered a serious heart attack. She was rushed into hospital and spent eleven days in the coronary unit, and a full month in hospital. Afterward, she continued to write when she could, but she never recovered full, robust health, and died in July 1983 at the age of seventy-four. Her triumphant sister Adele died in St. Boniface in 1998, at the age of 105.

After taking us to the Roy home, our Winnipeg guide Gordon Sinclair then showed us the site of the Battle of Seven Oaks, where the rivalry between the Hudson's Bay Company and the Nor'Westers and their pemmican suppliers among the Métis led to an 1816 clash where Scottish Selkirk settlers were killed by Métis buffalo hunters on horseback. These well-disciplined light cavalry troops were led by Cuthbert Grant, a "halfbreed" whose father had sent him east with the plan that he would be educated in Scotland. (And what was the name of the street where my show would be held, again? Ah yes, Grant Avenue. In Winnipeg, history is all around you, even in the shape of an old building downtown named after Thomas Scott, the man executed by men acting for the provisional government led by Louis Riel — whose gravestone Gordon also showed us, in the grounds of the St. Boniface Cathedral, to which Gabrielle Roy's father had been one of the original building fund donors.)

Finally, for old times' sake, he took us to the Fort Garry Hotel, where my Mavis Gallant incident had occurred. In conversation there I laughed about my trouble with writing my own damned book, and blamed Winnipeg's own Margaret Laurence. The story goes that at the height of her fame Margaret attended a cocktail party where she met a brain surgeon. "A novelist, eh?" he asked. "Well, when I retire from being a surgeon, I plan to take up writing novels."

"What an amazing coincidence," said Margaret. "When I retire from writing novels I plan to take up brain surgery!"

I've repeated this fine put-down many times, and laughed heartily. Yet it turned out that I had made the same mistake as the arrogant surgeon. I had thought that writing a book was just a matter of time — or, more precisely, of clearing the time to do it. After retiring from the world of publishing I had lots of time. But as the title of the rueful piece I wrote about it on my blog demonstrates, I found it "Harder Than I Thought."

I knew Margaret, and had been surprised to find that we had roots in common. Her maternal grandfather Simpson, the lawyer who moved to Canada to set up his practice in Neepawa, Manitoba (which became the basis of the fictional Manawaka), had gone to Glasgow Academy, the high school I attended much later. His traditional Scottish education, with lots of Latin, must have made him an impressive figure on the frontier, and it was clear that Margaret's family was at the top of the social tree on the almost treeless prairies. His former house, where Margaret grew up, is now the Margaret Laurence House, visited by admirers from around the world.

Her true publishing relationship was with Jack McClelland, but I came to know her in due course as a redoubtable figure. A British journalist once called her features "mannish but not unmotherly" — to Margaret's rage, as she revealed in a letter to her great friend Adele Wiseman. But he had a point. She had strong features, and large, thick-framed, dark-rimmed glasses that gave her a decisive, straightforward look. To me she looked almost shaman-like.

That, certainly, was the role she played when she acted as a sort of den mother to Canada's writers, whom she called her "tribe." And when she helped to create the Writers' Union of Canada, she was an inspiring leader.

Margaret Laurence (1926–1987)

She was a brave woman, pilloried by ignorant boors for writing "obscene" books (like *The Stone Angel* and *The Diviners*, for God's sake!) that should be removed from the local library system and kept out of the schools. She and the equally obscene Alice Munro (who nobly showed up to defend her at a Clinton meeting full of vocally Christian neighbours) were attacked by local religious extremists. (Thank Heavens they missed "Sex at the Cottage"!) Living in Lakefield as chancellor of Trent University must have been uncomfortable for Margaret when she was attacked by similarly small-minded folk in nearby Peterborough. But with the help of supporters like young Linwood Barclay and his Trent girlfriend Neetha she gamely served out her three-year academic term. Not everyone knew that she always wore a long dress for her speaking engagements — and there were many, as she received fourteen honorary degrees — in order to conceal the fact that her knees were trembling. In Christopher Moore's 2015 book, *Founding the Writers' Union of Canada*, Margaret Atwood says, "She was very nervous speaking in public. She had to sit down, she shook so much."

Her 1964 novel, *The Stone Angel*, was selected as the best Canadian novel at Jack McClelland's famous 1978 Calgary conference. The novel's narrator, ninety-year-old Hagar Shipley, is a tough, determined character, "rampant with memory," who in turn will not be forgotten by her readers. (If you watch the 2007 film version of *The Stone Angel*, look closely at the Winnipeg mansion scenes: they're set in the Ralph Connor House.) Among the characters who inhabited the fictional prairie town of Manawaka, Morag Gunn of *The Diviners* (1974) also lives on triumphantly, as does the novel's unforgettable opening line: "The river flowed both ways."

For many of us, *The Diviners* is Margaret's greatest book. Myrna Kostash (a writer we'll meet in the Alberta chapter) is fascinated by Cuthbert Grant, the man caught between two worlds, who worked for the Nor'Westers as a Bourgeois but also led the Métis. She reminded me how large the Battle of Seven Oaks looms in Margaret's book, for a small skirmish on the outskirts of modern Winnipeg. In his cups, Morag's stepfather, Christie, will proudly recount the story of his people, the penniless Scottish Highlanders evicted to make way for sheep. They find hardship here, across the ocean, but inspired by the legendary Piper Gunn (and the clenched-jaw clan war cry, "The

Ridge of Tears") they tough it out in the Red River, until their threat to the Métis pemmican trade leads to trouble.

There was a difference between the "halfbreeds," like Cuthbert Grant, who were English-speaking, with fur trade fathers and Native mothers, and the French-speaking Métis, who were the backbone of Louis Riel's rebellions in defence of their way of life. They were so distinct that they even had their own French-based language, Michif. Not only Alistair MacLeod admirers must regret that no great Michif writer has come to the fore.

In Christie's words, the settlers had hard times, with "winters so cold it would freeze the breath in your throat and turn your blood to red ice. Weather for giants, in them days. Not that it's much better now, I'd say."

Young Morag asks, "Did they fight the halfbreeds and Indians, Christie?"

He replies, "Did they ever. Slew them in their dozens, girl. In their scores."

Yet when Morag asks, "Were they bad, the breeds and them?" Christie's answer is uneasy:

"Bad?" He repeats the word as though he is trying to think what it means. "No," he says at last. "They weren't bad. They were — just there."

Later Morag's lover Jules Tonnerre tells the story of Métis resistance down through the years, against the intrusions of the English and "the Arkanys," the Orkney men who made up a huge part of the Hudson Bay workforce. As a folksinger, and the father of Morag's daughter, he proudly recreates the stories of Riel and Dumont, and he does it in song. We all remember history, our history, in our own way.

Margaret's friend and biographer, Clara Thomas, summarized her career well when she wrote: "She was much beloved and will be remembered for her works and her personal warmth, strength and humour, which she shared so generously." For example, she was the proud godmother of Andreas Schroeder and Sharon Brown's daughter, Sabrina, and took her role very seriously. Towards the end of her life she phoned their house in B.C. almost every week, passing on advice that would help Sabrina's writing. This regular contact meant that Andreas was aware that she was fighting an even greater enemy than the lung cancer that had struck her. She was "blocked," unable to write. This affected her terribly, attacking the core of her being: if she was no longer a writer, what was she? She would tell him, "I'm a writer who can't write anymore, yet here I am, giving advice on writing. I feel like a fake."

This, like her advancing cancer, preyed on her mind. She began to explore the road to a painless death. She collected the required ingredients, and researched the procedures. Andreas remembered a phone conversation that left him and Sharon feeling that Margaret's death was not far off. The next day, she decided it was time. She was found at her Lakefield home on January 5, 1987.

In happier times, she had met, and tickled, my baby daughter Meg, when we dropped by an early Writers' Union get-together in Toronto. More than a decade later, Meg was at high school on Bloor Street in Toronto when Margaret's funeral was held in a church right opposite the school, but teenage propriety ("I didn't really know her") prevented Meg from joining me at the historic funeral. The most moving part of the service was when a lone piper marched outside the church, playing a lament. Afterward, Ken Adachi, the *Toronto Star*'s soft-spoken books editor and the author of the book about Japanese Canadians *The Enemy That Never Was*, remarked to me that he wanted a piper at *his* funeral. It was not to be.

One of the most interesting authors I ever published was Winnipeg's George Swinton, the author of the 1972 classic illustrated book *Sculpture of the Eskimo*. Updated and revised and re-titled editions of *Sculpture of the Inuit* appeared, the last in 1999. When we visited Winnipeg I made a point of taking Jane to see him, not just as a great expert on the art of the North, but because he was a remarkable man.

He was born into high society in Vienna in 1917. He was twenty when Hitler's army marched in and took over Austria in the Anschluss of March 12, 1938. That night young George went to the opera. As a patriotic Austrian he cringed with shame when the orchestra began the evening by playing the triumphant German national anthem, "Deutschland über alles." Everyone rose to their feet, and stood at attention.

Not quite everyone: George sat there defiantly, his arms folded, all eyes upon him. At the end of the show, he received word that the

Nazis were after him, and would arrest him that night.

("Who warned you?" I asked him, when I first heard the story.

"Oh, a friend who was high in the Nazi party."

"A friend . . . ?" I spluttered.

"Yes," smiled George, the Viennese socialite, "we played bridge together.")

It was the role of a rich young idiot — a sort of Viennese Bertie Wooster — that got him out of Austria that very night. With a few young friends, he bought some bottles of champagne and went to the train station, where he purchased a ticket for Switzerland. Then, with no luggage, he reeled towards the entrance to the platform, manned by ugly men in leather coats who were on the look-out for someone like him trying to escape. He and his loudly drunken friends reeled around, offering champagne to everyone they staggered against, and got George through. A friend bribed the train carriage attendant to let the poor young drunk sleep it off, undisturbed, when they reached the Swiss border. And thus George escaped to freedom, and later, to Britain.

The rest of his life was equally remarkable, including the fact that as the owner of an undeniably Austrian passport, he was "Deemed Suspect" when war came and shipped out of Britain to a Canadian prison camp. There he and other German speakers like Eric Koch (my distinguished CBC friend who used "Deemed Suspect" as an ironic book title) were prevented from playing any part in the war against the Nazis who were killing their families. Finally, George, desperate to help, managed to persuade the Canadian army that, fluent in German, he could be very useful working in military intelligence.

They finally agreed . . . and sent him to Japan.

Later George wound up in Winnipeg and fell in love with Inuit art, making annual visits to the North and becoming one of the world's greatest authorities on the art and the artists. I asked him once why the Inuit people had been so open to visits to their camps from this outsider, this big white man. "Ah," George said, laughing, "I was very strong, so they were glad to have me around, and to use me." A new version of the white man's burden, fetching and carrying and dragging sleds.

The combination of his on-the-icy-ground knowledge of the

artists and his own artist's eye made George a recognized world authority on Inuit art. Indeed, the *Winnipeg Free Press* said the final version of his classic book "remains the best book there is on the subject, and a work of art in itself." Praise came from all over. The *Ottawa Citizen* reviewer called it "a wonderful catalogue of a style of art as uniquely Canadian as the paintings of the Group of Seven."

Canada was lucky to have him.

When Jane and I visited, we toured his Winnipeg apartment, amazed and delighted by the range of Inuit sculptures and prints that made it a superb art gallery. George told us that he was moving into a small apartment in a seniors' residence and would have to give up all but a handful of the choicest pieces of art.

We were horrified. How would he cope with having his beloved art removed from his everyday life? George smiled contentedly. "It's all up here," he said, tapping the side of his head.

The Winnipeg show was held in the café area of the Grant Avenue bookstore. It was very efficiently set up, with Jane, having helped with the PowerPoint in her role of "techie," watching nervously from the audience, as John Toews worked his technical magic.

I was not to learn until many performances later that café-style seating, with tables, is not ideal for audience involvement. A performer gets the best response when the audience is crowded into rows of theatre-style seating, as close to the stage as possible, giving people a sense of *shared experience*. Who knew? Actually, lots of people knew this, but my education in the ways of the theatre was just beginning. By the end I was still learning, but knew some details of local audiences, such as the tendency of Prince Edward Islanders to enjoy comic moments in shoulder-shaking near-silence.

What was remarkable is that the Winnipeg audience proved to be made up of old friends from various parts of my publishing past. Notable among them was David Friesen, the former head of the famous printing company down the road in Altona, who had printed literally millions of copies of books by the authors I was talking about. I remember, for instance, that the huge print run of Pierre Trudeau's *Memoirs* involved just about every living Mennonite in Altona.

But for me the highlight was the appearance in the audience of Don Starkell. To be precise, this was the dry husk of Don Starkell.

The mighty man who had taken a canoe south from Winnipeg in an epic journey later described in *Paddle to the Amazon* (1987) was long gone. So was the Northern adventurer who had boldly paddled and dragged a kayak from Churchill all the way through the Northwest Passage in *Paddle to the Arctic* (1995).

Readers of the best adventure travel books know that Don put an open canoe in the Red River, with his two teenage sons, and paddled it all the way south to Belem, at the mouth of the Amazon. During the 12,000-mile journey they took on the whole Mississippi, drug smugglers, soldiers, sharks, alligators, drought, starvation, and sickness, and benefitted from the kindness of strangers.

One of his sons (the sensible one) quit when they were being swamped again and again by incoming waves broadsiding them as they crept along the shores of the Gulf of Mexico. Yet Don and young Dana kept going, completing the longest canoe trip in history. And the book (assisted by the editorial hand of Thunder Bay's Charles Wilkins) still provides very exciting reading. A real classic.

Later, Don found it hard to settle back into everyday life in Winnipeg where he worked at the YMCA. So he devised another adventure: taking a kayak north from Churchill at the base of Hudson Bay all the way through the Northwest Passage, dragging the kayak across the ice when the sea froze. He made it *almost* unscathed (losing parts of his fingers and toes) and lived to write *Paddle to the Arctic*, another classic, and to continue paddling on the Red River. Early one morning years ago, I was scrambling beside the river near The Forks, trying to get the rising sun framed in the rose window of the ruined St. Boniface Cathedral when I saw a kayak in the shadows of the willows near the bank. *Early morning? Winnipeg? A kayak?* It had to be Don Starkell, as my shouted greetings soon established. We met and embraced on the bank before he paddled off up the Red River, to head west along the Assiniboine.

I thought that he was superhuman and would live forever. But when he struggled out to attend my show in Winnipeg in October, it was clear that the cancer was winning, and every movement was painful. We talked affectionately, and our handshake with his shortened fingers turned into a farewell hug. His death came the following January. Still, he *was* in many ways superhuman. I am very glad that, like all authors, he had found a way to cheat death.

CHAPTER 2

HOGTOWN HEROES

Reading in the Shadow of Queen's Park . . . Waggling with Robertson Davies . . . Lunch with Marshall McLuhan . . . Learning with "Uncle Norrie" (aka Northrop Frye) . . . Al Purdy, Larger Than Life . . . Storytelling at the Royal Ontario Museum . . . The Politics of Queen's Park . . . Visiting the Lieutenant-Governor . . . The Power Corner . . . Literary Bond Street . . . Grey Owl Fooled Everyone . . . Prime Ministers and Other Visitors . . . The Arts and Letters Club . . . Inside the York Club with Robertson Davies . . . Reading Michael Ondaatje's Body of Work . . . In Praise of Margaret Atwood . . . An Objective Critic

The very first event in My Life as an Author began at the annual Word on the Street (WOTS) festival in September 2011 in Toronto's Queen's Park. In my role as wide-ranging Canadian publisher I've attended WOTS events in Halifax (on Spring Garden Road, or down by the Historic Properties, right beside the salt water) and Vancouver (outside the main library, whole blocks away from the salt water), but most years I was in freshwater Toronto.

In the old days the festivities were held, literally, on the street (strung out along Queen Street West). When they expanded and moved, to cover the northern part of Queen's Park with a sort of literary tent city, nobody suggested changing the name to the Word on the Park, or Words and Readers Park. (Pun lovers may remember that Don Harron and Catherine MacKinnon, holding a summer tented show in Prince Edward Island, gave it the audacious title "Loitering Within Tent." Charlie Farquharson, no doubt, greatly approved, with his famous horse laugh.)

My very first public appearance as a *published* author was a fraud. My book, you see, had not actually been released in bookstores, but finished copies did exist and, like Peter C. Newman (who recalled carrying his very first book around in his briefcase so that he could pull it out every so often to check that it really existed, with his name on the cover and everything!), I sneaked constant looks at it. But because copies were around, my "reading" was to be followed by a "signing." Too much excitement! A little nervousness, too.

The tent where I was to read was devoted to authors who qualified as (I'm not making this up) "Vibrant Voices of Ontario." My less than vibrant voice was preceded by the respected author and teacher Antanas Sileika, reading from his new novel. I sensed this would be harder than being the publisher offering smiles of encouragement from the audience. I was brought to the stage and very respectfully introduced by our host Stuart Woods, then editor of publishing trade magazine *Quill & Quire*. Too respectfully, because a pall of silent reverence fell over the audience as I read what I thought was a laugh-along chapter in my book.

The epilogue to *Stories About Storytellers*, "What Happens After My Book Is Published?," is based on the handout entitled "Awful Warnings" that as a publisher I routinely supplied to first-time authors. My new authors always reacted with amusement as I predicted the terrible, Murphy's Lawless things that would happen to them, and their books, in bookstores, in newspaper reviews, among their friends, in interviews, and so on. About six months later, a much more thoughtful response — along the lines of "I thought you were joking" — tended to come back to me.

Little did I know, then, that in my role as author I was to experience indignities almost beyond imagining. One example: when I went to speak to the book club members of a prestigious, expensive downtown Toronto club, my wife asked me why I was taking the time to attend such a small-scale event. I told Jane that it would be a pleasant evening with a good meal in good company, and while the numbers would be small, everyone would bring along a copy of my book to be signed.

And so it proved. Except when I opened the copy proffered by the nice, rich lady to my left for me to sign, I noticed that it was *a Toronto Public Library edition*. "I can't sign this!" I objected, and she went away, offended. So did I, although it gave me a great story.

Now, in the WOTS tent, despite my best intentions, it was my turn to suffer. The audience reacted solemnly as I told what I thought were hilarious stories of author readings going askew, although Stuart Woods defied one of my rules by getting neither my name nor the title of my book wrong at the end.

After this funereal reception, I was ushered to the Authors' Tent to sign copies, and soon fell into the role of the seated, smiling professional, remembering to make eye contact and beamishly asking, "How would you like me to sign this?" In all of the signing sessions that loomed in the future I never solved the perennial author's problem of signing the book to an old friend whose name has slipped your mind. The usual fudge — "How do you spell your name, again?" — doesn't work well with irritated people named Mary or Tom.

Worse, I found myself grappling with signing decisions (Do I sign on the title page? Do I strike my pen through the author's name printed there, as Robertson Davies used to do, delicately replacing the printed name with the freehand one? Should it be signed "to" the buyer, or "for" them? Should I be "Doug," or "Doug Gibson," or "Douglas Gibson"? Should I, like Pierre Berton, avoid giving any hint of my cheque-signing signature? And what should the personalized message be?) Who knew that so many decisions had to be made on the fly — as opposed to on the fly leaf — by the signing author?

Even worse, I found that greed was affecting me as I sat there. To my horror, I found myself resenting the old friends who stood at the front of the (very short) line, chatting amiably *but not buying a copy of the damned book!* Oh dear, a new chapter in my life had just begun — the transformation from greedy publisher to greedy author.

Queen's Park, of course, is filled with literary memories. Robertson Davies, for example, used to stroll through the park, taking his morning constitutional walk from nearby Massey College, which lies just to the west. He was a striking Jehovah-like figure, his flowing white locks riding above a flowing white beard, and often topped by wide-brimmed, almost Cavalier-style hat. The effect was so striking, in fact, that dazzled observers claimed that he was wearing a cape. His family later denied this, explaining that the cape effect was given by the Inverness overcoat that he liked to wear, with the extra layer built in around the shoulders.

He was not unaware of the effect he created as he processed around the park, brandishing his walking stick. In fact, after a stick-waggling exchange of greetings, he once drew aside another cane-user, Reed Needles (a young man who had a bad knee), to give him a lesson on the proper use of a stick. "He did not think I waggled properly," Needles recalls in Val Ross's book *Robertson Davies: A Portrait in Mosaic* (2008). "And he thought that as an actor I should know these things. So one day he took me to the long covered walkway outside the Trinity College Buttery, and we went up and down and he showed me how to swing the stick properly. One puts it down every fourth step, not every second."

On his way back to his Massey College home, R.D. (even in this fond recollection of my old friend, "Rob" seems improper) would pass by Trinity College. I was the editor/publisher behind the decision to put the distinctive roof-line of Trinity, set against a summer night sky, on the cover of *The Rebel Angels* (1981). Catching the full moon as it passed through the window in the notable central tower proved to be a major challenge for me and Peter Paterson, the chosen photographer. Along with his sturdy assistant, we panted our way around Trinity, lugging heavy wooden boxes full of Peter's equipment, and somehow the mid-summer moon kept moving out of the shot.

Eventually we decided that the perfect place for a shot *in five minutes* was from a window upstairs. I dashed up and discovered that it was in a washroom, with windows that opened. The presence of urinals encouraged me to believe that it was a male washroom, so our midnight visit would not present a problem. Yet when we crashed through the door, behind our heavy cases, at the sink stood a terrified young female summer student in flimsy pyjamas, foaming at the mouth — no, wait, brushing her teeth. It was a bad moment for all four of us. But we pleaded literary necessity, set up our cameras, and got the shot out of the window. Ironically, the shot that graced the final cover was taken five minutes later, when we were retreating across the quad, still embarrassed by the intrusion that had so alarmed a nice young woman. You can still see the result on the hardcover edition of *The Rebel Angels*. And you can still see a number of fine portraits of Robertson Davies taken over the years by Peter Paterson.

Thanks to Canada Post, the stamp that was issued in 2013 showing Robertson Davies as photographed by Yousuf Karsh has reminded all Canadians of his distinctive looks. I was pleased to be present when the stamp was unveiled at Massey College, a few short steps away from Trinity.

A final note about the old College. I was a pallbearer for R.D.'s funeral at the Trinity College Chapel. It was an achingly cold December day, and I foolishly wore only a raincoat, as we stood on Hoskins Avenue, looking east to Queen's Park, and waiting for the hearse to do its solemn work. I was so cold that I recalled the bitter joke that winter funerals tend to produce a crop of other funerals. The very next day I bought a warm, navy-blue formal coat, and it has served me well at funerals ever since, including the January 2013 funeral for R.D.'s beloved wife, Brenda, in the same Trinity Chapel.

Marshall McLuhan (1911–1980)

Across Queen's Park to the east lay the territory of two world-famous University of Toronto professors, Marshall McLuhan at St. Michael's College, and Northrop Frye at Victoria. They were two renowned figures, working within shouting distance of each other. As members of the U of T's English Department, they even served on the same university committees, and sometimes shared a cab home. B.W. Powe, who studied under — and admired — both men, has written a thoughtful study, *Marshall McLuhan and Northrop Frye: Apocalypse and Alchemy* (2014), which rewards close attention. In summary, he rejects the argument that the two giant figures detested one another (as more than one critic has claimed); instead he argues that they were warily cordial, and that constant presence of the other inspired each of them, driving them onward, along their own very different career paths.

I got to know Marshall fairly well, thanks to the fact that his agent, Matie Molinaro, was a good friend from my earliest days in Toronto. After a few encounters with him (where I was struck by his very direct gaze) I was invited back to Marshall's Wychwood Park home. This family house, set in a very fine midtown neighbourhood carefully created within a park, was remarkable for the air of Southern hospitality that was wrapped around it by his charming (and the word is precise) wife from Texas, Corinne. She brought the warmth of the South to a central Toronto home even in the deepest midwinter. Earlier, when the six McLuhan kids were young, the *Globe's* Kay Kritzwiser recorded that visitors seeking an audience with this intellectual guru had to pick their way through "a tangle of bicycles."

Marshall was a wild card. Tom Wolfe once wrote a perceptive essay about him called "What If He's Right?" Even the title caught the problem that he posed to the world. Here was this obscure professor in Toronto whose Cambridge PhD thesis had been on "The Place of Thomas Nash in the Learning of his Time." (Not everyone knew that Nash, or Nashe, was an English dramatist and satirist who died in 1601, whose works included the promisingly named *Anatomie of Absurditie*, and who liked to marshal puns to help his case, as McLuhan did.) Soon the learned, prairie-born English professor, who had joined the English department at St. Michael's College in 1946, was studying what *The Canadian Encyclopedia* called "the linguistic and perceptual biases of mass media."

In 1962 he published *The Gutenberg Galaxy*. As the admired Canadian editor William Toye notes in his memoir, *William Toye: On Canadian Literature*, that book "contains the sentence 'The new electronic interdependence recreates the world in the image of a global village.'" Toye goes on to comment that Northrop Frye "was the chairman of the Governor General's Award committee that awarded the medal to McLuhan, not because they admired the writing, but because *The Gutenberg Galaxy* was already being celebrated as a ground-breaking, though idiosyncratic, interpretation of Western history, and they would look foolish if they didn't choose it."

Toye's interpretation is backed by Powe's revelation that one of Frye's private notebooks contains the entry "Global village, my ass." McLuhan over the years directed a few zingers towards Frye, once writing, in Powe's words, with his "voice drenched in scorn: 'It is heartening to observe Northrop Frye venturing into his first steps towards understanding media.'" Yet he also once wrote: "Norrie is not struggling for his place in the sun. He is the sun."

It was a complex relationship, two very large fish in a fairly small pond, colleagues and rivals.

In 1964 McLuhan brought out what was to become his best-known book, *Understanding Media*. Now it was clear that not only was he looking at stuff that nobody had thought worth studying, he was also throwing out provocative suggestions that changed the way people might look at the world — such as the idea that "hot" media like print and radio were essentially different from "cool" media like television and the telephone, so different, in fact, that they changed the message that was received. Hence the term that gave him the title for his 1967 book, *The Medium Is the Message*.

What made Marshall even more troublesome is that he scorned the usual reserved, dignified professorial role. Although he was a very devout traditional Catholic ("If there are going to be McLuhanites, you can be sure I'm not going to be one of them"), he enjoyed being a tweedy academic showman. It was no surprise to those who knew him when in the middle of Woody Allen's *Annie Hall*, Marshall himself shambled up on screen to join a movie-theatre lineup to adjudicate a discussion about McLuhanism. It was the ultimate cameo appearance.

Many readers were troubled by his aphoristic style, where declarative statements also made cameo appearances, not always linked to the thoughts that came before and after. Marshall was unrepentant; linear argument was for others. He was on to the next idea.

As for his classes at U of T, one of his former students, Damiano Pietropaolo, recalled him warning his class, "All the theatrics in this class will be provided by *me!*" Of his conversational style another colleague once noted, "Marshall's very polite. He always waits until your lips stop moving."

My old friend Donald Gillies was a Ryerson teacher who talked his way into one of Marshall's famous classes. Don found it very stimulating and became a great admirer. He described Marshall as "a committed, probing, engaging (though sometimes ruthless) teacher." He was present as the ruthless side emerged; a member of the class unwisely began his oral presentation "with a definition read from the Oxford Dictionary. Marshall pounced on him: "You can't quote an English dictionary to me. I have two BAs, two MAs, and a PhD in English!"

Yet the weekly evening classes were very popular. "One learned to arrive early to find a chair, or else sit on the floor at the feet of the master." Celebrities such as Pierre Trudeau and the CBC news-reader Stanley Burke were known to drop in — but presumably found a chair. In the end Don Gillies wrote: "To conclude in simple truth, my time with McLuhan both inspired and reconfigured my subsequent professional life."

As a Southam Fellow at Massey College, the writer Martin O'Malley was also pleased to sit in on these evening classes, which he found "friendly, and tweedy, and apple-juicy." He remembers Marshall once bringing along Tom Wolfe to a session, where things were very friendly. Less friendly was the exchange with the political science professor Jack McLeod (whose idiosyncratic description in *Canadian Who's Who* begins "polymath, writer, splendid person"). The splendid person once provoked Marshall's wrath. He found a furious note on his car beginning "*You are parked in my space!*" Jack returned it to the McLuhan car with a welcome apology, followed by the unwelcome sentence "This is the first thing you have written that I have ever understood."

For all his worldwide fame, Marshall obviously troubled the university administration. When his thin, high-browed face was staring out at the world from the cover of *TIME* magazine, and "McLuhanism" was on everyone's lips (with "McLuhanisme" on pouting French lips) and his theories were cropping up on every editorial page, it was clear that he was a star. So what did the university do? They gave him an office in a garage.

That's a little unfair, since it was officially a coach house, with the fancy name Centre for Culture and Technology, but in Tom Wolfe's words it looked "like an unused Newfoundland fishing shack." (Tom was very good at snap — and snappish — instant comparisons. Once, around 1970, I was involved in taking him to speak at York University, then a brand-new campus of large concrete buildings rising out of a bare landscape north of Toronto. He gazed around from the cab and said, thoughtfully, "It looks kind of like Brasilia!")

It was in that garage/coach house, still to be seen just off Queen's Park (at 39A Queen's Park Crescent, with the A significant), that I once visited Marshall to take him to lunch. He was pleased to see me, and he showed me around the paper-strewn space that he shared with a group of colleagues/acolytes, some of whom were enlisted as co-authors when publishers succeeded in persuading him to take on another project. Among them that day was his son Eric, and I was happy to agree to Marshall's suggestion that he should join us for lunch.

The next hour or so was extraordinary. Even as we walked to lunch, Marshall kept up a constant stream of comments on the passing scene. This man's briefcase demonstrated this, while that noisy red car revealed that, and so on, comments too fast and furious for me to quote exactly now. Inside the restaurant, I recall, he was interested in the sheer drapes, which allowed us to see out, but prevented people on the street seeing in. And he had extensive deductions to make about the lighting, the menu, the waiter's uniform, and so on. (I recalled from Tom Wolfe's article that on a visit to a strip club Marshall, in his professorial role, observed about the naked stripper: "Ah, yes, she's wearing *us*!")

What was most extraordinary to me was how his son reacted to all this. By this point Eric was almost middle-aged, well beyond the point of parental hero-worship. Yet he greeted every comment of Marshall's with vocal admiration. "Wow, that's amazing, Dad! How did you think of that?" or "What an astonishing insight! Nobody's ever put it so well before." I had never seen a son react in this way to a father, and I looked with narrowed eyes at Eric, to be sure that he wasn't being sarcastic, putting us on. But, no, he was obviously sincere. As the sincere compliments kept flowing, I found myself reacting by stepping into the usual son role, that of critic. Marshall's quick-fire comments seemed to me to be a mixture of the brilliant, the obvious, and the nonsensical, so I would try to challenge the last group, with "Wait a minute, surely . . ." objections. My comments went nowhere, submerged beneath the tide of "That's so true, Dad!"

I enjoyed our lunch, but never succeeded in publishing Marshall. Most traditional academic reviewers were lukewarm, or undecided, about McLuhan. Even Frye was deeply critical, on occasion, once writing that "McLuhan is caught up in the manic-depressive roller-coaster of the news media." The always-sensible literary scholar W.J. Keith summarized the general feeling well, writing, "Whatever the ultimate verdict, however, he remains one of those baffling but significant figures around whom circulate the dominant ideas of their age." And while Marshall was often criticized for predicting unbelievably wide-ranging changes . . . such as, to take a wildly unlikely example, the rise of the internet — we're left still wondering, *what if he was right?*

Just north of St. Michael's College, and the famous garage, lies Victoria College, the academic home of Northrop Frye from 1939 until his death in 1991. I barely knew Herman Northrop Frye (and very few people knew of the unused "Herman," a name not exactly popularized in Canada by Reichsmarschall Goering). But I knew *of* him as a major international literary figure, even if this lad from Moncton had first hit the big-time by coming second in a national *typing* competition. This brought him to Toronto in 1929, where he enrolled in Victoria College. After a brief interlude at Emmanuel College, where he became an ordained minister (delighting in his summer service at a parish on the Prairies where he once overheard local church women denouncing a recent rain as "not necessary"), and then a spell at Merton College, Oxford, he returned to Victoria, and spent the rest of his distinguished academic life there, without the benefit of any (now obligatory) PhD.

Northrop Frye (1912–1991)

Christina McCall summarizes Northrop Frye's fame perfectly in her posthumous memoir, *My Life as a Dame* (2008).

When I encountered him first, Frye was in his early forties, just settling in as chairman of Vic's English department, already acclaimed for *Fearful Symmetry*, his study of William Blake, writing his famous book, *Anatomy of Criticism*, attracting invitations to lecture at Princeton and Harvard and to publish in important learned journals in the U.S. and the U.K., early indications of his brilliant international reputation as a literary theorist that was to grow more luminous as he aged. At Victoria even then, his fame was harped on by older students so insistently that my cohort grew impatient with the hyperbole.

As Christina's publisher I got to know her well in full, glorious flight as the author of *Grits* (1982), and the co-author with Stephen

Clarkson of the two-volume classic, *Trudeau and Our Times* (1990, 1994). She was already an ambitious student when she attended her first Frye lecture. "He came into a classroom one September afternoon, wearing an academic gown that was rusty with age, stood behind the lecturer's podium, looked at us through his rimless glasses, and began to talk about John Milton in a voice devoid of passion. By the time he had finished speaking fifty minutes later, almost everyone in the room was in the grip of an intellectual excitement of a kind we had never known, and that night I wrote in a Commonplace Book I was pretentiously keeping, 'I think my head is coming off.'"

Foolishly, I never took the opportunity to see Frye lecture. I didn't even stop to reflect how amazing it was that this world-famous scholar continued to teach *undergraduate* classes; this despite the fact that his shyness with young students meant that, in Margaret Atwood's words, when he met you on campus, he seemed "to address his remarks to your shoes."

Yet this shy, precise scholar had moments of uncharacteristic elation. Powe has pointed out the following astonishing passage from Frye's private notebooks: "The Twentieth Century saw an amazing development of scholarship and criticism in the humanities, carried on by people who were more intelligent, better trained, had more languages, had a better sense of proportion, and were infinitely more accurate scholars and competent professional men than I. I had genius. No one else in the field known to me had quite that."

Others would agree, but in some surprise at the source.

I did once go to see him in his office. My friend Harry J. Boyle (the brave author whose 1972 book I named *The Great Canadian Novel*) was the Vice-Chair of the Canadian Radio-Television Commission, and he once spoke warmly about working with his fellow-commissioner, "Norrie" Frye. When I noted sadly that Norrie was among those Canadian authors who chose to be published by companies based elsewhere, with the books merely *distributed* in Canada, Harry encouraged me to visit his friend Norrie to make my case. At the CRTC, he said, Frye was keenly aware of the uphill fight Canadian media faced, against a system that favoured American distribution. In fact, I was pleased to find that one of his essays commented on a "Spring Thaw" sketch that ended an enthusiastic account of a new NFB film with the words: "Coming Soon to a Sunday School Basement Near You!"

In due course I visited the great man in his Victoria College office, just off Queen's Park (very near today's Northrop Frye Hall, and the statue of a life-size Frye sitting invitingly on a bench, open book on his lap). I remember that when I was ushered into his office it was quiet, very quiet. So was the bushy-haired, comfortably built man who greeted me courteously, then eyed me levelly through his rimless glasses as I made my case for his publishing in the future with a Canadian publisher, such as, oh, for example, me.

I ended with a flourish by suggesting that his current publishing arrangement was really only of benefit to the man who ran the Canadian branch plant!

"Ah yes," replied Professor Frye, politely. "I chose him because he's an old friend."

Loyalty can be very inconvenient.

My friend Cathleen Morrison was a former student of his who became much closer in 1998 when, as a widower, he married her widowed mother, Elizabeth. Frye gratefully described this marriage to an old friend as "a miracle." In a note to me Cathleen recalls:

> Their home in Toronto was just a couple of city blocks from ours, and Norrie and Elizabeth became regulars at our Sunday dinners. In winter Norrie liked a corner seat beside the fire, where he nursed a small glass of single malt Scotch.
>
> Participating in the life of our family may have been a challenge for Norrie, but he handled with indulgence the hail of small talk, much of which was focused on the children. The atmosphere was relaxed.
>
> "Uncle Norrie," asked our twelve-year-old nephew Alex of Montreal (for word had somehow spread around the children that this was how Norrie should be addressed), "Uncle Norrie, you have thirty-nine honorary degrees. How many *real* ones have you got?"

A postscript. In 2002, when I married Jane, I moved into her house in Toronto's Moore Park district. A three-minute walk away (and we walk it on many evenings, and I've just timed it) is the house that Northrop Frye lived in for many years. A tiny plaque beside the front door notes that he was there from 1945 to 1991.

Jane recalls that Frye's daily walk to the subway took him past our house. One of the world's great thinkers, perhaps fresh from a celebrated tour of Italy's great universities, on his way to his office, thinking great thoughts, and exchanging shy greetings with accountants and garbagemen and lawyers and skateboarding schoolchildren. It's a pleasing thought.

Opposite Victoria College, but set inside Queen's Park, is the marvellous black metal statue of Al Purdy, right at home among the literary tents. I knew Al well, and although I did not edit him, I was proud to publish his poetry, and his single novel, *A Splinter in the Heart*, set in the Trenton of his boyhood. He was a big, untidy man. I once described him as one of the few people who could shamble even while sitting down. The black statue, by Dam de Nogales and donated by Scott Griffin, catches this perfectly, with the characteristic hank of hair falling over Al's eyes as he leans heavily on one shirt-sleeved arm.

Like his statue, Al was a larger than life character, and I noticed that the pace of the McClelland & Stewart office seemed to pick up when he roamed the corridors. People were pleased to see this big, loud, friendly guy, who brought a whiff of Prince Edward County with him. In our office encounters he seemed to like me well enough, but what brought us closer together was an open-air reading he gave in High Park on the hottest night of the year. I was there, and went backstage to greet him. We were all bathed in sweat and he greeted me with such surprise that he clearly thought of me as just a fancy-pants downtown office guy who always wore a tie. He wouldn't have greeted me that sweltering night with more surprise and delight if I'd swum across Lake Ontario to get there. After that, we were friends.

Later, as I've recounted in *Stories About Storytellers*, he played a morose part as the straight man in Yevgeny Yevtushenko's explosive onstage performance at the Harbourfront Authors Festival. But normally he was the life and soul of any poets' party. In fact, his home-built A-frame house at Ameliasburgh was famous as the centre of many wild but inspiring get-togethers, involving poets like Margaret Atwood, Michael Ondaatje, Frank Scott, Leonard Cohen, and literally dozens of others over the years. Later, when *Beyond Remembering: The Collected Poems of Al Purdy* came out in 2000, the year of his death, both Atwood and Ondaatje wrote affectionate forewords about what he had meant to young poets like them. Ondaatje's tribute calls Al "this self-taught poet from up the road. What a brave wonder."

So important was that A-frame as a sort of inspirational club-house for generations of writers, that when, in 2012, it seemed the house would be sold and torn down, it became a national crisis. Fortunately, two heroes in British Columbia, Jean Baird the literary activist and Howard White the publisher, sprang into action and started a national campaign to save the A-frame. Because of my friendship with Al, I was glad to be invited to join a Toronto-based committee to raise the necessary funds. Led by my old M&S friend George Goodwin, our group studied how best to raise money. (I remember that before one meeting with a potential donor I went and sat beside Al's statue, for inspiration.) In the end, with the blessing of Al's widow, Eurithe, we decided to hold a big fundraising event at Toronto's Koerner Hall, on February 6, 2013.

I learned that when you stage a one-off concert you take your financial life in your hands. Although all of the poets and musicians and personalities like Michael Enright and Gordon Pinsent were contributing their time free, we still had to sell around 400 tickets *to break even*. Two days before the event we still had not reached that mark. This was despite the fact that we had personally stuck posters all over downtown. (I'm especially proud that the renovating architect Duncan Patterson and I succeeded in putting up a poster — erecting one, you might say — at the Condom Shack on Queen Street.)

With my friend Michael Enright's help (I saw the internal CBC memo, where he assured his colleagues that I was "a good yak" — a technical term, no doubt) I got on *Metro Morning*, the local CBC radio show, to talk about the glories of the next evening's event.

And it worked — either that or the Condom Shack's clients decided to postpone their amorous activity on that one evening to go to Koerner Hall. When the lights went down we had 700 people in the audience, looking at a backdrop of the A-frame and listening as Al's recorded voice began to read "The Country North of Belleville," reciting the roll-call of great, forgotten, back-country pioneer names. Then Gordon Pinsent slipped quietly onstage and seamlessly took over the reading of the next verse. It was breathtaking.

The evening, which included a memorable Enright-Atwood interview about the Purdy good old days, was just as fine as we had hoped. At the end, as all of the performers took their bow in a hurricane of grateful applause, I stood at the very end of the long line of poets and musicians with my hand on Gordon Pinsent's shoulder. He agreed that the audience seemed to like us.

And we made money, lots of money, although the campaign to turn the A-frame into a retreat for working poets continues, and a visit in fall 2013 confirmed that necessary renovations require more money. But that night Al would have been pleased — gruffly pleased. And in May 2014, I was glad to take part in a similar Ottawa fundraiser, where Bruce Cockburn (very shy and kind when I visited him backstage) attracted the crowd to the theatre at the National Library. I had the honour of reading Al Purdy's poetry. Once again "The Country North of Belleville" did its inspiring work on the audience, and had friends saying to me, "I didn't know you could do that!" Neither did I. But it was Al's magic that had entranced them.

Just north of Queen's Park lies that solid, ancient establishment, the Royal Ontario Museum. And since this book is about storytelling, I must tell you now that the ROM has officially recognized me as a "storyteller." Here is what happened.

Early in 2012 I was contacted out of the blue by a nice official at the ROM. She understood that I was a storyteller, yes? "Well," I mumbled, "my book is called *Stories About Storytellers*, and in my stage show I tell lots of stories, so I guess I am a storyteller."

"And you come from Scotland?" she went on.

"Yes," I replied, wondering where this was going.

"All right," she said, very pleased. "Then you're a Scottish storyteller!"

The logic seemed inescapable. She went on to ask if I could come to their Celtic Weekend in March as a "Scottish storyteller." I said that I knew some good Scottish stories, so, yes, I could come along and tell them to a mixed audience of kids and parents. (I had been drilled by the fierce people at my publisher, ECW, that as an author with a new book to promote I *must accept every public performance invitation*.)

A few days later, she was back with a further enquiry. This was a Celtic weekend, so could I tell Irish and Welsh stories, too? A little research provided good stories, so I said yes, and we were all set for two forty-minute sessions, at 12:00 and at 2:00, with me as a "Celtic storyteller."

On the great day, high in the hallowed halls of the museum, I sat on a throne-like chair in front of a collection of movable stools occupied by a group of kids, who included my grandchildren Lindsay (seven) and Alistair (five). When I told the Irish story, about Niall of the Nine Hostages who was "The Slave Woman's Son," I prefaced it with a word or two about slaves in different cultures, and unwisely referred to the Haida totem pole in the space just outside our room. I explained that a visit to the Haida Heritage Centre in Skidegate had revealed to Jane and me that the Haida were sea-raiders who took slaves, which allowed them (like Athenians) to have a slave-supported leisure society that could create great poetry and great art, like these totem poles.

This was too much for Lindsay, who dragged her nana off to see the nearby pole, from top to bottom, then loudly returned to interrupt my tale-weaving with the words "What did I miss, Grandad?"

The Welsh tale was "The Lady from the Lake," and the Scottish one (where Alistair proudly told his neighbours, "I know this one, I know what happens") was "The Goodman of Ballengeich." This almost perfect story is about a disguised king passing secretly among his people (doing mediaeval public opinion surveys in a very informal way), and being rescued from sword-wielding robbers by a brave young farmhand armed only with a flail.

Just before the second show, Jane and I were roaming around the main floor of the ROM, where an all-woman Celtic band was playing fine traditional music. When they paused to ask for a song from anyone in the audience, Jane called out to ask them if they knew the old Irish song "The Wild Rover." When they said yes, and invited her to start singing, she demurred, saying, "Not me, him!" and thrust me forward.

So it came about that the busy main floor of the museum resounded to three verses of me singing "The Wild Rover" while the audience joined loudly in the chorus "And it's no, nay, never (CLAP, CLAP, CLAP, CLAP). No, nay never no more . . ." Etcetera.

And then as I took my bow, still blushing in disbelief, the PA system cut in to announce, "The Celtic Storytelling Session is just about to begin on the fourth floor," and I had to rush off. Believe it or not, some of the audience actually followed me upstairs for my second storytelling session.

So clearly my résumé has to be updated, to include the sacred title "Celtic Storyteller." I think we'll leave out the entry about Irish drinking songs.

To most people in Ontario, Queen's Park stands for the government of the province, based in the massive legislative buildings in the centre of the park, aka "The Pink Palace." The politics that went on there almost put an end to my career in publishing.

In 1974, when I arrived at Macmillan of Canada as the new, young editorial director of the trade division (the people who produced books aimed at bookstores, rather than textbooks), I was horrified to find that almost no new books were under contract. So I moved fast to find new books, and was delighted to discover that Jonathan Manthorpe, the *Globe and Mail*'s man covering provincial politics, was just completing a book called *The Power and the Tories*, about the Tory dynasty in Ontario from "1943 to the Present."

It was a thoughtful, well-written book, but it was also full of wonderful, irreverent fun, and I tried to catch the irreverence by per-suading the legendary cartoonist Duncan Macpherson to produce a cover showing Tory premiers handing down the crown till at the end of the chain William Davis was handing down a blindfold that went over the eyes of John Q. Public. That superb cartoon hangs in our house, and I see it, with pleasure, every day.

Manthorpe's writing was equally entertaining. Of a hard-fought leadership convention he notes: "It may shock the idealistic reader to learn that not all votes were won by the exercise of sweet reason." On another occasion he talks about the way that William M. Kelly, the Tory Party's bagman, operated. When people who did business with the government had an audience with Mr. Kelly to discuss possible contributions to the party "they were astounded to find that Kelly's idea of what was generous exceeded their own by many thousands of dollars."

As for political portraits, in those Castro-Guevara days Manthorpe described the young NDP leader Stephen Lewis as unfortunately coming across on television as "an arrogant ruthless fanatic who would have the whole province cutting sugar cane given half a chance."

It was all lively stuff, but never better than when he explored why an incoming member of the Davis team was having trouble removing a "deadbeat" who was a hold-over from the previous Robarts regime, whose very senior position "appeared to bear no relationship to his rather limited abilities." The Davis new broom discovered that the man had protectors in high places. "More digging revealed that a small group of very senior people were very concerned that the man should be handled with all delicacy and deference. They feared him and what he could do to them because, to put it plainly, he had been procuring women for them."

The man is kept carefully anonymous throughout, and Manthorpe concludes with the words, "Lovers of fairy stories will be glad to know that everything was eventually resolved neatly and happily. The man was persuaded to accept a well-paying and prestigious post on the fringes of government in a city a long way from Toronto, and many people breathed a lot more easily."

The book was an instant success, and was flying off the shelves when we were hit by a lawsuit. A man, in a city a long way from Toronto, came forward and said, *That's me, and it's not true, and I'm suing you! Stop publishing this damaging book!*

Crisis! An emergency meeting of the Macmillan board was held, with me in the hot seat. Gladys Neale (the all-powerful head of the company's chief money-maker, the School Textbook Division) leaned forward and put in the question that would have ended my career at Macmillan. "Why was this book not checked by our lawyers?"

The company lawyer, Jim Mathews, spoke up: "It was. I checked it and approved it. We didn't foresee the possibility of this man stepping forward to incriminate himself."

I lived to publish again. But the board meeting had a discreditable ending. The market was loudly demanding a second printing of this bestseller, and in response we came up with a miserable compromise. We reprinted the book, but left the offending three paragraphs blank. Three blanked-out paragraphs, in the middle of the book, dammit!

In retrospect, since the lawsuit went nowhere, we fell for a scare campaign cooked up by Tory operatives who didn't like the light that this book was shining on dark places inside the party. They were determined to find some way to take the wind out of the book's sales, and they found a way that worked.

The outside northwest corner of the legislative buildings at Queen's Park contains a discreet stone staircase, flanked by six elaborately carved pillars, each one different in style, like an architectural textbook illustration. It leads to the chambers of the Queen's official representative in Ontario, the Lieutenant Governor. When my author, Jim Bartleman (a former career civil servant in the Foreign Affairs Department) became the Right Honourable James Bartleman, the new Lieutenant Governor, it meant that I entered an interesting new phase of being involved in a number of behind-the-scenes events.

A word of tribute here. Jim Bartleman was a hard-working author, whose books *On Six Continents: A Life in Canada's Foreign Service 1966–2002* (2004) and *Rollercoaster: My Hectic Years as Jean Chrétien's Diplomatic Advisor, 1994–1998* (2005) revealed his fascinating career as a diplomat. I remember with pleasure that in the first book he tells of the time when as Canada's Ambassador to South Africa he and Marie-Jeanne, his wife, visited the San people, a tribe of bushmen living near the Namibian border. They were having a fine visit, chatting and drinking coffee, when "the scene changed dramatically at the sound of an approaching bus. Our hosts hurriedly set aside their cups and stripped off all their clothes. 'We look more authentic this way,' one explained. . . . Sixty earnest German tourists were soon the unwitting participants in a very profitable charade . . ."

I was even prouder to publish *Raisin Wine: A Boyhood in a Different Muskoka* (2007), which gave details of growing up as an aboriginal kid, or, to use the language of the time, "a halfbreed." His father, a labourer with a Scottish background, brewed homemade raisin wine in "dry" Port Carling, to help finance the household run by Jim's Chippewa mother. Things were tough, but the local library inspired Jim's love of books. With the magnificent help of a cottage-owning American who told Jim, the local boy who worked around the property, "You get into a University, and I'll pay for it," this led, in time, to a university degree from Western, and a truly remarkable career.

During his term in the Lieutenant Governor's office I watched with admiration as he used its prestige to advance the cause of aboriginal Canadians, especially young ones (and his campaign to collect books and fly them in to remote reserves in the north is legendary, with eighty-two summer camps for reading now established in communities around Ontario). But he also bravely chose to speak about another cause dear to his heart: mental illness. The mountain he had to climb with that last taboo subject was made clear to me when I was invited to attend a meeting of the downtown Rotary Club. From the podium Jim was speaking very seriously about how prevalent mental illness is in our society, speculating that in a crowd this size there would be roughly fifteen people fighting mental illness.

"Where are you? Show yourselves! Ha, ha, ha," shouted a leather-lunged joker in the crowd.

Jim paused, obviously considered using the idiotic intervention as a teachable moment, an example of what he was up against, then graciously chose to ignore the loud-voiced moron. I assume, and hope, that the shouter got a tongue-lashing afterwards from his fellow-Rotarians, whom he had just disgraced.

That day I had arrived late at the National Club, where this event was held. In a miracle of split-second bad timing, just as I was trying to squeeze through the receiving line of Rotary officials, Jim Bartleman came up the stairway opposite and, seeing a familiar face, greeted me enthusiastically. "Doug! I didn't know you were a Rotarian," he cried, shaking my hand, while the dark-suited line of *real* Rotarians edged away from me resentfully. I managed to extricate myself in order to buy my lunch ticket.

When I emerged, with the instructions *The table at the front, on the left* ringing in my ears, I reached the entrance to the large, formal dining room, where everyone was seated. I was not to know that in another miracle of bad timing the chairman had just said, "So here he is, the Lieutenant Governor of Ontario, the Right Honourable *James Bartleman!*" There was a mix-up, causing a delay after the announcement, so Jim was not ready to enter. But I, arriving too late to hear the introduction, definitely was ready to go, and in I went.

I was surprised by the burst of applause as I strode in to the crowded room — *The table at the front, on the left* — and even more surprised when the applause turned to laughter. So I marched down the aisle, waving both arms above my head, in self-parody, until the real Lieutenant Governor arrived, to real applause. It was a *Zelig* moment, and Woody Allen would have enjoyed it.

And I did enjoy attending some fine events at Queen's Park, as Jim Bartleman's guest in the Lieutenant Governor's chambers, including the time that Princess Anne and I commiserated about the fortunes of the Scottish national rugby team. "Another 'building year,' I'm afraid," she said, gloomily.

The centre of power in Toronto is the corner of King and Bay. Flanked on all sides by giant bank towers, there is a shortage of sky. This is the hub of Canada's financial world, and countless corporate movers and shakers have offices clustered around it. So when, as a shameless publisher, I wanted to catch the attention of Corporate Canada, I staged a piece of street theatre right at that corner.

We had just rushed out a book called *The Bre-X Fraud* in August 1997 (by Douglas Goold and Andrew Willis of the *Globe and Mail*) and we wanted to get the financial world talking about this controversial new book on the Canadian gold-mining scam that had cost thousands of investors many millions. So I hired a young actor friend, John Gordon, as a sandwich-board man. He was well-dressed, in shiny black shoes, neatly pressed black pants, and a tie around his neck. What was missing was a shirt under the tie, or a jacket. The sandwich board above his naked torso explained that. Front and back it proclaimed I LOST MY SHIRT ON BRE-X, before announcing the new book in smaller type.

Through the warm August weather I walked from the M&S office at Dundas and University with the half-naked John, and along the way we were greeted by smiles, and nudges and nods and winks, even laughter. But as we approached the corner of King and Bay, the atmosphere changed. No more smiles. Just scowls, which seemed to say things like "Hey, this wasn't funny." "We were all fooled by Bre-X. People lost real money there!" "We're talking real money, $6 billion." "The biggest mining scam of all time, for God's sake! A penny stock that ended up at over $280, then the crash came and it all disappeared. *Not funny!*"

So John tramped around all four sides of that key corner, looking mournful, through the lunch hour, and in theory everyone went back to work talking about the new book. But clearly most of the financial crowd, the people Tom Wolfe called "the Masters of the Universe," were not amused by our prank. As John said afterwards, it was as if people came to work "with their game face on," and took everything about money very seriously. Standing nearby in my role of observer/protector, I was surprised by this humourless reaction, and was left thinking that maybe the view that the rest of Canada has about Toronto ("Hogtown," and a place that could produce a mayor like Rob Ford) as a solemn city that's all about making money — and takes itself far too seriously — is not all wrong.

Just ten minutes on foot from the power corner takes you to the part of downtown that I know best. Opposite the old Eaton Centre lies a public space lit by the dozens of flashing ads that mimic Times Square, and pulsate around the clock. Just beyond there, along Dundas two blocks east of Yonge, lies Bond Street. Despite its elegant London name, Bond Street is shabby now, and runs for only three short blocks, but it was once a centre of Canadian book publishing.

I worked there from 1968 to 1980, and it is full of memories for me that may interest the literary tourist taking shelter from the flashing ad boards on Yonge Street. Just north of Dundas, under the scowl of Egerton Ryerson's statue at Bond Street's north end, you'll find 105 Bond Street. That was for many years the home of Doubleday Canada, where I got my first job as a trainee editor. The three-storey office building is not much changed (although the giant warehouse is gone) and it is easy to imagine excited authors taking a deep breath before they swung open the door and mounted the stairs to meet their publisher for the first time.

You can imagine ghosts from across the country, like Harold Horwood or Cassie Brown from Newfoundland, Thomas Raddall from Nova Scotia, David Legate from Montreal, Blair Fraser from Ottawa, Arthur Hailey from Toronto, Harry J. Boyle from Alice Munro country, R.D. (Bob) Symons from Saskatchewan, George Hardy from Edmonton, and Ernie Perrault from B.C. all stepping in off Bond Street with a quiet sense of occasion.

This was where the famous Thomas P. Kelley came with his white-gloved wife, on a mission to sell me on the merits of his book on the Donnelly murders. This mission culminated in him jumping excitedly on top of my desk (which was ankle deep in papers) as he continued his rousing sales pitch . . . until I had to help him down. Here, too, Joey Smallwood, trying to impress an audience of two (me and a pop-eyed colleague) with the merits of his autobiography, became aroused by his own oratory in a way that I will tell in my final chapter on Newfoundland; I was delighted by the larger-than-life little man as he sprang from his chair and began to pace around, giving a speech, his thumbs in his lapels. And this was where I returned with Barry Broadfoot from the memorable lunch at a cheap restaurant on Dundas Square where he had showed me tantalizing sample material for his tape recorded book that he wanted to call *Ten Lost Years*.

The success of that book led me to make a big move — at least a one-minute walk down Bond Street — to number 70, in the middle block of the three, where Macmillan of Canada had its offices. Since Macmillan has disappeared without trace from the Canadian book scene, it's important to explain how central it once was. That is achieved brilliantly by Ruth Panofsky in her 2012 book, *The Literary Legacy of the Macmillan Company of Canada: Making Books and Mapping Culture*. The London-based company expanded around the world from its 1843 beginnings, with offices in London and New York, and branch offices in India and Australia, to the extent that by the turn of the century Frederick Macmillan could be described, by Shafquat Towheed, as "almost certainly the single most influential man in the world of Anglo-American letters in the period."

In 1905, they decided to open a Canadian office. By 1910, in Ruth Panofsky's words, "business had grown sufficiently to warrant construction of Macmillan's own stately five-storey premises, with an above-ground basement, at 70 Bond Street." That grandly faced building is still there, and likely to impress the literary tourist. I worked there from 1974 until 1980, when Macmillan moved elsewhere. We left with appropriate ceremony, out of respect for the 70 years' worth of new books that were born there. A piper played a lament, and I made a farewell speech into the roar of traffic. But 70 Bond Street still stands, and is well preserved by the current occupants. I hope they are aware that those stone stairs and lime-wood panelled halls saw the passage of authors like Stephen Leacock, Mazo de la Roche, Frederick Philip Grove, Morley Callaghan, Robertson Davies, Donald Creighton, W.O. Mitchell, Hugh MacLennan, Alice Munro, and Mavis Gallant.

Archibald Belaney/Grey Owl (1888–1938)

Even Grey Owl, the Englishman who successfully posed as a Native man, and was revered by all, used to stalk softly up these steps in buckskins and moccasins. In his 1978 memoir, *Fun Tomorrow*, the former Macmillan publisher John Gray remembered his time as a young sales rep chauffeuring Grey Owl around town, one seat in the back of the car reserved for his feather war bonnet. When he was revealed after his death as Archie Belaney, from Sussex in England, John Gray was taken aback: "For a time I clung to a theory that if he wasn't an Indian he really believed he was, for I could still see the jabbing upright finger and hear the strong voice, 'I am the custodian of the ancient dignities of the Indian people.'"

The Grey Owl story is stranger than fiction. We now know that he was an English lad who became fascinated by Canada's First Nations people, and came to settle in Northern Ontario at the age of seventeen. In due course he invented an impressive background as the son of a Scot and an Apache mother. He married an Iroquois woman named Anahareo and adopted the name Grey Owl, along with the long hair and the buckskins that became his trademark. His first book was published by Macmillan in 1931, and *Men of the Last Frontier* became a huge success. Then, encouraged by his wife, the former trapper became a spokesman for conservation, as well as the needs and desires of his people. He worked out west on conservation programs in Riding Mountain National Park and Prince Albert National Park, the setting for three other books: *Pilgrims of the Wild* (1934), *The Adventures of Sajo and Her Beaver People* (1935), and *Tales of an Empty Cabin* (1936).

On the lecture circuit he was a huge success, touring Canada, the United States, and Europe as the personification of everyone's romantic dreams of "the noble Red Man." In England, at Leicester, his talk on the need for conservation had a huge effect on two young brothers in short pants in the audience, Richard and David Attenborough. In London, he was even received by the King and Queen and the little princesses at Buckingham Palace, which did his reputation no harm.

His stirring oratory as "the custodian of the ancient dignities of the Indian people of Canada" took everyone in. (Except, I must record, Morley Callaghan, who told me that when he was reverently introduced to this other Macmillan author, he "knew right away that this guy wasn't an Indian.") But with rare exceptions like Morley, everyone swooned before him, and accepted him as a spokesman for Native people. Amazingly, other Native people seemed to accept him. Here's John Gray's account of a lecture by Grey Owl at the King Edward Hotel, where the speaker had magically evaded John's guiding arm outside the Crystal Ballroom.

As I approached the doors I could see that the room was crowded and still. On the platform Grey Owl, who it seemed to me now must have entered by the roof, was just beginning. Over at one side sat an Indian whose bare copper arms and shoulders gleamed beautifully above a purple blanket draped gracefully around him. Grey Owl introduced him as his friend Little Beaver from the St. Regis reservation, and Little Beaver, standing up, unsmiling, raised his hand palm outward in the ancient and dignified greeting.

Later, John Gray puzzled over this support.

I was one of those who didn't, couldn't, believe the exposé. As for the conclusion that he was a fake, a con artist, I could only weakly disagree; what about the Indians, like Little Beaver, who gathered around him wherever he went? Out of loneliness or admiration they had hunted him out in the cities where he was lecturing and together they would have long talks about their problems, and then try to forget them in dances up and down hotel corridors to the beat of skin drums, and the terror of other guests.

Even his biographer, "Rache" Lovat Dickson, a lean Albertan who had forged an impressive career in the London publishing world and had worked with Grey Owl, found his real identity hard to believe. I knew Rache, the author of *Wilderness Man*, in his retirement years in Toronto, and he always seemed to be, metaphorically, still shaking his head in disbelief at the universal success of Archie Belaney's fraud, especially with himself.

As for Macmillan, the company stayed loyal. The front lobby, right beside the tiny elevator, continued to display a fine copper etching of the noble "red" man, and in my day we continued to sell his books by the thousands. I may even have had a hand in updating the cover copy for the paperbacks, especially as the world caught up to the good sense of his conservation message.

I remember that his wife, Anahareo, and their daughter, Dawn, once dropped in to see someone at the Macmillan building, which meant me. They were very pleased to find the plaque still on display, and I was thrilled to meet this distinguished, gentle old lady, a link with a storied past. I was amused when the movie world, always fascinated by larger-than-life heroes, persuaded pale-faced Pierce Brosnan to play Archie Belaney in the 1999 movie *Grey Owl*, directed by a somewhat older Richard Attenborough.

At the Giller Prize dinner in 2014 I asked Tom King, the thoughtful writer about aboriginal-white relations in Canada, what he made of Grey Owl's popularity. Tom noted that in Grey Owl's time white Canadians were very clearly keen to hear from the aboriginal side, but in this particular conversation "had no idea that they were just talking to themselves."

I should explain that if you're the editor or publisher of a famous publishing company based in downtown Toronto, you're likely to find the world coming to your door. Sometimes the visitors are welcome, like Anahareo, or the great western historian James H. Gray, who wanted to show his grandson around his publishing house. That went well, but when Donald Jack (the author of The Bandy Papers series of comic novels) did the same thing, in the hope of impressing *his* visiting daughter, fate intervened. When I threw open the boardroom door — "And *this* is where we make our publishing decisions" — the two visitors walked in, then recoiled, squealing. Barring the way on the sober green carpet was a moist dog turd, artistically coiled.

I explained that this was not a usual part of the editorial discussion setting (or in any way an editorial comment on any book under consideration), and the embarrassed assistant who had brought her sick dog into work soon cleaned it up. But it was life imitating art, with Donald Jack experiencing a blundering Bartholomew Bandy moment.

Sometimes total strangers (such as "Mr. Brown," alias Igor Gouzenko) managed to talk their way in to see me. I remember one woman, very smartly dressed, whose writing desk at home had been cunningly wired by CIA agents to administer electric shocks whenever she wrote a sentence that criticized their country. I remember, too (and the common theme of administering jolts had never occurred to me until now) an enthusiastic middle-aged man with a Dutch accent who promised to write a book for me about his recent discovery of a surefire way for a man to bring his female sex partners to ecstatic heights *"Every time! Every single time!"*

Unfortunately shyness — or possibly fear that I would steal his successful formula, and become rich, and very, very popular — prevented him from revealing his secret, at least until I had given him a lot of money to put it on paper. I regret that his formula remains secret to this day, making the world a less exciting place.

Stories from the distant past cluster around that building. When Mazo de la Roche was a young writer, her worldwide success with *Jalna* (1927) far in the future, she was thrilled to receive an invitation to visit Hugh Eayrs, then the publisher at Macmillan, at 70 Bond Street. She was so flustered and excited that she failed to dress with her usual care. When the great man ushered her into his office and offered to take her coat she remembered that she was still wearing a ratty old sweater to protect her good dress. So she politely declined his offer, saying that, no, thank you, she preferred to keep her coat on. As their conversation continued, she became uncomfortably hot. When Hugh Eayrs slipped out of the office to get a book for her, she tore off the coat, then the sweater, rushed to the window overlooking Bond Street, opened it wide, and tossed the sweater out. She had just regained her chair when Eayrs returned, saying, "What a pretty dress."

When the time came for her to leave the building, going down the steps, she furtively looked around for her sweater. It had gone. Bond Street, you see, has always been on the edge of a seedy part of town.

A number of prime ministers, current and former, strode up those Bond Street steps. I remember John Diefenbaker visiting the office in 1974 to launch the first volume of his autobiography. When we shook hands he didn't mention that he remembered me as the youth who had sat down so crushingly on his wife's fragile straw hat.

Once, before my time, the building was visited by a British prime minister and the owner of the company, Harold Macmillan. I'm told that in honour of his impending visit the operator of the tiny elevator was presented with a smart new blazer instead of his usual greasy sweater. The elevator guy's hard life involved slow horses and medium-paced women, and when Macmillan arrived the fancy blazer was gone, never to return. When the lordly visitor from London departed in his limo, the over-awed staff lined the windows overlooking the street, confident that their time in the spotlight was over. Yet with a politician's instinct, he turned for a last wave, and they all ducked beneath the windows, slowly popping back up again like shy, embarrassed gophers. What this meant for relations between Britain and Canada is not recorded.

The most unfortunate case, as I've told elsewhere, was that of

Canada's prime minister Mackenzie King. As he left the building he announced that he wanted to go next door, to pay his respects to the former home of his ancestor, William Lyon Mackenzie. (The house is still there, in fine condition as a museum, well worth a visit.) The bachelor prime minister was not aware, as his appalled companions were, that the house had fallen on hard times and was now occupied by, ahem, ladies of easy virtue. As the prime minister stood reverently on the sidewalk outside his ancestor's house, one of the ladies, eager to coax him out of this shy hesitation, opened the window and invited him in, with very explicit promises. The prime minister's group departed at high speed.

Mackenzie King was not a notable ladies' man. William Toye learned that his author, Norah Story, had accompanied the prime minister on a number of formal dates in Ottawa. How romantic was he, the mischievous Toye asked? Not very. The most romantic thing he ever said to her was that she "had eyes like Mussolini."

Just down Bond Street, on the east side, stands St. Michael's Cathedral, a replica of Salisbury Cathedral, but with no cows grazing around it. That was the setting for one of Canada's greatest literary funerals, when the formal High Mass for Morley Callaghan ended with an uplifting outbreak of Dixieland jazz. "Just a Closer Walk With Thee" and "St. James Infirmary Blues" pealed out from a band concealed above the cathedral doors as we all moved through them out to Bond Street.

Yonge Street just north of Dundas has a distinctly raunchy side to it, especially just north of where Sam the Record Man hung his historic sign. After a late evening at the office I was once passing one of the strip clubs there (perhaps Zanzibar Club) when a friendly female voice called out "Hey, Doug!" It came from a good-looking young woman, lightly dressed in what looked like a dressing gown, who was enjoying a smoke in the warm summer air just outside the club. She seemed familiar and, yes, it was "Denise!" I knew her as a nice girl who had worked in the Doubleday warehouse. She told me that, you know, working as a stripper here paid much better than the job in publishing, and I really should come in and see the show. When I pleaded that I had to get home to my wife, she told me that I should bring her along to the show, too, for a night out sometime. We never got around to it, and I'm sorry about that. I'm also sorry that I lost touch with "Denise," who was both bright and good-looking, and shy in a way that was the opposite of brash and brassy. I hope that life has treated her well.

Opposite the strip club section lies Elm Street, which houses the ancient white Barberian's Steak House. There, in the Cold War 1960s, the legendary *Toronto Star* cartoonist Duncan Macpherson found the Russian ambassador dining with his bodyguards. Their table was laden with baked potatoes and heavy steaks and capitalist, rich, red wine. Duncan, a great enthusiast when he had a few drinks under his belt, insisted happily ("No, just sit where you are!") on showing his friend the ambassador his new party trick, where he took hold of the white table cloth, like this, and with a sudden pull whisked it right out from beneath all the . . . It did not go well, and Duncan had to make a hasty retreat, before the bodyguards' guns appeared.

Across the street stands the Arts and Letters Club, a fine old dark red-brick building from pre-war Toronto . . . as in pre-1914. The club still actively honours its artistic and literary legacy, but its heyday was a century ago when it was the Toronto hangout for Tom Thomson and the artists of the Group of Seven, as recorded by historic club photographs.

On the main floor, past the comfortable Members' Bar, there is a grand, dark, wood-panelled room, a sort of mediaeval banquet hall (decorated with whimsical coats of arms for original members), with a stage at the end. This hall is the venue for club lunches and dinners, and occasional theatrical performances. And this was where my own stage show was born in the spring of 2011, under the encouraging direction of Mike Spence. Indeed, this was where I gave the very first public performance, before an audience. That audience was politely encouraging, although I learned the useful lesson that an intermission will always take its toll on attendance. But it was a very good place to start a long journey.

In mid-winter it is foolhardy for a Canadian author to plan to do much travelling, so after 2011, I devoted myself in those snowy months to visiting local venues, such as churches, libraries, or clubs. They all were interesting places to visit, like the ancient National Club on Bay Street (not far from the corner of King and Bay, and across the street from the best downtown bookstore, Ben McNally Books,where I launched my book); or the Heliconian Club, a historic club for women interested in the arts that's based in a fine old wooden building (the former Olivet Baptist Church) in Yorkville; or the Women's Art Association, also based in a fine old wooden building, of clapboard as if from the South End of Halifax, but just west of Yorkville.

I also "played" the Badminton and Racquet Club, and the Cricket, Skating and Curling Club. Fortunately, no cricket was in progress, so I had no nightmarish memories of the cricketing disaster in Scotland when my swift, athletic throw in the field, a thing of balletic beauty, felled the knee-capped umpire and set the Perth crowd threatening a field invasion. "UMPIRE HURT AT NORTH INCH" was the local paper's headline, and it was a good reason for me to escape to Canada.

The most hip location was the Green Door nightclub, way west on Ossington, where cool new restaurants now sit alongside cigar factories and auto repair shops. My friend (and for a time my theatre agent, as he was for *the* Stuart McLean) Bob Missen arranged a Sunday afternoon show at the Green Door, where I perched on a bar stool to give my show to forty-five brave, paying customers.

But I remember most vividly my visit to the York Club. That is, the York Club of Eric Arthur, Frank Lloyd Wright, and Robertson Davies. It's the mysterious red Romanesque building — all arched windows and carved sandstone and turrets beneath rich shingles — set grandly back on its own grounds from the corner of Bloor Street and St. George, beside the subway station. In his classic 1964 book, *Toronto: No Mean City*, Eric Arthur, the famous professor of architecture, wrote about the astonishing interior of the club, which had originally been a private mansion belonging to the Gooderham family, and was full of magnificent woodcarving details: "Standing in the hall or reading room, one does not feel the presence of the original owner and his family so much as those humble craftsmen who wrought with such skill and apparent delight the woodwork in mantels, stairs and trim in a variety of woods," which, he recalled, the visiting Frank Lloyd Wright especially admired.

Because the club lies close to Massey College, Robertson Davies was a regular visiting member. (One friend, Mark McLean, tells of finding him reading *Vogue* magazine there; when challenged about this he noted simply that it had "by far the best horoscopes.") When the omens were good, he used to take me to lunch there. We would begin with a drink in one of the turret rooms and then proceed (perhaps the word is "process") through the ancient panelled hallways to the dining room. That dining room is the setting for a scene in R.D.'s final novel, *The Cunning Man* (1994):

> Thus it was that we three got together at my club, the York Club, a famous refuge of the beleaguered well-to-do, and dined in the handsome dark chamber where a few others were eating and engaging in muted conversations. I had feared that talk might be difficult, but it flowed freely. . . .

A little too freely, in fact, as secrets begin to emerge from the two men who are dining with the woman whose affections they have shared. Voices are raised, until the ultimate York Club offence becomes a danger.

> "The people at other tables are beginning to glance this way," said Brocky. "Pipe down, Nuala, this isn't your club and you may get Jon a bad name here. Rowdy guests."

The guests were not rowdy the night that I performed my show after dinner at the York Club, and I was pleased to be introduced to the assembled "beleaguered well-to-do" by my lawyer, Aaron Milrad, and to see that my old friend Betty Kennedy had brought along a table of friends. Betty wrote two books for me, including an account of Hurricane Hazel, the 1952 storm that reshaped so much of Toronto's landscape. Betty, always gracious, remains a good friend. Her outdoor swims in her Campbellville pool go on later than seems shiver-free, but for a veteran of *Front Page Challenge*, perhaps "First Frost Challenge" is nothing.

Just south of the York Club, hidden away in an alley, lies the legendary Coach House Press. Under Stan Bevington — bright-eyed, and fiercely bearded like a circuit-riding Methodist preacher six generations ago — it occupied an honoured place in the small press world, which was far from my own Big Bond Street Publisher experience. Michael Ondaatje came out of — and is still very loyal to — that world, and he retains links with his friends at Coach House. He was also a filmmaker (one of his films was *The Clinton Show* about, yes, Alice Munro's town). And after great success with a number of prize-winning poetry collections he became a novelist, with *Coming Through Slaughter* in 1976. But he really hit his stride in 1987 with *In the Skin of a Lion*.

At this point, our paths crossed, since I became his publisher at M&S. But I can claim absolutely no credit for the success of his poetry collections, or for the novels that were published in my time, like *The English Patient* (1992) and *Anil's Ghost* (2000). They, like *Divisadero* (2007), were all edited and well looked after by my esteemed colleague Ellen Seligman. Michael and I have always remained on good terms but have never been especially close, although I remember how he laughed at my story of the novelist who tried to sell his book to me at Hugh MacLennan's funeral. His eye-rolling laughter seemed tinged, however, by sad familiarity with the desperation authors sometimes display encountering someone who might help them to get published, such as a publisher, or a famous novelist.

As his novels became worldwide successes, it was fun for me to be along for the ride, printing and reprinting many copies. But I admired the fact that he managed to keep Hollywood-style fame at arm's-length, even when the film of *The English Patient* won the Oscar for the Best Picture. That would have tempted all too many authors into a Monte Carlo life of parties and paparazzi. Instead, Michael has stayed resolutely low-key. He devotes his time, outside writing, to supporting a few good causes, like the Griffin Prize, and to occasional books that pay tribute to favourite authors, like Mavis Gallant. For M&S he selected his favourite Gallant stories for a book called *Paris Stories* (2002), and said admiringly of her work: "Gallant's subject is the comic opera of character . . . Before we know it she will have circled a person, captured a voice, revealed a whole manner of life in the way a character avoids an issue or discusses a dress."

He works hard at his writing. When he was creating *Divisadero*, with some scenes set among professional gamblers, he consulted David Ben the magician to give him "hands-on" demonstrations of how card sharps cheat. David tells me that he found him "very respectful, and a pleasure to deal with, even when I was telling him that gamblers wouldn't talk that way." And admirers of his wife, Linda Spalding's prizewinning fiction (and Michael, of course, has won every award going, including the Booker, the Giller, and several Governor General's awards) respect both of them for managing to create fiction in the same house, at the same time.

As an Ondaatje admirer, I have a humble suggestion. I think we can get more out of his books if we learn to read him in a special way. All authors write with their eyes: we see what their characters see. Fewer authors can also write with their ears; we hear what goes on around their characters, and how they sound. Even fewer write with their nose, so that smells, good or bad, seem to arise from the book. Almost none write with their bodies, letting us sense what their characters are feeling and touching, and what, literally, they may be rubbing up against.

Michael Ondaatje, I'd suggest, is our great writer of the senses. Sports writers sometimes tell us that a player, on a given day, was "playing out of his skin." I find that Michael, always, every day, is "writing out of his skin."

Think about it. How often do we find the word "feel" or "feeling" in his work? How often do the bodies of his characters notice the warm stone, or touch the rough brick, or feel the rain in their hair, or wrap this piece of clothing around them? All of this — although far removed from love play, which he can describe very ably — is "sensual" writing. Sometimes the sensual writing hits our own bodies hard, as when in *Coming Through Slaughter* Buddy Bolden slices off a male nipple with a straight razor, and you jump as you read it. How, literally, chilling is the early scene in *In the Skin of a Lion* where Patrick has to work in the cold river, trying to get a rope under a drowning cow. By contrast, in *Divisadero*, how comforting is the feel of the father's checkered shirt as his daughter lies against him on the couch? And in *The Cat's Table*, how often does the feel of the wind, or the movement of the ship, affect the passengers' bodies, and how they feel?

His use of smell is so strong that in *The Cinnamon Peeler* he has the title character become, in effect, a smell. And even contemplating the title *There's a Trick With a Knife I'm Learning to Do* is bound to set many readers thinking of hands, and cuts, and blood, and pain. But usually his strength lies in his ability to engage *all* of our senses. That

Margaret Atwood (1939–)

being so, it's amazing that the central character in *The English Patient* is a man so badly burned that he is almost beyond having any sense of touch, as we understand it. But of course he remembers, with his wounded lover in the cave in the desert: "I leaned forward and put my tongue against the right blue eye, a taste of salt. Pollen. I carried that taste to her mouth." And in *Anil's Ghost*, Michael handicaps himself by introducing so many bodies that have died so horribly that the reader's senses almost shut down. But it is always worth reading onward. Reading with our bodies.

I associate the University-and-Annex part of Toronto with Margaret Atwood. Now *there's* a famous figure to consider, and reconsider. Not only has Margaret Atwood written many books, but she has also had many books written about her. There will be many more. Her roles are so wide-ranging — poet, novelist, short story writer, anthologist, opera creator, critic, economist, librettist, political organizer, nature lover, defiant computer geek, inventor, and much more — that she is almost impossible to classify. But it is fair to say that for many people, in many languages, Toronto's (and Canada's) most important artist is our own Lady Oracle, Margaret Atwood.

I know her fairly well. I have never edited her, but have enjoyed publishing her. Over the years I have acquired a number of stories about her. If your distant view is of a politically correct, very clever woman with a cool, level stare that is intimidating, and with an even, deliberate speaking style that is intimidating, and with frizzy hair that becomes fashionable every ten years or so and is itself intimidating, some of these stories may surprise you.

The first story is from her youth, in what she describes as "my first moment of truly public embarrassment." When she was growing up in Leaside (a few years before another typical Leaside kid named Stephen Harper), the woman next door, for whom she babysat, was the producer of a CBC TV show called *Pet Corner*. Margaret, then aged fourteen, was asked to bring along her pet, a praying mantis named Lenore, and talk about her. (I pause for a *New Yorker* praying mantis cartoon, wherein the female says to the male, "Before I make love to you, then kill you and eat you, can you help me with this shelf?" There will be no more praying mantis jokes, I promise.)

Margaret's account of what happened next is to be found in *That Reminds Me*, a book of author horror stories:

> Lenore was such a hit that *Pet Corner* decided to have me back. This time I was to be merely an adjunct. A woman was coming onto the show with a tame flying squirrel. I was to be the person the flying squirrel flew to, a sort of human tree.
>
> All went as scheduled up to the time of the flight. Flying squirrels were explained, this one was produced (close shot), then raised on high, aimed and fired. But flying squirrels are nocturnal, and it was annoyed by the bright television lights. When it landed on me, it immediately went down my front.
>
> At my school we wore uniforms: black stockings, bloomers, white blouses and a short tunic with a belt and a large square neckline. It was this neckline that the squirrel utilized; it then began scrabbling around beneath, and could be seen as a travelling bulge moving around my waist-line above the belt. (Close shot.) But it was looking for something even more secluded. I thought of the bloomers, and swiftly reached down the front of my own neckline. Then I thought better of it, and began to lift the skirt. Then I thought better of that, as well. Paralysis. Nervous giggling. At last the owner of the flying squirrel fished the thing out via the back of my jumper.

After that, minor author interview problems like having a sudden nosebleed or falling off the podium (two real examples from her life) seemed like kid's stuff to Margaret.

I admire the fact that Margaret rolls up her sleeves to get things done. When the Writers' Union of Canada was just a gleam in a few authors' eyes, she and Graeme Gibson (no relation) were heavily involved in setting it up. She and Graeme were living together on a farm north of Toronto, which allowed William French, the *Globe*'s book man, to describe them as "co-agriculturalists" (a term that has never been employed since, to my knowledge). Here, from Val Ross's book *Robertson Davies: A Portrait in Mosaic*, is the perceptive piece that Margaret wrote about approaching the magisterial figure of Robertson Davies in 1974, when he was being recognized around the world as a major literary figure:

In the early 1970s, I'm with Graeme and I'm in my early thirties. Davies is in his early sixties. We were forming the Writers' Union of Canada, and Graeme and I went to his office at Massey. He was sitting in his Masterly chair, and he was backlit. The light was shining through his beard. And you could see the face underneath. It was a very different face from the bearded presence. The face under the beard was sensitive, vulnerable, anxious, not the magisterial presence, the magician who says "I command you" — none of that.

Graeme and I said our *blah-blah-blah* Writers' Union speech, and when we'd finished, without missing a beat, Davies replied, "I'll join." Right away! He knew the situation of writers in Canada. He knew how we were treated.

I remember a fundraiser for writers at the St. Lawrence Centre on Front Street when Margaret and R.D. presented a surprising double act. Margaret produced an ear-splitting Annie (Get Your Gun) Oakley version of "Anything You Can Write, I Can Write Better," with R.D. gamely playing along ("No, you can't." "Yes, I can.") Film may even exist.

When I was in Orkney, north of the Scottish mainland, helping out as part of an Adventure Canada cruise that also featured Margaret, I was stopped on the street in Kirkwall by an excited stranger who blurted, "My wife thinks she has just seen Margaret Atwood!" I confirmed the sighting. The Scottish couple were thrilled. Margaret went on calmly about her business.

A few short weeks later, I was able to tell this story to a Toronto crowd that was rallying in support of Toronto's beleaguered librarians. They were under assault from the Don't-Waste-Taxpayers'-Money-On-Stuff-Like-Books Ford brothers (called "The Twin Ford Mayors" by Margaret), and she had sprung to the defence of our libraries, like the writer engagé she is. Her unwelcome entry into the fray had produced the belittling boast from Doug Ford that he wouldn't recognize Margaret Atwood if he saw her on the street. My story contrasted his proud ignorance (a worrying Ford family trait) with the recognition she sparked among strangers on a street on a remote Scottish island. Intelligent strangers.

Another scene shows another Margaret. She and Graeme live in an old house in the middle of Toronto's Annex, just north of the university and the York Club. It's an area of winding streets, and full of the large red-brick Romanesque Victorian houses that form Toronto's most interesting architectural heritage. Jane and I were invited there to a Boxing Day Party, and we brought along Jane's mother, Louise, then in her late eighties. Inside, near the front door, Louise sat on a chair amid the clutter of snow boots that mark any Toronto winter party. She had never met Margaret before that afternoon, but Margaret kneeled on the floor to help her put on her indoor shoes. It was all done very naturally and easily and without a hint of intimidation, which is why I tell the story.

One last story, about Larry Gaynor, to whom Margaret's 2013 novel, *MaddAddam*, is dedicated. Larry was in every sense a larger than life character, and also a friend of mine. His life intertwined with Michael Enright's long before Michael became the voice of CBC Radio's *The Sunday Edition*. They were young and foolish together, and had to leave Canada after the fire-breathing trick in Guelph went wrong onstage. In England they kept a bear in their London flat, because, well, Larry was working for a circus. I won't tell the story here because it will certainly appear in Michael's eagerly awaited autobiography. I've seen enough of it to know that will be a wonderful book.

But I can tell the story that I produced at Larry's wake, organized by his friend Michael in 2010. Larry was staying in Edinburgh with his old pals Graeme and Margaret in the flat that Graeme was given as the University's Writer in Residence. I was also visiting Scotland's capital city, and had been invited to join them there.

Now it's important for you to know that Larry was a gigantic man, with a chest like a barrel and a voice to match, trained on Canadian military parade grounds. His friendship with Graeme and Margaret had seen him through many careers, which were rumoured to include a time spent as a bouncer in a Soho night club, and even a spell as a gun-runner. Certainly, over the course of his life he did time as a CBC script-writer, as a novelist whose book almost made it into print, and as a travelling circus man — "a carnie" — in both Britain and Canada. He once took my pop-eyed four-year-old daughter Katie behind the travelling carnival scenes, throwing open a tractor trailer stuffed to the roof with pink and purple plush toys, saying, "Pick any prize you want, kid." I remember that during the carnie years the police found that one of his employees was, in Larry's words, "selling smack out of The Birthday Game." Larry was delighted, when he appeared in court to defend his shiftless assistant, to be able to describe him — with a straight face — as "a victim of society."

In the Toronto media world, the stories flew about him. "Were you there when Larry broke the desk at that magazine party?"

"Did he sit on it?"

"No, he got mad, and picked it up *and smashed it over his knee!*"

This was the man who was staying at the flat in Edinburgh, sometimes taking Graeme and Margaret's daughter, Jess, to her little play group, to the surprise of the other intrigued "mummies." On the evening in question, however, Graeme and Margaret were going out for dinner, so when my brother Peter arrived to take me out to dinner, rather than leave Larry sitting there, we did the polite thing and invited him to join us. As the three of us walked towards the restaurant, I was trying to find a way to warn my brother that Larry was gelignite, likely to explode unexpectedly at any moment. But he was chatting politely as we walked along, and Peter went unwarned.

As luck would have it, Peter had booked dinner at Hendersons vegetarian restaurant, surely the most quietly respectable restaurant in the most quietly respectable city in the world, where people spoon their yoghurt with their pinkies raised. As we stood there in the entrance, waiting to be seated, Larry took in the air of whispery gentility. Without any warning, he threw his massive head back and bellowed, "I used to be only five foot tall and weighed only seven stone UNTIL I BECAME A VEGETARIAN!"

There was a stunned silence . . . and then people began to laugh. Peter and I reeled about, drooling and colliding with the cash desk, and the laughter grew and grew. As we were shown to our table there was no doubt where every eye, and every ear, was directed. Larry certainly gave them value for money, regaling us with circus tales that began with lines like, "Have I told you about the night the giraffe fainted?"

In Toronto, Larry fell on hard times, and eventually emphysema took hold. But he was still defiantly good, smoky company. His old friends Graeme and Margaret stood by him. Like Graeme, Margaret, although she was juggling dozens of book projects around the world that kept two full-time assistants busy, found time to visit Larry. In fact she was the last person to visit him before he died.

And then she dedicated her next book to him.

Margaret is also very generous in her treatment of other writers. The literary world is not short of malicious gossip, as we saw when Alice Munro won the Nobel Prize. Because Margaret's name had often been mentioned as a possible Nobel contender, there were some small-minded people eager to find evidence that she must resent this win by another Canadian that would, the way the world works, set back her own prospects. Anyone searching for such evidence must have been disappointed when they read the triumphant, admiring piece that Margaret wrote about her friend Alice in the *Guardian*.

There was no surprise there for me. Some of the best, most perceptive things written about Alice's work have come from other writers — and the introduction to *Alice Munro's Best* (the 2006 selection of stories) that was written by Margaret Atwood is perhaps the best appreciation of Alice's work that I have ever seen. And when Farley Mowat died, the most thoughtful and gracious short tribute to him that I saw came from Graeme and Margaret.

A remarkable woman, Margaret Atwood. It may take Canadians a long time to wake up to just what a remarkable person she is, internationally. Just after Alice Munro's Nobel award, a Canadian in London was celebrating the news with friends in the British capital. She found that she had to argue hard to convince them that Margaret Atwood was also a Canadian. She was so constantly present at the centre of British culture that they had always assumed that she was one of them. A world figure, in fact.

I began this chapter in the centre of Toronto, in Queen's Park, so it seems right to end it just north of the park, in the Gardiner Museum. In 2011, on St. Andrew's Day, I was lucky enough to be the first speaker in a lunch series hosted by the *Literary Review of Canada* and the museum. While people munched their paper-bag lunch, I whizzed through the Tony Jenkins caricatures, then asked the audience for suggestions about which authors they'd like to hear about. The requests came thick and fast, and I was able to be a polar bear gutting James Houston's husky, and so on.

At the end I signed a dozen copies or so. As I was about to leave, compliments still ringing in my ears, I was approached by an elderly member of the audience. Always eager to meet my admiring readers, I stooped graciously to accept her comments. "I notice," she said, severely, "that you frequently use 'who' when it should be 'whom.' 'Who' is the subjective, and 'whom' the objective case."

I thanked her, as objectively as I could.

CHAPTER 3

SASKATCHEWAN PIONEERS

Pioneers in the Family . . . Bookstore Tales . . . David
Carpenter, Author and Teacher . . . Saskatchewan's Adopted
Son . . . Near the Bessborough Hotel . . . Just a Regular Guy
Vanderhaeghe . . . Mordecai and Guy . . . Leaving Saskatoon
and Finding George Bain's Lilac . . . Spreading Time for
Sarah Binks . . . The Festival of Words in Moose Jaw . . .
The Mae Wilson Theatre . . . Birding with Trevor Herriot . . .
Finding W.O. Mitchell's Home

"Saskatoon, Saskatchewan."

John Diefenbaker used to tell the story of two bewildered tourists crossing Canada by train who peered out of the window at a night stop and asked a man on the platform where they were. When they received that two-word answer they commented, "Well, they obviously don't speak English here!"

It's true that the names came from the Cree language. But it's also true that they've been speaking English in the area for quite some time now. Certainly, members of my family were speaking a Scottish-accented version when they arrived in Saskatoon on Hallowe'en night in 1901. Jean Young, of Stewarton, Ayrshire, was my grandmother's sister, and when she married Archibald Wallace Robertson they set out at once for the Canadian West, to live and work in Saskatoon for three years.

In 1904, a year before Saskatchewan became a province, they "filed" on a homestead near Arelee, northwest of Saskatoon, roughly where Eagle Creek runs into the mighty North Saskatchewan. There was a little money (from Scotland) in the family, so they were able to hire help from the nearby "Russian" settlement. But they faced the usual harsh pioneer problems. The family history, written by their son Archie (the man who sponsored my 1967 entry into Canada), reads in part: "In 1906 the folks had a bit of a set-back when the horse disease, Glanders, went through the district. A veterinarian and a policeman rode through testing all horses. Any that failed the test were shot on the spot. Dad was left with one foal."

This, please note, was in a world where horses were needed for *everything* from ploughing to harvesting the wheat, and even for getting off the farm. In the words of Archie's brother, Tom (Thomas Young were his first names, just like my own father), to get to the Raspberry Creek School, "We walked the four miles to school, and in the winter we didn't attend until we were old enough to drive a horse ourselves."

They had other prairie pioneer problems. "With a sod roof," Archie recalled, "a heavy rain would come through a couple of days later." On one occasion, a prairie fire got out of hand. An ember blew across the fire guard line, and burned down the barn.

Most dramatic of all was the time father Wallace took a horse-drawn load of grain in the sleigh across the frozen North Saskatchewan to Radisson. He almost made it. Then the ice broke, and the team and the sleigh went through. Fast work allowed him to get the pin out, and the horses and he were able to scramble ashore. But all the grain was lost. As he waded through the chunks of ice, I assume he didn't have time to reflect on the irony that he and his father-in-law, Thomas Young, who had been a very prosperous Scottish grain merchant, were at opposite ends of the same business. The shards of ice cutting his shins would have shown him who was at the sharp end.

In Scotland we grew up with these tales of our Saskatchewan cousins, and welcomed the family when they came back. My father's cousin Ian, for example, spent his RCAF leaves with my parents in Dunlop, until he failed to return from a bombing raid in 1943. That was the year of my birth. He was twenty years old.

We followed with interest as the family spread to the other Western provinces, but Saskatchewan was the home base, and I've always felt at home there. One notable moment for me was joining my cousin Bill on the tractor when we combined oat straw at the farm, until we were interrupted by an October snowstorm. Ah, Saskatchewan.

My *Stories About Storytellers* show in Saskatoon was hosted by the kindly folks at McNally Robinson, at their store on the southeast side of town. As you step inside the store you know at once that Paul and Holly and their people have succeeded in what all good independent booksellers strive to achieve — the sort of clubhouse feel that makes the place a hangout for intelligent folk in the local community, a place full of interesting events, from children's book readings to guitar concerts — or even former publishers chatting about their authors.

Paul and Holly are so good at this that I once said grandly that what Canadian publishing needed was more McNally Robinson bookstores. But bookselling seems to require many local variations on a formula successful elsewhere. The great success of the stores in Winnipeg and in Saskatoon is balanced by the closure of their store in downtown Calgary and in far-from-downtown-Toronto Don Mills.

Time for a digression in praise of booksellers. It's a tricky business, running a bookstore. Let me tell you a story, from my early days of authorship. Being a first-time author is a humbling experience. You are pathetically grateful for any praise from readers. Sentences like "I love you and want to bear your children" or "Congratulations, this is the Lotto Corporation calling to tell you that you have just won a million dollars!" pale in significance compared with the magic words "Hey, Doug, I'm really enjoying your book!"

That was the greeting I received from Ron Graham (the well-known author and, obviously, highly intelligent and discerning reader) as I entered Toronto's Massey College. He could have followed up with a request for a loan, certain of success, and I would happily have stooped to shine his shoes. In fact, I was so thrilled that I went on to confide to him my shy first steps as an author, doing things like trying my hand at autographing books *in a store.*

He told me of his first visit to a bookstore to see a pile of his just-published first book, lying there, throbbing. He hung around, sensing that something was bound to happen. Sure enough, a young man, browsing through the store, came to his book and picked it up. He leafed through it, read a couple of passages, and then, to Ron's almost audible horror, put the book down and walked away. A minute later he came back, and started to leaf through it again. Ron, quivering with excitement and unable to stand the suspense, was at the point of going up to him and offering to buy the book for him. Before he could do that, however, the young man looked around, slipped the book into his bag, and walked briskly out of the store.

Ron, left standing there with his mouth open, is still not sure what he should have done. Being an author is hard. And being a bookseller is very hard.

Another story: I once dropped in on Book City's Danforth Avenue store, fresh from buying Tofurkey for the vegetarian troublemakers around our Christmas table. The elder statesman of the Toronto chain, the eminent Frans Donker, happened to be in the store, and greeted me warmly. He urged me to sign the two copies of my book on hand, then went looking for a third copy out on the shelves. He returned, shaking his head over that copy. The flap had been carefully folded over to mark a place two-thirds of the way through the book. Some anonymous browser had apparently been working his or her way through the book, and was nearing the end — without any messy expenditure of dollars or the risk of overdue fines at the local library.

Or this next story. In March 2014, the Book City branch on Bloor Street closed down. This was a source of sorrow for Toronto book-lovers, but especially my family, because my daughter Katie had enjoyed her summer job there. But now for the drama. In the words of the *Toronto Star*: "Lightning hit a metal newspaper box outside the front door about fifteen years ago, shot down the store's centre aisle to the raised desk at the back where it fried the printer and crashed the computer system. No one was hurt. Customers still talk about 'the orange ball of fire.'"

The life of a Canadian bookseller. It goes with being part of "The Perilous Trade."

Among the people who risked their lives, stepping into a bookstore, to see my show that night in Saskatoon was the locally based author David Carpenter. I've never had the pleasure of editing any of Dave's more than a dozen books (novels, short story collections, essays, memoirs, even a poetry book, and most notably *God's Bedfellows*, *Writing Home*, and *Courting Saskatchewan*) but I've admired "Carp's" role as a central figure in the province's writing life, and we've known each other so long that I can't remember when we met, although I know that he had hair then. He taught for many years at the University of Saskatchewan, and on that famous weekend at Old Fort William in Thunder Bay, I even saw him in action.

Like Jack Hodgins (whose class I've also visited, and who once taught Dave), he's a natural teacher. It was humbling for me to see the difference between someone like me, who gets up and talks (interestingly, I hope) about writing, and a true writing instructor who works from a carefully designed plan, the product of years of hard thought and practice.

Dave's a very genial fellow, always good company, and he chuckled happily at my show that night, along with a select crowd of friends, including Dr. Stuart Houston (who has banded more than 140,00 birds over the years, and knew Bob Symons well), and relations like Peg Robertson, whose email includes the handle "cowdoctor." But it came later, in fact, in his role as the editor of *The Literary History of Saskatchewan* (2013) that David paid me a more serious compliment: he invited me to contribute to this important Saskatchewan book. His written dedication in my copy says, "Thanks for joining us." It was a great pleasure for me to write the entry about my very first author, R.D. (Bob) Symons, of Silton, Saskatchewan. The honour of being appointed as a sort of adopted son of the province was even greater.

Now, this "adopted son" stuff may sound like sentimental nonsense coming from a hopeless romantic who took his kids to lie in the Métis rifle pits at Batoche; or to stand beside the buffalo rock near Eagle Creek, to feel the waxy surface of a rock rubbed smooth by thousands of bison down through the centuries; or to climb down from the level prairie near Prince Albert to the deep trench where the North and the South Saskatchewan rivers join at The Forks, in order to watch the swirling river flow silently in one wide stream all the way to Hudson's Bay. But the province that featured in so many letters to our house in Scotland has always felt like a home to me, and has welcomed me.

For example, the Saskatchewan Writers' Guild once invited me to come in and address their Annual Meeting. (That year it was held at the Hotel Saskatchewan in Regina.) In the past I've been welcomed as a visitor to Robert Kroetsch's writing class at "Fort San" (you'll meet this gentle, soft-spoken, bearded teacher and writer later, when he roars into action to tackle a wild elk in Banff), and to the Sage Hill writing group farther up the Qu'Appelle Valley (where I lent my enthusiastic voice to support Philip Adams when he drilled into the writers there the vital lesson that every reading they're invited to give is *a performance*, and must be polished till it becomes a professional one). I've served as a jury member for a Saskatchewan Writers' Guild award. I've even been received informally in the premier's office by Roy Romanow, thanks to our mutual friend, the excellent Gail Bowen. But all of this pales beside being honoured by Dave, and

Nik Burton at Coteau, when they invited me to take part in helping to write the comprehensive literary history of Saskatchewan, which triumphantly came out in 2014 with a proud assist from me.

Between downtown Saskatoon and the river stands the grand old Bessborough Hotel, full of literary memories. I and McClelland & Stewart's gifted designer, Kong Njo, set up shop there in 1998, after W.O. Mitchell's death. The other members of our team were Orm and Barb Mitchell, there to select the text from W.O.'s work that would enrich a large book entitled *W.O. Mitchell Country*, based around landscape photos taken over the years by the remarkable Courtney Milne.

Courtney was there, in from nearby Grandora, with his partner, Sherrill Miller ("researcher, writer, and fellow-traveller extraordinaire"). Much more important, though, was the fact that this famous photographer, the man behind successful books like *Prairie Light* (1985) and *The Sacred Earth* (1991), was there with many fine photographs — more than 18,000 of them!

Day after day, with me in the role of Solomon, we went through a screening of all of Courtney's slides, choosing the 200 that would appear in the coffee table book, with Orm and Barb choosing the selections from W.O's writings that would blend best with these fine, never-before-published photographs. It was as hard as you can imagine, but when Kong and I flew back we knew that we had an exceptional book to publish, which we did, in 1999. It was very popular and very beautiful, and is still. This "magical blend of text and pictures that is greater than the sum of its parts," is a fitting memorial to two great artists, Mitchell and Milne, both sons of Saskatchewan.

Just south of the Bessborough stands the courthouse where on Tuesday, November 6, 1984, Colin Thatcher (powerful rancher, ex-cabinet minister in the Saskatchewan government, and son of premier Ross Thatcher) was found guilty of arranging the murder of his wife, JoAnn. It was an amazing story, and it took up months of my life. Maggie Siggins was the Regina-based author with the courage to take on the book, when many other writers in the province were nervous about dealing with Colin Thatcher's story. (Thatcher, you may recall, later lost his appeal for early parole when his RCMP escort informed the court hearing that he had just threatened her.) In recognition of the scale of the case we gave the 1985 book the title: *A Canadian Tragedy* (with the subtitle: *JoAnn and Colin Thatcher — A Story of Love and Hate*). It was, and remains, a remarkable story of a justice system unable to deal with one of its own ("Surely he would never . . ."), a man who would go on breaking rules, until a woman was dead. A superb book.

Later, when Maggie came across another murder on a Saskatchewan farm, the murder itself seemed a little too uneventful to make a whole book. Maybe, Maggie and I decided over Chinese food, the setting — *the farm itself*, down through the years — would be worth researching as the basis of an interesting book. Maggie set to work and struck gold, finding that successive waves of Canadian history had washed over this one, typical farm. *Revenge of the Land: A Century of Greed, Tragedy, and Murder on a Saskatchewan Farm* won the Governor General's Award for Non-Fiction in 1992. There is more than one way to shape a good story.

Just north of the Bessborough (and before you reach the Mendel Gallery, and the colony of White Pelicans on the river) is a fine park, with one of the most surprising First World War memorials I have ever seen. It shows a young man, in his team uniform, standing with his foot on a soccer ball.

It commemorates the young sportsmen — in this case, soccer players — who rushed to join up in 1914. I'm proud that Daniel Dancocks wrote for me a fine, bitterly titled book about the early days of that war: *Welcome to Flanders Fields* (1988). Young Canadians were so excited by this great contest in Europe that many were rushing, as one of them wrote, "to get in on the fun."

That soccer statue hits me hard, because soccer, or "football," played a large role in Gibson family history. My great-grandfather, Robert Gibson, must have been an amazing man. A fatherless boy, born out of wedlock, he somehow rose in Victorian Scotland to become a factory owner in the town of Kilmarnock. "Hannah and Gibson" made tweed (a fine Scottish tradition) and were so successful that one of Robert's sons was stationed in Denver, selling to the American market. (I later found his grave there.)

Another son, Robert (my grandfather), was his sales manager. But this factory owner's son was not only a recognizable rich kid in town, with a factory's name attached to him. He was also a gifted soccer player. So gifted, in fact, that he played at the top level in Scottish professional soccer, turning out for the Kilmarnock team against the big football teams like Rangers and Celtic.

This displeased his father, who knew that there were no sales managers in the tough world of Scottish football, peopled by former miners and steelworkers. In that world, his father knew, his son would be a marked man. Some day, he warned, they would get him: he really should give up playing the game, be sensible, and settle down. But young Robert, who still lived at home, defied his father, and kept on playing for Kilmarnock, in the world of roaring crowds, flying boots, and crunching tackles.

One day his father's warnings came true. In the course of a big Saturday game, "they" got him, and a flying tackle broke his leg.

In those days before emergency wards and plaster casts, he persuaded his pals to take him to a bone-setter. When the leg had been set, he then persuaded them to carry him home, and set him up on the couch in the living room. His plan was to conceal his injury from his father, and to crawl about secretly, as required, until his leg healed.

The fierce old man (a town councillor and a Justice of the Peace, and such a power in the Liberal Party that when Prime Minister Gladstone's nephew came to Kilmarnock to run in an election, he stayed at the Gibson house) arrived home from his workaholic day, armed with the evening paper. How did the game go? My grandfather, from the couch, shrugged a non-committal reply. His father unfolded the hot-off-the-press paper.

Silence.

Then an explosion.

"*It says here you broke your leg!*" Not for the last time, a member of the Gibson family found that the power of the press can be very inconvenient.

First, the way to pronounce Guy Vanderhaeghe's name. It rhymes with "Buy Van Der Haig." Some people are thrown by the Flemish ". . . aeghe" (especially when it's pronounced Flemish-style, with lots of throaty phlegm involved) and give "Guy" the French sound. In reality, our man is just a regular Guy.

But he is also a superb writer, one of Canada's finest.

I don't have a chapter on Guy in my *Stories About Storytellers* book. That's because I restricted that sort of lengthy treatment to authors whose work I actually edited. Guy worked with Anne Holloway and then Ellen Seligman as his editors, never with me. But I've been involved with publishing him, right from the start. And during that time he's always been based in Saskatoon.

I was the publisher of Macmillan of Canada back in 1981 when Anne and other editors there started urging me to read a new collection of short stories that had just been submitted by an unknown young writer from Saskatchewan. I was very busy with grand publishing issues, and it was only when I caught the flu and had to stay home in bed that I had time to read this unknown's manuscript.

The accompanying letter was not promising. In my memory it was addressed to "Dear Sirs," ran only to a couple of paragraphs, and shyly mentioned that some of the stories enclosed "for your consideration" had appeared in this or that literary magazine. So when I tell you that I started to read feverishly, I'm using a medical term, and not referring to any level of excitement.

Yet within a few pages I knew this was something exceptional. Very soon I knew that my colleagues had been right to pester me to read this. By the time of my second hot drink I knew that we had to rush to publish *Man Descending*, and that we would do very well with it.

Here I must confess that at the Writers' Union of Canada meeting in St. John's in 2014, Guy had the perfect platform to project how terrible it was to be a lowly writer, endlessly waiting for word, while this remote figure named "Doug Gibson" lay around (presumably languidly eating grapes, or figs, from a silver salver), taking his time to reach a decision. In his Margaret Laurence Lecture, Guy recalled with great precision that *he* finally gave *me* a deadline, which I just managed to meet. When concerned friends later asked me for my side of the story, I said that Guy's version was too good not to be true.

Guy was only thirty-one when his first book came out, and it changed his life. He was an archivist/teacher, patching together a living with writing grants, along with his artist wife, Margaret, in Saskatoon. After the book came out, his life continued to be a patching process, but now the patches were larger, and a little more predictable. Short story writers tend not to become rich, but

Guy Vanderhaeghe (1951–)

Guy was on his way to becoming famous. The tough, clear prairie voices (often of working-class young guys, who are rarely heard in "Literature") rang out from every page, and readers everywhere were impressed.

Canadian reviewers sat up and took notice that a major new writer had just appeared on the Prairies. The *Montreal Gazette* said: "If his ability to create rich human beings is impressive, even more stunning is his narrative ability." *Books in Canada* said: "These are stories to be read and remembered." *Maclean's* summed up the general excitement about this new kid: "*Man Descending*, with its felicities of language and characterization, launches a writer whose ascent is likely to be well worth tracking." Later, as the book was published around the English-speaking world, in London the *Spectator* called Guy "an energetic, eloquent, bitterly indignant wit, a Canadian Gentile Philip Roth."

Man Descending won the Governor General's Award for Fiction in 1982. The prize was given in Quebec City that year, and much later — in March 2013 — Guy and I happened to be there together at the fine local literary festival. We were able to compare happy memories of how he and his wife, Margaret, and I (along with the Non-Fiction Prize winner, Christopher Moore and his wife, Louise) enjoyed the awards ceremony in the Laval University buildings dating from the Ancien Regime, and then they enjoyed the formal evening dinner at the Citadelle mess hall of the Royal 22nd Regiment, "the Vandoos," surrounded by military waiters in bright red uniforms.

It was a long way from the small town of Esterhazy, in southeast Saskatchewan, where Guy grew up, the grandson of a Belgian immigrant who came to Canada in 1910. His father was a good man with horses, even competing in rodeos. His mother, by contrast, urged him to read books. Guy recalled small-town life in Esterhazy to Noah Richler in his 2007 book, *This Is My Country, What's Yours?*: "Until I was six or seven years old any work that wasn't on a farm was part-time. Then suddenly people could work twelve months of the year." The potash mines had arrived . . . but of course, as Guy (a true son of Saskatchewan) gloomily notes, "potash is not a renewable resource." But what did prove to be a renewable resource was the life Guy saw around him, so that his short stories feature visits underground, or teenage fights in pool halls.

His career continued to make steady progress. I was proud to publish *My Present Age* in 1984, in which Ed, the unbalanced anti-hero, wages war on a neighbour in the apartment downstairs with the help of equipment from his shot-putting days — depth-charge style. The novel also takes us on a memorable tour of the Prairie city as Ed seeks out his fleeing, pregnant wife. A second novel, *Homesick* (1989), travelled so well from its Prairie setting that it won the City of Toronto Book Award.

I never did see either of Guy's plays (*I Had a Job That I Liked*, *Once* and *Dancock's Dance*), but every one of his books reveals the dramatist's mastery of dialogue, with the lines snarling or whooping off the page. You can see that in every story in his 1992 collection, *Things as They Are*, whether the people involved are old ranchers bucked off and dragged on the prairie, or the fierce Grandma Bradley cutting enemies down to size, or the teenage boys setting up a boxing match that is sure to end in disaster. All wonderful stuff.

Then, out of the blue, Guy changed direction completely. He turned his historian's training to look hard at our past, and started to reclaim Canadian history for all of us. He wrote three historical novels: *The Englishman's Boy* (1996, which won him a second Governor General's Award), *The Last Crossing* (2002, which won many prizes), and *A Good Man* (2011, which deserved to). All of them were dramatic lessons that were bound to smarten up anyone who believed that Canadian history was boring, and that the Canadian West was settled in a peaceful way, without any violent incidents.

Here let me draw attention to one of Guy's greatest skills as a writer. No other Canadian writer can match his skills when it comes to scenes of action, of violence. One example: early in *The Englishman's Boy*, our skinny young hero is grabbed at the saloon bar by the bully who runs the hotel. ("Stevenson grinned in his face. 'Hello,' he said, and suddenly struck him a savage blow to the ear with his fist.") The out-matched teenager manages to get his knife from his boot and sticks it in the bully's armpit. He keeps it stuck there, as the bigger man, on tip-toe, twists in spitted agony, his blood "pouring down the blade like rainwater down a drain spout." When eventually the boy realizes it's time to back out of the bar, there's a special Vanderhaeghe moment:

The boy stepped over the body to where the black silk hat had rolled and trampled it savagely under his dirty boots. No one moved as this was accomplished. "None of this was my doing," he told the room, brandishing the pistol above his head for all to see. "I'm walking now. If this bastard has any kin or friends setting here making plans — you've seen my gun. It's cocked." He took a step toward the door, then pivoted on his heel and kicked the senseless body in the head.

"Hello," he said to it one last time.

One other example of Guy's mastery of violent scenes. In *The Last Crossing*, there is a dramatic account of the best-known nineteenth-century Native battle on the Prairies, when more than a thousand Cree and Assiniboine warriors clashed with Blackfoot fighters. It ends badly for the "halfbreeds" on both sides. Jerry Potts, for instance, one of Guy's main characters (and a notable mixed-blood figure in the old West, the scout who led the Mounties on their march west) arrives to find his Cree rivals, the yellow-haired Sutherland brothers, now at bay. "The brothers sit back to back in a puddle of blood, unable to stand. Both men's legs are useless, broken by bullets. Their carbines are empty, but they have drawn their knives, prepared to fight to the death, to sell their lives dear. Potts swings down from his pony, hurries up to the ring circling them." When one Sutherland brother sings his death song in Cree, the other, remembering his Hudson Bay Company father's teaching, sings the slow Scottish psalm "Praise God, from whom all blessings flow . . ."

In person Guy is a quiet man. Noah Richler describes him well: "Vanderhaeghe, a diabetic, is a tall man of good build who had only recently decided against the punishment of playing hockey with kids twenty years his junior. He spoke quietly in that soft-spoken but resolute, mesmerizing prairie manner that dictates its own pace and attention from those who listen."

What's missing there is the Vanderhaeghe chuckle. All through the years I've known him, I've felt certain that within a minute of our phone call's start, we'd both be chuckling. Maybe I started it, but it was more likely to be our joint memories of funny stories and encounters in the past. It might be the tale of Guy and his rink-rat friends featuring in a Ken Dryden hockey film for the CBC. Or about the time I was delayed en route to a Saskatoon dinner with Guy and

Margaret (described in my earlier book) when a very big man who had just left a bar in a great hurry pointed at his own large feet and asked me the alarming question, "Are these women's boots?"

All great, shoulder-shaking stuff.

And then Margaret fell gravely ill. It was a terrible, downhill progression. Guy, nursing her around the clock, became so exhausted that he too was taken to Emergency, and sheltered by friends. All of the good people around them did what they could to help, but Guy's experience with the medical system was a series of infuriating disappointments. When Margaret died in 2012, all of his friends worried about him. No more shoulder-shaking laughter.

David Carpenter, one of those staunch friends, has reported that Guy is back to playing golf and returning to everyday life, and Guy has confessed that he is indeed mistreating golf balls again. We all wish him well. We all rejoice in the news that there is already another book, *Daddy Lenin and Other Stories*. And, in due course, we hope, much more of the Guy Vanderhaeghe chuckle.

A final word: it's not widely known, but one of Guy's greatest admirers was Mordecai Richler. The mutual admiration between the Jewish kid from St. Urbain Street and the Prairie boy from Esterhazy was perhaps unpredictable — until you realize that these were two master craftsmen who recognized rare talent when they saw it. They became friends. Indeed Charles Foran's quotable 2010 biography, *Mordecai: The Life and Times*, recounts their friendship in some detail, from the time in Saskatoon when "the shy young novelist . . . initially balked at bringing a courtesy bottle of Scotch to Richler's hotel room, fearing his notorious bark. David Carpenter persuaded Vanderhaeghe that Mordecai Richler had been asking to meet *him*."

They became such good friends, in fact, that in September 1991 Mordecai flew out to Saskatoon to appear at a fundraiser for local writers. He was there when the biggest literary bomb to hit Canada in decades went off. The *New Yorker* published Mordecai's scathing attack on Quebec's language laws under the title "Inside/Outside" (later expanded in book form as *Oh Canada! Oh Quebec!*). In Foran's words, "No single article published by any Canadian had ever achieved such instant notoriety — or impact."

The *New Yorker* sold out instantly in Quebec, and the response was almost hysterically hostile, with one Quebec provincial politician wanting the author arrested for treason. Mordecai was having a Scotch at Guy and Margaret's house when he called home to Montreal. That was when he learned about the threatening calls his wife was receiving. On the spot, he cut short his visit and flew back into the storm.

In future years, Charles Foran notes, Guy went on to receive "the sure signs of Richler affection: a 'good word' put in on his behalf with publishers and editors internationally, and brief, jokey faxes." They remained such close friends that Guy served as a pallbearer at Mordecai's Montreal funeral in July 2001.

An unexpected final story about Guy. In September 2013, I mentioned Guy's name to Joanne, a teacher at a Toronto school where I was giving my show. She reacted very strongly. "*Guy Vanderhaeghe*! My mother-in-law stayed alive until I could finish reading *The Last Crossing* aloud to her. Then she died."

The last crossing, indeed.

Before we leave Saskatoon it's time to quote Charles Gordon again. In the acknowledgements to *The Canada Trip* he says kind things about me. "In his editing, Doug consistently amazed me with his knowledge of what is where in Canada. Many times he was able to tell me that I could not have been looking at what I thought I was looking at from a given spot — a sunset, a mountain, an ocean — because I was facing the wrong way. This invariably sent me back to my map collection, and invariably forced me to conclude he was right — except maybe for once in Saskatoon." (Ah, yes, the Idylwyld highway, reliably north-south until it turns east-west after the river, dammit. But isn't it nice to see another editorial role revealed: *make sure the author is headed in the right direction*.)

Which brings us to Lilac.

George Bain was the superb Ottawa editorial columnist for the *Globe and Mail* for many years. A small, neat man, and a former bomber pilot, he never lacked courage. He was a lone voice protesting that the imposition of the War Measures Act in 1970 was an overreaction to what should have been a matter for the police. This principled stance led to a move to have him barred from the Ottawa Press Gallery — strange but true — a move that fortunately failed, as the defenders of press freedom finally came to their senses.

Not surprisingly, George welcomed the chance to take his readers out of Ottawa, alerting them to the importance of Lilac, Saskatchewan, "Jewel of the Wheat Belt." Between 1965 and 1973 he would punctuate his usual columns about the parochial affairs in Ottawa with weekend letters of wider interest sent to him by his friend Clem Watkins Jr. of the "Lilac Advance." In 1978, I was proud to help George Bain advance the causes that Clem Watkins held dear by publishing the collected *Letters from Lilac* by Clem Watkins Jr. (edited and selected by George Bain, illustrated by Duncan Macpherson).

Lilac emerges as perhaps the most important small town in Canada. Not only is it the point of balance for an unsteadily see-sawing nation (there is more land to the east, of course, but the Rockies weigh more), politically it is equally pivotal. Thanks to Clem Watkins, those with eyes to see were able to detect what issues were swaying the grass roots and which way the political wind was blowing. Without fail, in every national election held during those years, Lilac followed — or, more properly, led — the national trend.

Thanks to George's "editing," Lilac's history comes in for full attention, including the Hitler-defying creation of the Icarus Elementary Flying School. The exciting 1968 run for the Liberal Party leadership (won by the upstart Pierre Trudeau) by Harry Melfort, the local MP, is widely discussed in the Round Table Room of Irvin Mervin's Commercial Hotel, or in the Legion. Local worthies include Knut Svensson who, in the absence of any local Scandinavian group, has risen to be head of *both* the Sons and Daughters of Scotland *and* the St. Andrew's Day Society.

To the embarrassment of the editor, George Bain, his own name sometimes enters the discussion. Once, when Clem Watkins Jr. is discussing a vacancy in the Senate he quotes a letter from the Bertrand Russell Branch of the Canadian Legion in Lilac, sent to the prime minister. It reads, in part: "However, if you wanted to take a chance on a boy in his forties, I'd suggest to you George Bain. He's young, I admit, but he can sit there at times so you'd swear he was dead. Senate timber if ever I saw it." Stephen Harper might have used similar advice.

In his Introduction, George Bain tackles the question of Lilac's location. "I should say something about Lilac, Sask., itself because people have tended over the years, for reasons which never have been clear to me, either to confuse its location, or, in a few cases, even to suggest that it does not exist — which, of course, is absurd, as Watkins' letters prove."

Later he gives precise directions: "Actually, if you take the map of Saskatchewan and trace along the first fold about six inches, and then let your finger travel obliquely about another . . . well, it is a little difficult to explain, but if I were there I could point it out to you in a second. That is the Lilac of C. Watkins Jr., lettrist."

It seems to me that Clem Watkins Jr. deserves to stand in literary history alongside the unforgettable Sarah Binks, the "Sweet Songstress of Saskatchewan." Culturally, any Lilac poetry competition is certain to reveal that the spirit of Sarah Binks still pulsates in several local bosoms (especially that of Miss Mildred Keats, the librarian, author of the Centennial poem, "Soul and Sinew, We're Yours, Canada"). Sweet Sarah's creator, Paul Hiebert, is one of the few people in the world to be described in a reference book as "chemist, humorist." But whatever formula the University of Manitoba professor applied to create his parody of literary biography, it deserves to be reapplied elsewhere. I have presented his 1947 book *Sarah Binks* to many friends as *sui generis* (totally unique) . . . although perhaps that should be "sooky," in deference to Sarah's famous pig poem, entitled "Hi Sooky, Ho Sooky."

The Afterword of the New Canadian Library edition of this humorous classic is written by, of course, our friend Charles Gordon. He abandons his usual understatement in his praise of *Sarah Binks* and its author. "On the basis of *Sarah Binks* alone, he should have been rich and famous and never have had to teach chemistry again."

And even for urban readers who rarely use the word "manure," as Sarah dances around exulting over the joys of "Spreading Time," there is a warm pleasure in knowing just what it is that is being spread over the fields. And as a translator, Sarah reaches new heights. One supreme example: the German love poem by Heine, "*Du Bist wie eine Blume*" becomes "You are like one flower." Translation is truly an art — or perhaps one art.

We didn't drive to Moose Jaw via Lilac, or Sarah's Willows (or Gordie Howe's Crocus). We flew there the following summer, to take part in the Saskatchewan Festival of Words, arriving in Regina (admiringly described by Paul Hiebert as "the Athens of Saskatchewan" and a place where Sarah, a simple girl from Willows, found herself abashed by "its polish, its sophistication, and its long rows of boxcars"). Jane and I, in our rented box-like car, were struck by how, unlike the rolling parkland to the north, here Saskatchewan is flat, flat, flat — watch-your-dog-run-away-for-days flat. It's all too easy to forget that the Cypress Hills (where *The Englishman's Boy* is set) are the highest point between the Lakehead and the Rockies. In summer the constant contrast between the bright blue of the sloughs, fringed with green trees, and the yellows and golds of the growing crops, and the blue-tinged flax fields had us exclaiming over the patchwork of colourful beauty.

The fine and famous festival has been held in Moose Jaw for almost twenty years now, but 2012 was the first year that I was able to attend. Right away I saw why my authors had always reported that they enjoyed it so much. Invited authors/performers are housed at the downtown spa hotel, built around some natural hot springs full of healing waters. We found that every day had to involve at least one wallow in the soothingly warm pool on the top floor, where people sunbathe then swim, drink cool water, then repeat the dose. I was right at home, because the little café beside the pool was named the Morningside Room, recognizing the fact that Peter Gzowski (a proudly sentimental graduate of the Moose Jaw *Times Herald*, just down the street) chose to stage his last *Morningside* broadcast from the hotel, and a photo of my friend Peter hangs on the café wall.

The festival itself is set a short walk away, in the library and art gallery on the edge of Crescent Park. This is Moose Jaw's central park (and indeed its Central Park) and is a fine blend of beauty and endless activity, which we explored every day.

I gave three readings, adapting my chosen excerpt to fit with my co-reader. For example, matched with Harold Johnson, a truly impressive Cree-speaker who is a Crown prosecutor in Laronge and has a master's Law degree from Harvard, not to mention a long, single braid down his back, I chose to read about Saskatchewan's own R.D. Symons, my very first author, who had also mastered Cree. I was so impressed by Harold that I bought a copy of his novel, *Charlie Muskrat*. The trouble with literary festivals is that you hear so many fine readings that you end up buying lots of books. An occupational hazard. And Harold has become a friend.

The second reading teamed me with John Vaillant, the superb Vancouver-based writer. It was a natural fit for me to read about James Houston, since that chapter leads to my visit to Jim's place at Haida Gwaii, and has a mention of the famous Golden Spruce tree there, which allowed me to regret in print that I had not been given the chance to publish John's superb prize-winning book *The Golden Spruce* (2005). It was a neat introduction to . . . John Vaillant!

And if you're looking for thrilling stories, consider John's two books of non-fiction. *The Golden Spruce* tells the story of a freak of nature, a giant spruce tree that was bright gold. It stood out in the Haida Gwaii forest (which John portrays brilliantly) so that it was a revered object to the Haida people, and a source of wonder to visitors to the island. Then a crazy (or deeply eccentric) logger, a man of remarkable physical powers, decided to make a statement about the great trees that were being lost. He swam in at night, towing a chainsaw, and cut the tree down. Faced with a furious Haida nation, he chose to risk a kayak ride across Hecate Strait from the mainland to attend his court case. He never made it.

As for John's second book, *The Tiger* (2010), I can only advise you not to read it at night. It tells the true story of a Siberian tiger in the Kamchatka Peninsula in the very east of Russia that started to hunt down the hunters who had hurt it in the past, apparently ignoring other humans it came across on its trail of vengeance. As we follow the tiger's progress, and the Russian game officer hunting it, the story is hypnotically exciting.

For my final reading in Moose Jaw, I saw no obvious link to my fellow reader. This was a very good thing. Jalal Barzanji's book *The Man in Blue Pyjamas* is a prison memoir of his days in Saddam Hussein's Baghdad, before he and his family finally managed to make it to Canada. Happily, I had no similar stories to write about. So after praising the PEN Canada help that brought Jamal to Edmonton, I simply chose to honour Saskatchewan's own W.O. Mitchell, from Weyburn, just east of Moose Jaw. Any reading that includes a selection of stories about the unforgettable W.O. is bound to be popular.

This selection from my chapter on W.O. Mitchell was no exception.

People love to hear about this remarkable "Character, and Creator of Characters." In his fine 2010 book, *How the Scots Invented Canada* (now there's a title!), Ken McGoogan recalls seeing more than 1,000 people in Calgary give W.O. a standing ovation, "and in the audience I found myself asking, How does he do it? . . . getting this whole crowd laughing at what many of them would normally denounce as crude, vulgar, indecent, and even blasphemous." Ken goes on to give a shrewd answer:

> Mitchell the stand-up comedian was also a man of serious purpose. In book after book, while wielding his humour like a broadsword, attacking everything uptight and straitlaced with the ferocity of a born satirist, he took special aim at the puritanical moralism that Canada had imported from Scotland, and which, decades ago, had threatened to stifle his boyhood. By cursing and swearing, caricaturing and gesticulating and making people laugh, W.O. Mitchell was celebrating his regional identity — this could be nowhere but the Canadian prairies — while waging a one-man war against the vestiges of Presbyterianism.

We were going to look for those vestiges soon, in his hometown of Weyburn, after my big show.

Saturday was a busy day for me, climaxing with my show at the Mae Wilson Theatre on Moose Jaw's Main Street. This is a grand old Edwardian theatre, with all the elaborate plaster trimmings, where touring music hall stars like Scotland's Sir Harry Lauder have appeared through the ages. I did my show against a truly massive screen, perhaps fifteen feet by thirty feet, which meant that the author caricatures were clear to everyone in the 300-person audience. While I waited nervously in the wings ("This is the biggest crowd I've had so far!") that audience was set up by a very generous introduction by the fine local author Bob Currie.

One new part of the show was a special surprise for my good friend Terry Fallis (author of *The Best Laid Plans*, *The High Road*, and now *Up and Down* and *No Relation*). Tony Jenkins had kindly provided a new caricature of Terry, since I knew that he would be in the audience at Moose Jaw, although he had seen my show before.

(Terry is that kind of friend.) I gave his picture the subtitle "Saint, Little Red Hen, and Prizewinner," and explained each part of the subtitle as Terry gurgled and blushed in the audience at his unexpected appearance. The poor man had just explained to his seatmate that, no, he was not part of Doug's show, when his picture appeared onscreen.

If you're after amazing stories, consider Terry's career launch. He and his wife, Nancy (a former colleague of Jane's), are such good friends of ours that we often have dinner parties together. But when Terry started to try writing a novel, he never once traded on our friendship. He never once asked me to "take a look at" his novel. Not even when he couldn't get any agent or publisher to even read this political satire set in — oh, no! — Ottawa.

Terry published the book himself, it won the Stephen Leacock Award, and I belatedly came along to publish it, as it went on to fame and fortune, winning the Canada Reads competition in 2011. So far, this despised and rejected manuscript that nobody would even look at has sold far more than 100,000 copies. And thanks to Terry's tireless promotion, and the publication of his other fine books — which led the Canadian Booksellers to make him *Author of the Year* in 2013 — the Terry Fallis market continues to grow. As they say, it couldn't have happened to a nicer guy.

Once, I was given a private tour behind the scenes in Parliament by Erik Spicer, the former parliamentary librarian. On another occasion James Houston took me and some others through a special exhibition of Inuit art, recalling when he watched this piece being sculpted, and what his sculptor friend was chatting about as he worked on that other piece over there. You have the same "behind the scenes" feeling when you set out with Trevor Herriot to look at birds in Saskatchewan. Trevor is a superb writer about nature. Prairie readers know his book about the Qu'Appelle Valley, *River in a Dry Land*, which almost won the Governor General's Award for Non-Fiction in 2000. It inspired Sharon Butala to write that "this impassioned wide-ranging book carries me back to my Saskatchewan childhood, to the grass and the sky and the exhilarating smell of the wild that was always there on the wind." There, and in *Grass, Sky, and Song* (2009), also nominated for the award, and in *The Road Is How* (2014), which

Trevor Herriot (1958–)

Margaret Atwood called "a profound and moving journey over our wild, fragile planet," Trevor writes about everything: minerals, pioneers, politicians, and birds. Beautifully.

If you don't know his work, try this early April scene, from his first book. "An elm tree east of me, longing for colour, reaches up and snags a piece of sky. I have seen this before: turn to the wind, fold wings once, twice, then sing. Sing the wild notes a mountain bluebird always sings on a day like this. Softly, to the hillside."

Trevor is an expert birdwatcher, so good that he has hosted a CBC Regina radio show that helped callers to identify birds they saw in their yard with, for example, a yellow stripe at the back.

His own keen ears can identify different types of sparrow chirps at a hundred paces, and his long-range camera skills are remarkable. I knew this because a couple of years earlier he took me out from Regina to do some birding near Last Mountain Lake, and it proved to be a very memorable morning. That was R.D. Symons territory, and Trevor had been inspired by Bob's work.

So he encouraged us, after our stay in Moose Jaw, to explore Silton, in search of memories of Bob Symons (whose own memories of his boyhood home in Sussex included a visit by Rudyard Kipling — "a good listener"). Our Silton trip was pleasant, but not very successful. The man at the store (always ask at the store!) remembered Bob and his wife, Hope, but confirmed that their house had been knocked down, with only the garage remaining, which we looked at, unimpressed.

Our search for Meadow Lark Cottage near the lakeshore at Pelican Point was no more productive. But a photograph of Bob's painting of the old cottage reveals that it was an ancient cottage even fifty years ago, in 1962, when it was painted, and must be unrecognizable now. That painting is one of many contained in a marvellous tribute, *Robert David Symons, Countryman, Artist, Writer, Naturalist, Rancher* by Terry Fenton, published in 2013. The lavishly illustrated book reminds us that as a child Bob once sat on the knee of John Singer Sargent, the American who became, in the words of *Chambers's Encyclopedia*, "the most fashionable and elegant portrait painter" in late Victorian England. Even better, as a young man in the West Bob actually met the great cowboy artist Charles Russell. The new book about Bob, who was not your average cowboy, has an introduction by none other than Trevor Herriot.

At one point Trevor talks about Bob Symons and his love of his adopted land: "His life was nothing else if not an example of the colonizer's struggle to stop colonizing and start living as though he belongs." Later Trevor tells a story, from the botanist George Ledingham, "of the night when Symons demonstrated his knowledge of prairie places. They were together at a slide presentation of landscapes from around the province, and Symons, to the amazement of all in attendance, provided exact locations for each photograph, right down to details as to where the photographer was standing . . ."

Jane and I were not disappointed by our time roaming around in Symons Country, and were glad to share our stories when we arrived in Regina to stay with Trevor and Karen and the family.

When Trevor suggested that Jane and I (eating their super-fresh garden raspberries for breakfast) head south with him and his birding friend Bob Luterbach to see what we could find en route to Weyburn, we were thrilled. It is as if the word spreads through the bird community that "Hey, Trevor Herriot's here!" and they flock (so to speak) to see and be seen by this great celebrity birdwatcher. If you think that's unlikely, look at the list of birds we saw that morning (sorry, another wild Gibson enthusiasm is coming up!), which was enhanced by the fact that a lush Prairie summer had lured uncommon visitors north from the parched American Plains states. We saw a white-faced ibis (as in Egyptian pyramid art), perky burrowing owls (now endangered), black terns at the sloughs (and one angry Forster's tern), Baird's sparrows, grasshopper sparrows, lark buntings, bobolinks (with a yellow neck at the back), chestnut-collared longspurs, and an amazing range of exhibitionist bitterns, normally heard but never seen. All of these were first-time sightings for Jane and me.

Of course we also enjoyed watching Swainson's and red-tailed hawks, not to mention lots of mallards and eared grebes on the sloughs, the usual gangs of redwinged blackbirds and cedar waxwings, and a lone upland sandpiper. Wonderful!

Later, after all of this birding excitement, Jane and I made a Mitchell pilgrimage to Weyburn. Armed with information provided by Kam and Megan at the library, we walked the streets of the little town, which now has roughly 10,000 people. As everyone who has read

W.O. Mitchell (1914–1998)

Who Has Seen the Wind knows, when W.O. was a boy the open prairie lay just a couple of blocks north of his house, which now stands close to the centre of town. The second page of the 1947 novel catches the prairie setting:

> Just before the town the river took a wide loop as though in search of some variation in the prairie's flat surface, found it in a deep-cut coulée ragged with underbrush, and entered the town at its eastern edge. A clotting of frame houses inhabited by some eighteen hundred souls, the town had grown up on either side of the river from the seed of one homesteader's sod hut built in the spring of eighteen-seventy-five.
>
> Now it was made up largely of frame buildings with high, peaked roofs, each with an expanse of lawn in front and a garden in the back; they lined avenues with prairie names: Bison, Riel, Qu'Appelle, Blackfoot, Fort. Cement walks extended from First or Main Street to Bison Avenue which crossed Sixth Street at MacTaggart's corner; from that point to the prairie a boardwalk ran.

Thanks to the library's leaflet we found the Mitchell residence at 319 Sixth Street. Nobody was at home, so we took photos and were just giving up and leaving when a car stopped outside. It was Jamieson, the son of the household, who kindly invited us in and showed us around the ground floor. It was exactly as we had hoped — all maroon furniture against a background of old oak panels — befitting a grand old house that was perhaps the best in town in 1903. Even the bevelled glass windows and doors in the book cases, and the Art Nouveau metal light fixtures, spoke to the careful standard of excellence from that time.

We also saw the Knox Presbyterian Church that the Mitchells attended (and we thought of Ken McGoogan!), but we did not get to see the inside stained glass, "all grapes and bloody." We peeked in at the ancient Royal Hotel (once opposite the now gone railway station, although Railway Avenue remains), and visited Bill's father's grave in the cemetery just south of town. I must confess that there was no sign of the cheeky gopher at the edge of the tombstone ("O.S. Mitchell. Loved by all who knew him") that so offended young Brian/Bill when the family solemnly visited the grave.

The Weyburn Museum (the "Soo Line Museum") contained many photos of the town from W.O.'s boyhood days and one of his father, and of his pharmacy. We roamed the banks of the Little Souris River, in search of the famous swimming hole where W.O. and the other boys swam naked. We even saw some descendants of the cattails that provoked such naughty behaviour from some of Sadie Rossdance's girls.

In the evening, having walked the streets to absorb W.O.'s Weyburn (and please note that all of the "Prairie names" that he quotes as street names have already occurred, quite naturally, in this book), I gave my show in the public library to about fifteen appreciative local people, including one smiling author, my friend Joanne Bannatyne-Cugnet (*A Prairie Alphabet*). As usual, my show ended with a heartfelt tribute to W.O., and in Weyburn that seemed just right.

CHAPTER 4

ALBERTA AND THE MOUNTAINS

Edmonton's Magic Carpet . . . The Mighty Peace . . .
Alberta's Search for a New Novelist . . . Pauline Gedge
and Ancient Egypt . . . Myrna Kostash and Creative Non-
Fiction . . . Calgary's Ken McGoogan, and a Leonard
Cohen Moment . . . Alistair MacLeod in Alberta . . . More
About W.O . . . Elk Stories to Ponder . . . Facing Grizzly
Charges with Andy Russell . . . Into B.C. . . . Saying Yes to
the Kootenays, and Elephant Mountain . . . Hot Times in
Kelowna

There are many Albertas, and Edmonton is just one of them — and a very atypical one, at that. For a start, in contrast with Calgary, the mountains are far away, hours along the road to Jasper. In Calgary, like so much of the province, the foothills and the mountains are the constant edge of the frame on the West, and provide an inspiring target as you drive into the setting sun.

Flying into Edmonton, however, the landscape is prairie turning into industrial machinery parks ("Cranes for rent"), then becoming suburban sprawl. Apart from the odd glimpse of a grain elevator or a nodding horsehead well, the only real point of interest is the deep North Saskatchewan Valley that separates downtown from the south side. The river, of course, was the setting for the original Fort Edmonton in the fur trade days (here he goes again!), and one of my best Edmonton memories involves walking through the construction site mud, the smell of new pine poles filling the air as men with hammers built the new Fort Edmonton tourist site along traditional lines. Down by the river it was a muddy, noisy, smelly, authentic eighteenth-century Western experience, and my Edmonton cousin, Graeme Young, and I half-expected the factor to come roaring out of the big house to chase us away from his fort with a musket.

In Edmonton, I had my very first experience with the "magic carpet treatment" that authors receive from literary festivals when we were met at the airport by the friendly volunteer Jean Crozier. She promptly whisked us in her car into the south side of town, past Old Strathcona, then across the famous fur trade valley to our downtown hotel. In less than an hour I was in a nearby mall, perched on one of those bar stools apparently reserved for TV talk shows ("Where do I put my feet?") and trying to interest the passing crowd of shoppers (not to mention people nipping out from the office to get cash at the bank machine) in the prospect of coming to my show at the Edmonton Festival, in the Milner Library Theatre that evening.

The amiable CBC host/interviewer got the name of my book wrong, but recovered swiftly after I happened to mention the right title in the course of my reply. The first of my Awful Warnings to Authors coming true to life — in my own life.

That evening the show went fine (although I was struck how perfectly Chaucer's phrase "the craft so long to lerne" applied to stage craft). Afterwards I got to relax by sitting at a table in the foyer, smiling in a relieved way and signing books. They were supplied by Audreys, the fine store on Jasper Avenue run by my old friends Sharon and Steve Budnarchuk. Sharon had worked in sales at McClelland & Stewart, and yet despite her knowledge of the harsh realities she wasn't afraid to get into the bookselling game with Steve. Long may they run!

Some of the books were signed for relatives (like Graeme's son Scot) but others were for apparently sober civilians, who said kind things. Kindest of all was the festival's head, David Cheoros, who wrote that onstage my "lifelong passion for these great writers is contagious." I hope it comes out on every page here.

Then it was back to the hotel for a come-down session. If you wonder where the speakeasy or late night "booze-can" came from, consider this: any performer — any actor, or a dancer, or a musician — has to get "up" for a performance. But what goes up must come down. And after even a modest sixty- to ninety-minute show like mine, I am really "up," and need to work at coming down if sleep is to be an option. That seems to apply across the board with performers, which is why they seek out late-night haunts, and why they often end up in trouble with the booze or other stuff that goes along with them. And this applies not only to hard-living jazz or rock musicians. My friend and neighbour Dianne Werner is a well-known concert pianist, and after a performance that ends around ten o'clock, she tells me, "I can forget about sleep till after three in the morning." She says that after a grilling evening, professional chefs have the same problem. Adrenaline. Who knew?

That evening in Edmonton I "came down" with a group of relatives, mostly Robertsons originally from way up in the Peace River Country, where the father, Archie (my sponsor to Canada), had been the mayor of Fairview. It was good to catch up, though my cousin Fraser had been too busy with the harvest to come all the way south from the Peace to Edmonton. Another year, maybe.

Peace River Country, of course, is a whole other Alberta. During the Dirty Thirties it was held up as a land of milk and honey — or at least, rain — to prairie farmers who were "droughted out." Barry Broadfoot's *Ten Lost Years* tells many such stories, including the one about the family fleeing north by wagon until the mosquitoes kill the horses. The farmer remembers touching the horses' flanks: "My hand would come away positively black and red. Black was the crushed bodies of the mosquitoes. Red, well you know what the red was . . ." The horses lay down and died, leaving him and his wife and kids to walk out with what they could carry. He ends the story bitterly: "We were way off the main road, miles off, shooting off to a place nobody goes and a storekeeper in Peace River told us, he was laughing, the fool, that if we had waited till winter some sleighs and lumberjacks, loggers, would have come along. Appears we were on a winter logging road and there was no farm land up that way at all. I lost two good horses and all my patience finding out, and now I kill every mosquito lands within half a mile of me. I'm pure hell on skeeters."

Certainly, it's a major surprise to travel hundreds of miles northwest of Edmonton through endless bush, in the comfort of a car, then near Grande Prairie to find yourself in . . . Manitoba! A fertile, green, open land of fields and grain elevators!

As I got to know the area from my father's cousin's family base in Fairview I was amazed to find that at Dunvegan, the old fur trade fort on the mighty Peace River, they've had a rich vegetable garden, all these miles north of Edmonton, *ever since 1805.* The area looms so large in Gibson family lore that when my parents toured Canada in 1981, they visited not only Banff and Calgary and Edmonton, but also Lethbridge in the south and Fairview in the north. Many Albertas, indeed.

I stumbled into the Alberta writing community very early in my career thanks to a remarkable man named George Hardy. Generations of students at the University of Alberta knew him as a perennial professor of classics, from 1922 to 1964. Ah yes, a lifetime devoted to teaching Ancient Greek and Latin; we all know the type. No, you don't: George, born in 1895, had fought in the First World War, and was such a tough, active guy that he rose to be the president of the

Canadian Amateur Hockey Association. Ah yes, you say, you know *that* type.

Not quite. He was also a bestselling novelist. His big, brawling, traditional book about ancient Rome *The City of Libertines* (1957) reportedly sold more than a million copies. Very late in his life, when he was well over eighty years old, he wrote for me two epic swashbuckling novels about Julius Caesar, *The Scarlet Mantle* (1977) and *The Bloodied Toga* (1979). ("Then Brutus was in front of him. Brutus! And a dagger in his hand — raised.") They are full not only of accurate history and fascinating details of ancient Rome, but also of adventure and violence and sex.

The old soldier came by his knowledge in these matters honestly. When he visited Toronto (he liked to stay at the long-lost Lord Simcoe Hotel) he would astonish me with his continuing involvement with fleshly pleasures. I remember him, in his eighties, sitting and puffing placidly on his pipe, telling me, "As a man, I still get the urge. And when I do" — puff, puff — "I do something about it."

And then he would reveal to his astonished visitor that his hotel suite was being shared by a girlfriend — somewhat younger, still only in her seventies — who was similarly inclined. It was an education for me.

His constant visits to see the sights and the sites of ancient Greece had gained him some good friends among modern Greeks. His best friend died in the brutal civil war between the Communists and the Royalists that tore Greece apart in 1946. "Doug," he told me, his old soldier's jaw clenched on his pipe, "they sawed him in half."

In addition to his other pursuits, he was a keen member of the literary community, and for a number of years he was the very active president of the Canadian Authors Association. Now, in the days before the highly professional Writers' Union of Canada was formed, the CAA was the only game in town. But its amateur members left themselves open to the cruel fun poked at them by F.R. Scott in "The Canadian Authors Meet," which includes a line about "virgins of sixty." George, of course, was the man to change that, and he worked hard to raise the standard.

Closer to home, he worked to help Alberta's writers develop. With the help of a gallant sparkplug named John Patrick Gillese (who on a freelance writer's pay had somehow managed to raise a family, including his daughter, Eileen, a Rhodes Scholar who went on to become a judge on the Ontario Court of Appeal, supervising a young articling law student named Katie Gibson, and later marrying Katie and Cindy), he created a provincially funded program for an Alberta "Search for a New Novelist" competition. He sold Hugh Kane of Macmillan on the idea of being the lucky publisher of whatever was swept up by the contest, so when I joined Macmillan in 1974 I found that a large part of my time and energy was taken up by this quixotic search.

I found myself in Edmonton attending political events where literary oratory ran free. A cabinet minister named Horst Schmidt bellowed out optimistic speeches about "zis zearch!" and everyone applauded. Paul Hiebert's Sarah Binks admirer, the Hon. A.E. Windheaver ("and what about the roads"), would have been right at home. I, with my status mysteriously upgraded to "Dr. Gibson," tried to tamp down the hopes of great discoveries who were bound to go on to fame and fortune, but it was an uphill fight. Everyone believed that this great government plan would flush out a brace or two of truly fine novelists.

And it worked.

In the few years that we ran the competition, and published the winners, we discovered, among others, L.R. Wright, Fred Stenson, and Pauline Gedge.

If you were to fly around the world looking for a place that did *not* remind you in any way of the land of the pharaohs and their pyramids beside the Nile, there's no doubt that Edgerton, Alberta, would rank fairly high. Yet Edgerton, close to the border with Saskatchewan near Lloydminster, is where Pauline Gedge lived, turning out historical novels set in ancient Egypt. They have made her a world literary figure. Thanks to her long association with her Toronto literary agent, my old Macmillan colleague Bella Pomer, translations of her fourteen novels have appeared in German, Dutch, Italian, Spanish, Swedish, Finnish, Turkish, Norwegian, Danish, Portuguese, Greek, Czech, Slovak, Polish, Romanian, and Russian.

And in French. When Pauline's presence on a boat cruising down the Nile became known, her French fellow tourists became noticeably excited. Later, her 1978 novel set in ancient Britain, *The Eagle and the Raven*, won the Jean Boujassy Award from the Société des Gens de Lettres de France.

Although she has written some science fiction, fantasy, and even horror, it is for her novels of ancient Egypt that she is best known around the world. They have sold millions of copies. And it all started with the Alberta "Search for a New Novelist."

As Pauline, who was born in New Zealand and raised in England and Canada, approached the age of thirty, she was uncertain what to do with her life. She had done some teaching and was divorced, and was now a single mother with two kids and on welfare — long before Harry Potter's creator had provided an encouraging precedent. In the past, Pauline had entered the competition, but her two previous entries did not win. Now she was staying with her sister in Calgary and feeling that her dream of being a writer was over. She had given up. She was facing the flight of steps up to her sister's place, when . . . well, here's the story as she tells it on her website:

> I vividly remember standing at the foot of those steps, looking up towards her door, and feeling as though my life had no purpose. I began to climb. By the time I came to the top a miracle had taken place in me. I knew exactly what I was going to write about — or rather, who — an ancient Egyptian woman I had studied about and admired since I was eleven. It was an experience that every writer longs for once in a career, that flash of inspiration, and for me it happened at the moment when my future seemed dashed.

At the time, Pauline knew little about the one and only female pharaoh, Hatshepsut, and yet she was able to research her life in detail thanks to the wonders of inter-library borrowing. Pauline, her fingers flying, wrote *Child of the Morning* in only *six weeks*. Her whole family became involved in the race to finish the book and get it off to the competition in time. For revisions her mother read the first draft aloud, while Pauline reworked the text. When the final page was ripped from the typewriter (this was before computers) Pauline's father drove the five hours to Edmonton on winter roads to get the book in on time — unaware that we had extended the deadline because of a postal strike.

Pauline Gedge (1945–)

The rest is history . . . ancient Egyptian history. Here's a brief excerpt from the novel, about the great female pharaoh travelling along the Nile:

> It was but half a day's journey from Giza to Heliopolis, true heart of Egypt, and they reached the city at noon. Dignitaries came aboard, crawling over the deck to present their welcome, but the royal couple did not disembark, for here Hatshepsut was to receive her first crown in the temple of the Sun. She sat on her little chair while they kissed her feet, remote from them, gazing over their heads at the shining towers of the city. Behind her, on the west bank, more pyramids marched; and from where she sat, they seemed to be all around her head, a crown of power and invincibility.

The book was a worthy winner. I'm embarrassed to recall that when I met Pauline before the grand official dinner in Edmonton for the announcement, I gave her grandfatherly advice to ignore all of the political speeches predicting amazing worldwide success for her and her book. She listened politely, a quiet, self-contained woman with a level gaze. All of those ridiculous, outlandish predictions came true.

I'm sorry that I never had the chance to show her the white-faced ibis that Trevor Herriot found for us on the prairies. She probably would have known the ancient Egyptian word for the ancient bird.

When I joined Macmillan in the spring of 1974 I soon found myself in a race to get some new books to publish. I heard that five bright young women were keen to write a book together, each contributing two profiles of other women. I met with them and the result was an exciting book called *Her Own Woman: Profiles of Canadian Women* (1975). The authors were a fascinating group, and their lives have taken them in a variety of directions.

Heather Robertson went on to great success as a prolific non-fiction author, a novelist (*Willie*), and as a brave defender of authors' rights when newspapers and magazines tried to sweep them away in an electronic tide. Her name is known at the Supreme Court, and revered by other writers. When she died in March 2014, writers — and readers — across Canada mourned her loss.

Winnipeg's Melinda McCracken has also passed away too young. After her death, Heather continued their last joint book project, *Magical, Mysterious Lake of the Woods*, which came out in 2003.

Valerie Miner Johnson has moved, first to Britain (where she was a close friend of my brother Peter), then to San Francisco, where she is now a university professor, with a memoir (*The Low Road*, 2001), and several novels to her name.

Erna Paris has become a major non-fiction writer, specializing in international issues of war, peace, and justice, with books such as *Unhealed Wounds: France and the Klaus Barbie Affair* (1985), *The Sun Climbs Slow: Justice in the Age of Imperial America* (2008), and, most recently, *From Tolerance to Tyranny: A Cautionary Tale from Fifteenth Century Spain* (2015). For me she wrote *Jews: An Account of Their Experience in Canada* (1980), and we have stayed friends. In 2010, as chair of the Writers' Union of Canada, she had the pleasure of telling me that I had been made an honorary member. (Her exact words were, "Did nobody tell you?" but it was definitely the thought that counted.)

And there was Edmonton's own Myrna Kostash. Every time I go to the city I look forward to seeing Myrna again. And just about every time I try to see her she is off somewhere else, pursuing one or more of her many careers.

You can trace those careers by looking at her books. *All of Baba's Children* (1978) tells the story of Two Hills, Alberta, a Ukrainian Canadian settlement. *The Canadian Encyclopedia* notes that "with her first book Kostash became a prominent voice in public debates about ethnicity." It was a good fit with her own birth in a Ukrainian Canadian home in Edmonton, and her master's degree in Russian language and literature from the University of Toronto.

Career number two was predicted by *Long Way from Home* (1980), which revealed her interest in counter-cultural movements. The next book, which she wrote for me, *No Kidding: Inside the World of Teenage Girls* (under the DG Books imprint in 1988), like *Her Own Woman*, reflected Myrna's burning interest in feminism. Other passions are for her place as a prairie dweller and, in the words of *The Canadian Encyclopedia*, "her enduring fascination with the politics, histories, and peoples of Central and Eastern Europe." So when I contact her to get together in Edmonton, she's likely to be off in somewhere like Turkey, as when she was researching her 2010 book *Prodigal*

Daughter: A Journey to Byzantium (this may well be the first time that "Byzantium" appeared in a Canadian author's title, not used as a metaphor or a fictional setting).

But this is only a small part of Myrna's life. She is such an organizer, and so community-minded that she constantly founds groups (like the Periodical Writers Association of Canada, or the Creative Non-Fiction Collective Society, to give two examples). It has even been suggested that it was Myrna Kostash who invented the term "creative non-fiction," a type of writing she has practised with distinction, and advocated with missionary zeal. And if your organization needs a hard-working committee member — and which one doesn't? — then you can count on Myrna, even to be your chair, as she was for the Writers' Union in difficult days, bravely ushering the Union through a tidal wave of political correctness that threatened to swamp it.

It was in 1993 that a group of minority writers approached the Writers' Union with the complaint that they didn't feel fully accepted in the mostly white Union.

Crisis! The result was that the guilt-stricken Union agreed to run a conference in Vancouver in 1994 that was restricted to non-white writers. Naturally, the idea that a writers group would restrict entry by skin colour outraged many of the members, among them Pierre Berton, a former union chair, who spoke and wrote eloquently against it. Yet — now it can be told — when the Canadian government put the conference in danger by withdrawing its funding support, on the understandable grounds that it didn't fund conferences that excluded people because of their skin colour, Pierre secretly stepped in to provide the funds. It was a stunning example of a man who genuinely believed the saying, usually (and wrongly) attributed to Voltaire, "I disapprove of what you say, but I will defend to the death your right to say it." A remarkable man, Pierre Berton. I was proud to publish him when he was alive, as I am now to spread this excellent story about him.

As you'd expect, the crisis (with tricky issues like "appropriation of voice" given an airing, and words like "racist" thrown around) was a very difficult time for the Writers' Union. But thanks to Myrna's steady hand, it's now regarded as an important milestone for the Union, which goes marching on, glory hallelujah, with Myrna still on at least one committee.

Myrna Kostash (1944–)

The list of committees that Myrna has worried her way through is almost as impressive as the prizes she has won, the most recent of which was the 2010 Matt Cohen Award. (I was delighted to see her at the party before the ceremony and hailed her: "Myrna! What brings you to Toronto?" The prize was supposed to be kept a secret, so she hedged, very uncharacteristically. All was soon made clear, and I was delighted for my old friend.)

Did you notice my phrase "worried her way through"? Myrna is a serious person, engaged in lots of serious work, on dozens of committees, with a worried frown on her face, which might alarm a stranger impressed by her credentials. What you need to know is that this serious, hard-working person needs to be teased, and will soon be chuckling, and even giggling. I like her a lot and am glad to pay this tribute to her. And I look forward to finding her in Edmonton some day.

Alberta is split in every way between Edmonton, the provincial capital, and Calgary, the commercial capital to the south. During my time as a publisher, Calgary was not only where W.O. Mitchell lived, it was the centre of a flourishing literary scene. It had two terrific bookstores — Sandpiper Books, near W.O.'s home, and Pages, the Kensington shop owned first by Peter Oliva, before he became a writer, then by Cathy MacKay. When Cathy died, I flew to Calgary to speak at the funeral of my old M&S friend. The university had a lively faculty, including the novelist Aritha van Herk, and a huge budget to spend in acquiring the papers of Canadian authors. It had a lively literary festival (held in Calgary and Banff) headed by my friend Anne Greene. In *Stories About Storytellers* I tell the tale of the time I stepped in to chair a festival session for 400 kids, where I introduced James Houston as the man who created the towering sculpture at the entrance to the nearby Glenbow Museum. Jim then stepped forward and went on to steal the show.

And above all, at the *Calgary Herald*, it had Ken McGoogan.

From 1982 until he resigned in 1999, Ken put Calgary on the Canadian literary map. When we penny-pinching publishers were planning promotional tours across the country, we would weigh the cost of a stop in this city as opposed to that one, and carefully consider the publicity that each city would provide. With Ken on the job, Calgary became an essential stopover. We knew that we could count on him to produce a thoughtful, lively interview with each author, and publish it in time to promote any local public author event. Because the publicity was so good, crowds turned out for the readings, and because the crowds were so good, other events were held, and because of all this, every author would try to come to Calgary for a chat with Ken. A virtuous circle. Then a bitter strike at the *Herald* turned into a lockout (I paid a sad visit to the picket line), and when the dust settled, Ken was gone.

The result was depressing evidence that one man can indeed make a difference to a city's literary culture, and Calgary suffered from his absence, even if Canada benefitted from his transformation into an author of books about the North, and the fine book that contains a kind final shoutout to me, *How the Scots Invented Canada*. Fortunately, we have a record of Ken's work in those Calgary days, including many author profiles, in his 1991 book, *Canada's Undeclared War: Fighting Words from the Literary Trenches*. There he argues passionately that what our authors do really matters, since what we have here is "a culture — a way of thinking and being, a nation-wide set of values and preoccupations — worth defending." He deals with themes I know all too well, about the constant pressure exerted by the big international distributors, whether of movies or books, and the uphill fight faced by Canadians in those areas.

Ken is also a great storyteller, and the book is full of Calgary encounters with visiting major authors. Try this one:

"The strangest thing happened to Leonard Cohen in Calgary in 1984. He was sitting in an obscure little restaurant talking to an interviewer when a waitress slipped him a note. 'Dearest Leonard,' it began. Cohen stood up, went over to the waitress and asked her who had sent it. The woman was gone."

Ken was the interviewer, so he got the whole story. One of the most famous Cohen songs is "Sisters of Mercy," about two young women he knew in 1966. In Ken's words, "The note Cohen received was written by one of the original Sisters of Mercy — who now lives in Calgary and who somehow ended up in Flix at precisely the same time as Cohen."

Leonard was amazed. "What a coincidence! Why didn't she come over to our table? Maybe she didn't want to intrude. Delicacy! What incredible delicacy!"

Most people don't know that Alistair MacLeod, the soul of Nova Scotia, was born in Saskatchewan and raised in Alberta. The reason lies deep in the roots of the Cape Breton way of life. His father was a miner, and went to where the jobs were.

In his fine book *This Is My Country, What's Yours?* Noah Richler quotes him about that experience:

I started school in a place called Mercoal, Alberta. It was one of those typical company towns. We lived in company houses that were built on stilts, and when the price of coal dropped, the town went away.

I remember, a number of years ago, driving from Banff to where Mercoal was, and there was absolutely nothing there. I drove into this little clearing and I said to my children, "This is where I started school." And they all laughed. They thought, "Here is Dad being funny." They were thinking, "Well, where's the school?"

He concludes the story: "We had come from a place that was very rooted, and here was this very different kind of place. There are people who come from there who cannot find where they were born, because it was a company town that just *vanished*."

Alistair's father brought the family back to Nova Scotia as often as possible, but there was a spell when the teenaged Alistair worked as a milkman in Edmonton. His employer, a kindly man, worked hard to persuade him that he had a good future in the milk delivery business. Alistair decided to try something else.

I once travelled on the Yellowhead Highway in Anne Stevens's M&S car with Alistair from Edmonton to Jasper, where we both spoke to the Alberta Library Conference at Jasper Park Lodge. The Yellowhead has its hazards, as Jane's brother, Peter Brenneman, knows only too well. On a mid-winter night he got an emergency call at home in Grande Cache. One of his workers had just hit a wild horse on the Yellowhead and was in hospital in Edson. Peter jumped in the car and drove east. At one point, the snowy night landscape became dreamlike, full of moving shapes. He realized that a ghostly herd of wild horses was racing along beside him. Then — *bang* — a horse was on his hood and through his windshield. Peter jammed on the brakes, and the horse dropped off and disappeared. Peter had to inch the rest of the way into the hissing sub-zero winds with no windshield. After he made it to Edson and reported the accident, the police found no evidence of the horse. In Alberta, even the wild horses are tough.

There's a link with Alistair MacLeod here. Do you know where these wild horses came from? There used to be scores of horses at work in the Alberta coal mines. When the companies closed the mines, they turned the horses loose, to fend for themselves. To this day their descendants roam the mountain country like ghosts.

Alistair MacLeod has a very funny W.O. story from his time in Banff. I sometimes had to coax it out of him, as I did at the Eden Mills

Festival near Guelph in 2012. He and W.O. taught writing together each summer at the Banff Centre. The famous centre, perched just above downtown Banff, a celebrated tourist town surrounded by mountains, has played a huge part in developing Canadian artists of all sorts, from musicians to ballet dancers all the way to ambitious young creative writers. It was at its peak in the summer, and I spent at least a week there, teaching at the Banff Publishing Workshop, every summer from 1981 to 1988. You may even find the remains of a tepee built in the woods there by my daughters.

But Alistair's story concerns a winter ride that he and W.O. took from the Calgary airport to Banff, to discuss major policy issues with the Centre people. When Alistair flew in late in the evening he thought that he and W.O. would stay overnight in Calgary. But W.O. was impatient to get to Banff, only ninety minutes away to the west. So they hailed a cab, got into the back seat, and gave the driver directions to Banff.

Unfortunately, the driver was new to Calgary, and to Canada, and did not know the way. Alistair had to direct him through Calgary towards this mysterious place called "Banff."

Even more unfortunately, it began to snow. Heavily. Very heavily. The driver, who had grown up in a much warmer climate, was clearly not used to snow. Soon they were driving along the Trans-Canada at a walking pace. W.O., who was dozing in the back seat, would look up occasionally and growl, "For Crissake, what the hell is going on?" and Alistair would continue to urge the driver onward. The poor man was appalled by the fact that whenever the snow cleared briefly, there were no lights or houses visible. Alistair would assure him that, yes, up ahead lay Banff, a town with lights and buildings and every-thing. Beside Alistair, W.O. dozed on.

Suddenly, out of the storm a large animal reared up before them. The driver turned the wheel, the elk disappeared, and the car hit a patch of ice and began to spin. Alistair, mindful of the instructions for an emergency like this in those days before seatbelts, put his arms around W.O. in a protective hug, and tried to wrestle him down to the safety of the floor.

W.O., roused from sleep by a hugging assault from the man he thought a platonic friend, came awake, struggling and snorting, "What the hell . . . !" He was not pleased.

The car spun to a stop, still on the highway. The driver began to cry. "*Oh, gentlemen,*" he wailed. "*I do not believe there is a Banff!*"

Alistair, leaning forward encouragingly, talked him onward. There was a bad moment when they reached the edge of the park and the official entrance, which was full of "Banff" signs but was dark and unattended in the middle of the night. This revived the driver's despairing belief that "*there is no Banff!*" But they made it eventually, and all three survived to tell very different tales. And "Mitchell's Messy Method" of teaching writing continued to inspire and inform many more writers down through the years at Banff.

You'll notice that an elk played a part, even if it was only a trot-on part, in that story. When I taught at the Banff Publishing Workshop, the drifting herds of elk were a prominent part of the campus, and in rutting season (October, and thus writers' festival season) there were many problems. I remember Roddy Doyle complaining to the audience that he had experienced a lot, touring the world to promote his books, but, as he put it in his worried North Dublin accent, this was the first time he had been in danger "of being focked by an elk."

Another elk story will follow soon. In Banff, my own WordFest event was introduced, to my delight, by my old friend Fred Stenson (author of *The Trade* and many others), who was famously another successful product of Alberta's Search for a New Novelist. Since I had just told the story of my notoriously unsuccessful attempt to interrupt a Mavis Gallant reading, at the end Fred came onstage to interrupt me, crouching, hands protecting his head, terrified by his role. It was very funny. And I did stop.

Later, in the same splendid new centre building that has replaced the old Donald Cameron Dining Hall, I had fun chairing the final session (featuring the fiction quintet of Germany's Thomas Pletzinger, my old friend Madeleine Thien, Scotland's Stuart MacBride, and our own Helen Humphreys and David Bezmozgis). Earlier we heard from Guy Vanderhaeghe. Guy's Saturday night reading from *A Good Man* was the high point at Banff, where he alluded to "an elk story," without elaborating. I know the story, and can reveal it here.

Some years ago (possibly even before Roddy Doyle's complaint), Guy was staying at the centre during rutting season. After breakfast with his friend Robert Kroetsch in Donald Cameron Hall, Guy came out of the hall alone and noticed that a herd of elk had drifted across to block his path back up to his residence, with the male looking aggressive. So he prudently waited at the foot of the stairs, which provide a sort of a barrier to any elk that lacks Fred Astaire training on staircases. A confident young woman came out from breakfast, and Guy politely suggested that it might be best to wait for ten minutes until the elk moved on. She took this suggestion badly.

"I will walk wherever I please!" she announced, and strode towards the herd.

The male elk had not read the proper consciousness-raising books. So she ended up behind a tree, yelling for help. Guy modestly describes what happened next, in a scene starring the fine Western novelist and teacher Robert Kroetsch: "That's when Kroetsch arrived on the scene and took charge. He tore off his jacket, advanced on the elk roaring like the Bull of Bashan, beating clouds of dust out of the ground with his windbreaker. It was a truly impressive, primal sight. I followed along in an entirely cowardly support role, tooting in my high tenor voice, and feebly waving my jacket the way the Scarlet Pimpernel fanned the air with his lace handkerchief. When Kroetsch succeeded in driving off the elk, he got no thanks from the young woman." Guy ends with the words "she simply fled for the residences, sobbing."

And the woman did not seek out Guy, the Scarlet Pimpernel, to thank him.

Another wildlife encounter, this time near Jasper. Once, when I was staying at my cousin Graeme and his wife, Ann's cabin in August, I did a very foolish thing. I knew that the old fur-trade route to the Pacific ran west on the Athabasca River, then up the Whirlpool. Then the portage route went alongside the Whirlpool all the way to the watershed, and into British Columbia. This was sacred fur-trade territory, and I planned to hike part of the way along it.

I set off alone, stupidly not telling anyone where I was going. As I walked along beside the well-named Whirlpool it was such a beautiful, peaceful August day and I was so far from anyone else that it seemed a noisy intrusion to keep ringing my bear bell. I silenced it, and drifted peacefully along the trail, enjoying the rich crop of raspberries. I came around a corner, and there in front of me was a great pile of bear scat, still steaming. There was no bear in sight.

But when I walked past the spot, now ringing my warning bear bell very energetically, I felt sure that he was somewhere just off the trail, watching me through the thick bush. The hair rising on the back of my neck told me that we have primitive senses that lie dormant, except in emergencies. My hike, now loud with the sound of the bear bell rung by my sweaty hand, was spoiled by the prospect of passing that spot again, and by my realization that if there had been an incident, days could have passed before help arrived.

If I had been confronted by the bear, I hope I would have been able to remember Andy Russell's advice. Andy, the author of *Grizzly Country* (which I did not edit) and *Memoirs of a Mountain Man* (which I did), was a grizzled old outfitter, guide, and rancher from the foothills country down near Pincher Creek, and a great friend. To prepare for his book on the despised Oldman River Dam (*The Life of a River*) Andy and I once followed the river all the way from its start as a little stream in the Rockies to "The Gap," where it swirls on to the prairie, then to the dam site itself (supply your own "not by a dam site" joke here), where we scrambled through the protective fencing around the dam, unchallenged by man or bear. The life of an editor contains many surprises.

Andy, a craggy, lean, wind-burned guy in a buckskin jacket and under a Stetson, was not a boastful man, but when I asked him about grizzly bear attacks, he told me that in the course of all his years in the foothills and the Rockies he had "stopped" more than twenty grizzly charges.

"*Stopped?*" I quavered. "How do you stop a grizzly charge, Andy?"

"Well, first you stand your ground." (I suspect this may be the hardest part . . . but running is not a good tactic against an animal that can run faster than you, and can casually kill you with one swipe to the back of the neck.) "Then," he said, "you talk to them."

"*Talk* to them? What . . . what do you say?"

"It's not that important. I'll say something like 'I'm Andy Russell, and I know that you live here and want to get from where you are to over here, so I'm not going to face you down but just sort of step aside here, like this, and let you through . . . ' and that usually works."

More than twenty times it did work. On reflection, maybe the key line is "I'm Andy Russell."

I've called this chapter "Alberta and the Mountains," so I feel able to move us west of Banff. I remember once, as a favour, escorting the English author D.M. Thomas from the Calgary WordFest to the Banff part of the moveable feast. I took him (theme alert!) to see a herd of elk at the Banff golf course, then up to the top of Sulphur Mountain. As the author of *The White Hotel* and other books, he was obviously an intelligent man. But when from the Sulphur lookout I showed him the scores of snowy mountains marching off to the horizon in the west, he had real trouble accepting my assurance that these mountain ranges, split by valleys, *ran for hundreds of miles to the west*. For a man grounded in green Cornwall, all this wasteful, rocky Canadian space was almost literally unimaginable.

Not far west of Banff, along the Trans-Canada Highway, you come to the border with British Columbia. Physically, it's not very dramatic right there. But it is, in fact, one of the most astounding borders anywhere in the world. Heading almost due north/south, the border runs along the summits of the highest peaks in the Rockies. No foot has ever trod along that border for huge stretches, and none ever will. Thanks to the invention of planes we can now fly across it, look down, and marvel.

The Alberta-B.C. border is also a spectacular watershed. South of Banff, rain or snow that falls on the eastern slopes will flow into rivers like Andy Russell's Oldman, merge with the South Saskatchewan, then the Nelson, to end up in Hudson Bay. Some sun-seeking snow-flakes will melt to flow southeast in Alberta into the Milk River, and from there south to join the Mississippi system, to end up in the Gulf of Mexico. Isn't our geography exciting?

The western slopes send *their* rain and snow into the Pacific, and I once was a thrilled participant in the process. In the 1980s I took off from teaching the art of publishing at Banff to ride a white-water raft down the Kicking Horse River into Golden, B.C. I was part of a group of strangers who paid money, got into life jackets, and pushed off in a big rubber raft clutching paddles. The guys in charge were experts. They rehearsed us on what to do if we fell out into the churning white-water. Even better, they managed to convince us that the safety of the raft depended on each one of us digging hard with our paddles as we hit the white-water stretch, and fought our way through.

I was in the bow at one side, and when we plunged into the white stuff, SWAAASH, I was hit in the face by bucketfuls of icy water that took my breath away. But through all the roar and the bucking, foaming spray I kept paddling fiercely, blinking through the icy spray, because the safety of the raft depended on it. Soon the roaring died away, the water levelled out and turned dark again, and we had made it. When we reached the bank and staggered out we whooped and embraced our fellow survivors. We had come through this together!

After they dropped us off in Banff the rafting crew presumably went off, *yawn*, to pick up the next group of tourists, and to impress on them how important it was for each of them to paddle hard, if the raft was to survive. I went back to the publishing workshop and was so enthusiastic that several others signed up for the white-water trip. I have a tendency to let my enthusiasms show, as you may have noticed. And most writers, and editors, will do well to remember to "just keep paddling."

But what has all this to do with being an editor? Within a couple of years I was editing Don Starkell's book, with passages such as this: "As we approached the rapids, we cut through some large standing waves and roared downhill into the V of the flow. *Orellana* shot through the water like an orange missile . . ." Experience helps editors. Experiences, too.

I wish I'd been able to take D.M. Thomas with me in the summer of 2014, when Jane and I flew southwest of Calgary to Castlegar. This was in the middle of the Stampede, and at the Calgary airport even the most dapper Air Canada agent was required to wear a Stetson and yee-haw his way through the workday. Our flight south on Central Mountain Air took us down to the foothills, then west through the Selkirks. It is an amazing stretch of mountain country, Crowsnest Pass territory, then the Kootenays. The sudden swoop down through the jostle of mountains to land at Castlegar caught our attention. It was a little like landing on the deck of an aircraft carrier.

The novelist Anne DeGrace (a friend from the Writers' Union AGM in St. John's) met us and took us along winding roads past the rivers that would flow south into the United States as the mighty Columbia River. Soon we were in Nelson.

For a few years now Nelson has hosted the Elephant Mountain Literary Festival, and I'm delighted to report that, led by Lynn Krause, they bring in worthy authors like, well, me . . . not to mention Gail Bowen, Eleanor Wachtel, Angie Abdou, and others, including Sid Marty. My old friend Sid, the big, burly folksinger, poet, and author of non-fiction classics like *Men for the Mountains* (1978) and *The Black Grizzly of Whiskey Creek* (2008), lives in Lundbreck, in the foothills, about as close as you can get in Alberta to Nelson. How long did the drive into the Kootenay country take him? Six hours.

For me, to stumble across Nelson was a piece of amazing good luck, since it's a very unusual place. First (and second and third) there's the setting. Elephant Mountain ("See, that's the trunk!") lies across the west arm of Kootenay Lake, and the town climbs steeply up from the lakeshore opposite the mountain. About 10,000 people live in the town, but it's in the centre of the Kootenays, so that many thousands of others flock in to do their shopping and other community things there, always surrounded by mountains.

There are about forty (count them) restaurants in town, and I can report that the local co-op store has a wide range of environmentally friendly products that you'd have trouble finding anywhere else in Canada. A reason for that is the Nelson background as a favourite destination for idealistic draft-evaders during the Vietnam War years. There is also a thriving "underground economy": a grandmotherly figure at a festival event told me about the details of the homegrown marijuana business (with "two light" setups for grow-ops being really small-scale, but "ten lights" being impressive). Apparently the town is full of amiable professionals who will help you to manage your crop, and when they send in someone to "bud" the plants, it's likely to be your friendly Sunday-school teacher tapping at the door.

Anne DeGrace is a calm, understated, middle-aged woman now, but she told us an amazing story about Nelson neighbourly help. In "hippy" days, when she first came to the town from Ottawa, she was a young, pregnant woman on her own, and she started a book and record store called "Packrat Annie's." When the baby came, two local Quaker women showed up out of the blue, with sleeping bags, and told her that they would run the store until she was able to return. Total strangers, and as good as their word. Anne still says that they changed her view of human nature. Now she works at the Nelson

Library, has published four novels, has found a good husband, and quietly gives a great tour of the town.

You may know Nelson without being aware of it. The Steve Martin movie *Roxanne* was set here, and gives a hint of the delights of the old mining town, which boomed in the 1890s. We were there in midsummer, at the time of the full moon, which had a supernatural appearance, rising over the encircling mountains. Strangers stopped in the street to gape at it, chat, and speculate if it was the biggest moon ever.

Certainly, July 2014 saw some of the hottest weather ever recorded in the B.C. Interior. At the festival, after Gail Bowen and Eleanor Wachtel had given successful Friday evening talks, with Sid Marty, Donna Morissey, and Angie Abdou to come later, I was due to give my show on Saturday afternoon in the Civic Theatre. The weather was scorching, and the town beach on the lake was a major counter-attraction. The *Nelson Star* warned its readers about the record-breaking heat, "with afternoon temperatures from the mid-30s to 40 degrees." But we were comforted by the news that air conditioning at the Civic Theatre was due to be installed.

No such luck. The gallant audience sat fanning themselves as I did my stuff on the stage. In the wings the heroic Jane slaved in the air-less dark over red-hot electronic appliances. After the ninety-minute show, when I took off my blazer-and-tie "publisher's uniform" back in our hotel room, Jane complained that my shirt was so sweat-soaked she could wring it out. The heat was something we remembered with head-shaking affection a few months later when my December show in Collingwood, Ontario, at the foot of the Blue Mountain ski hill, was interrupted by the roar of a snow-making machine. Local hazards. Ah, the life of a literary troubadour!

But also, ah, Nelson. Unforgettable, all the way from Gyro Park with its lookout over the lake (and great Saskatoon berries!) to the Japanese garden near the old train station at the other end of town, where in the early days the whole population used to show up to see who had rolled into the booming town.

The next day we were driven to Castlegar to pick up our car, which we drove west — and up and down — through some of the most beautiful country in Canada. Our car crawled over ear-popping high mountain passes, then raced down, down, down to the next river bridge, then coasted along beside farm fields before the next groaning climb. It was always fascinating ("Wait a minute! This is where the Doukhobors settled!" "Big White! I used to ski here!") as we drove to stay with Jane's brother Peter and his wife, Heather, in Kelowna.

That's a special city for us. Peter and Heather lost their home there in the great fire of 2003, when 27,000 people were evacuated with no jammed roads, no looting, and no panic. In my role as publisher of M&S I was very pleased to be able to combine forces with the local Kelowna paper to produce *Firestorm: The Summer B.C. Burned*, a big, illustrated book that sold very well. It raised lots of money for reclamation projects, although it was nothing compared to the estimated 250 *million* trees lost in the fire. (I remember being flown across the Kelowna fire scene in a small plane when the pilot showed us one house, where his buddy's "outdoor thermometer had stuck at sixty-nine degrees Celsius." The house survived, although far more than 200 in Kelowna did not.)

After Nelson, when I dropped in to visit Mosaic Books in Kelowna, it was great to be warmly remembered as "the fire storm guy."

CHAPTER 5

THE COASTS OF B.C.

The Vancouver International Writers Festival . . .
Unconventional Memories of Carol Shields . . . Bill
Richardson Sets Me Dancing . . . Almost Exposed at the
Improv Theatre . . . A Pitch for Alan Twigg . . . Jack Hodgins's
Island . . . Sir Francis Drake and Comox . . . The Delights of
Denman Island . . . Sunshine Sketches of a Little Coast . . .
At Home with Andreas Schroeder . . . On to Haida Gwaii . . .
A Mile in James Houston's Waders

Hal Wake has had a huge impact on Canadian writers and readers. For many years he was the man on the book beat at *Morningside*, which meant that after surveying scores of books he decided Peter Gzowski should talk with this new author and not that, or that, or that one. Often the chat with a young poet named Lorna Crozier or a new novelist called Jane Urquhart or Nino Ricci (to take just three examples out of many) changed their lives and affected hundreds of thousands of readers. I know very well just how immediate and massive the impact on book sales was in Peter's heyday. In my role as publisher I received many phone calls from booksellers pleading to be told when an author would be featured on *Morningside* (so that they could stock up on the book in question).

But all good things come to an end and in 1990 Hal Wake, the big, curly-haired guy originally from Ottawa, left his Toronto home to take his family back west to Vancouver. Soon he was no longer in the studio backrooms. As CBC Radio's morning man he was wakening farmers in the Fraser Valley, hailing sailors at Tsawwassen, and soothing commuters stuck on the Lions Gate Bridge on their way downtown through Stanley Park, where joggers around the seawall were listening to him on their iPods. Hal's friendly, level voice was a constant reassurance, even when the day's news, and the interviews he conducted, revealed that not all was right with the world, even in the Vancouver he loved.

One of the reasons that he loved his new Vancouver home was the writers' festival that had been set up there in 1988 by a Scottish whirlwind named Alma Lee, who had previously herded the cats of the Writers' Union of Canada. Year by year the festival had got better and better, attracting a loyal local audience, including lots of excited kids, and producing a spreading international reputation among major authors everywhere. (Once, they even roped me in as a host of a reading involving Jack Whyte and Diana Gabaldon, so they had very high standards.) Then Alma decided to retire. Hal, a long-time supporter and former board member, applied for the job, and got it, starting in 2007.

Once again, he was fully immersed in the world of books. To my delight he asked me, in the fall of 2011, to bring my show to Vancouver Writers Fest. The previous year I had played an offstage part in the festival's celebration of Alice Munro. When all of the international cast of writers there to pay tribute were assembled by Hal in a fine Indian restaurant it was my happy duty to thank them all on Alice's behalf. In answer to a question about my editorial role I shrugged and said that my main role was to tell Alice to stop rewriting and polishing the manuscript endlessly, and to grab it from her. At this there was an explosion from the quiet man sitting beside me. *"Ah,"* said Alistair MacLeod to the group. *"He's very good at that!"*

When Jane and I flew in from Banff we were whisked to the Granville Island Hotel, the centre of the festival. We were in time to attend the opening night gala dinner, a Bollywood-themed extravaganza. I watched the energetic Indian dancing, marvelling that people the world over have managed to arrive at folk dancing styles that have so much in common.

I was very pleased to be seated at a table alongside Anne Giardini. A lawyer by training, she is a remarkable combination of a major business tycoon (she runs the Canadian branch of the giant West Coast lumber company, Weyerhaeuser) and an enthusiastic patron of the literary arts, as she was proving that night in her role as the chair of the board of the Vancouver International Writers Festival. (She is also a board member of PEN Canada.) But she comes by her interest honestly. She is the author of two novels, and she is the daughter of Donald and Carol Shields.

I knew — and even published — Carol Shields. In 1982 we brought out her fourth novel, *A Fairly Conventional Woman*. The plot centres on a middle-aged woman attending a conference, where the possibilities of romance intrude. I know all about this from my own life, and how our society has come to terms with special rules. When Jane and I met, like two fire-engines colliding, at the Couchiching Conference, a friend who is an experienced political operative — and who may wish to remain anonymous here — was appalled by my swift plans: "Doug, this was *at a conference* — you don't have to *marry* her!"

Interestingly, while Carol dealt with the matter much more

Carol Shields (1935–2003)

sensitively in her novel than my laddish friend, the theme seemed to matter to her. *Happenstance* (1980), which was cleverly packaged with *A Fairly Conventional Woman* in 1994, offers another perspective on the novels' central marriage — that of the middle-aged historian husband, whose anxiety about the book he is trying to write reaches a crisis while his wife is off at the convention. Like *Larry's Party* (1979) it's the perfect demonstration that Carol was able to write convincingly from a male point of view.

That's fascinating, because she's famous for the perfect pitch that she had for the ears of her female readers. As evidence I'd present the *Dropped Threads* book projects that were so deservedly popular with women's book clubs. Carol told an interviewer that she and Marjorie Anderson, her co-editor, felt "that women are so busy protecting themselves and other people that they still feel that they have to keep quiet about some subjects." The usually hidden subjects included work, menopause, childbirth, a husband's terminal illness, the loss of a child, getting old, the power of sexual feeling, and much else. *Dropped Threads* went into several editions, topped the bestseller lists, and spoke to millions of women.

It also revealed a surprising side of Carol Shields. In her afterword in the first edition, she revealed that at her college graduation ceremony in high summer "under our black academic gowns my girl friends and I wore, by previous agreement, nothing. Nothing at all. This was considered high daring in those days, 1957."

It raises eyebrows even today.

Almost as surprising is the fact that Carol's supportive husband, Donald, read her works for the first time only when they appeared in the bookstore. The families of writers develop coping systems that make life simpler for them.

Carol's 1982 novel for us was full of quiet virtues, with not a hair out of place, and the plot and dialogue were smoothly polished. It's interesting, I think, that she once wrote a book for Penguin on Jane Austen, noting the significance of "glances" in her heroine's understated work. I greatly enjoyed all of my publishing encounters with this friendly, lady-like Winnipegger with a gentle overbite who managed to combine writing with teaching and raising five children (including Anne, the future lumber baron). In her low-key way she was cheerful, and straightforward, and blessed with a lively sense of humour. (Naked under her graduation gown?)

Yet *A Fairly Conventional Woman* managed only modest sales, and she moved on, without rancour, to publish her books elsewhere. And other, wiser publishers, went on to publish her next books, leading (just eleven years later) to *The Stone Diaries*. That book won the 1993 Governor General's Award, the National Book Critics Circle Award, and, in light of Carol's Chicago birth, the Pulitzer Prize.

Another one that got away.

Carol was of an age with Alice Munro, and they became very good friends. I know that after 1999 Alice would visit Carol at her home in Victoria, and that she stayed in close, affectionate touch during the long fight against breast cancer that finally took Carol away in 2003.

Our MC that evening at the Vancouver Writers Fest Gala was the unique Bill Richardson. A former Winnipegger (theme alert!), he has gone on to an enviable career as a CBC Radio star, hosting programs like *Richardson's Roundup*. He is also the author of half a dozen books, including the Stephen Leacock Award winner *Bachelor Brothers' Bed & Breakfast* (1993), and a similar number of books for lucky children. "Playful" is the precise adjective here; I suspect that he is the only person in *Canadian Who's Who* ever to list his hobbies as "polo, juggling, and playing the cello."

He also has a flourishing sub-career as an MC at events such as our Vancouver gala, and that night he and I laughed recalling an earlier encounter when he ran a Toronto Libris Award night, a sort of untelevised, unglamorous Oscar night for the Canadian book world.

Early in that Toronto evening Scott McIntyre had bounded with typical energy onto the stage to receive from Bill's hands an award for Douglas & McIntyre. But something was wrong. Pointing in distress at his throat Scott croaked that he had such bad laryngitis that he really couldn't speak. For the voluble Scott, this must have been as frustrating as a symphony conductor strapped into a straitjacket. Bill responded very creatively: "But surely, Scott, this is why Interpretive Dance was invented?"

A good joke, and the theme came up again that evening. Then, thanks to Alice Munro, I found myself invited to the podium to receive an award. Alice had learned about the environmental advantages of printing books on recycled paper, which was more expensive. Greedy publishers like me knew that it was totally inappropriate ("More *expensive?*") for big, bestselling books like Alice's forthcoming 2001 collection, *Hateship, Friendship, Courtship, Loveship, Marriage.* The shrewd environmental campaigners, however, saw Alice as a promising target, and reached her, and persuaded her. When Alice in turn persuaded me, kicking and screaming, to use the paper on her book, recycled paper suddenly became the norm. Alice's polite but firm stance changed the whole picture of printing in the Canadian book trade, forever.

Now, out of the blue, Bill Richardson was summoning me to the stage to receive an environmental award for good works.

I was speechless. So I said, "Interpretive dance, eh, Bill?"

And the astonished audience saw me miming elaborate gratitude to the great big sun up there, and demonstrating my love of all the little birds and other lovely things that make our world so beautiful and leave a sensitive person like me wanting to clasp them all to my bosom. It was disgusting, and must have been physically painful to watch.

I did manage to mention Alice's role, in words, before the appalled Bill thanked me and waved me off, noting that generations of stern Caledonian ancestors were now rolling over in their graves — and not, I suspect, in a well-choreographed way.

Hal Wake had set my show for Tuesday evening at the Improv Theatre on Granville Island. There was a fine, bare stage, with an array of café-style tables in front. Paul Whitney, the distinguished librarian, was all set to introduce me. What could possibly go wrong?

With five minutes before showtime, in the Green Room I told my kind volunteer handler that I should visit the washroom. "Not that one," she said, "it doesn't flush. The one down the corridor." Nobody added the words: "But don't close the door, or you'll be trapped inside."

You can imagine the rest, including the two-fisted beating on the door until the stage manager finally came ("Didn't anyone warn you about the door?") and released me, panting, just in time.

After Paul gave me a very nice introduction, Jane's jaw dropped as I strode manfully onto the stage with my zipper at half mast. She thought, for a moment, that nobody would notice, but she caught Janet's eye, and her friend nodded mournfully. For the next seventy-five minutes I paced around the front of the bare stage, unaware that many eyes were following, not me, but my zipper's dramatic progress. All part of the excitement of an unscripted show.

In September 1967, I came to Canada on the ferry from Seattle to Victoria. Since then, I always try to arrange to arrive in Victoria by ferry. This time it was by bus and ferry from Tsawwassen, with the usual delight in the birds ("Pigeon guillemots!"), then the swing through Active Pass and the bus trip from Sidney that landed us downtown at the Victoria bus station, to be met by Jack Hodgins, in accordance with tradition. Hotel hospitality suites are fine in their way, but there's nothing to beat staying at the home of old friends like Jack and Dianne. The whole house was one big hospitality suite, and we also got to check on whether the deer were still getting into the garden.

A fine, relaxing day, in fact, until it was time for the evening show at Bolen's bookstore. Munro's Books (started in 1963 by a young couple — the wife, Alice, went on to a career as a writer, while the husband, Jim, was awarded the Order of Canada in 2014 for his years of dedicated service to Victorian book-lovers) and Bolen's, farther out from downtown, are two of the best bookstores in the country. At Bolen's that evening my simple request "Which of these authors in my book would you like to hear about?" worked well. The only person who didn't seem to enjoy it was Jack, who hates public appearances, even as part of the audience, so much so that I tried to persuade him to go off and buy a book. But a large part of his agony came from the fact that I might be asked to talk about *him*, which I'm always pleased to do, but which embarrasses him. He got off lightly that evening.

In the small crowd in Bolen's were people from my past, including my old friend, Ralph Hancox, whom I got to know well when we were working together on the committee that created the Simon Fraser Publishing Studies program. Ralph, the former head of *Reader's Digest* in Canada, was a colleague and friend of Robertson Davies in his *Peterborough Examiner* days. It was Ralph who passed on to me R.D.'s confession to him that *Fifth Business* was a different, much franker book than its predecessors because his parents were dead when he wrote it.

Working with Ralph on that SFU committee put me in touch with many people who have since become good friends, notably Rowland Lorimer, who has made the Master of Publishing program (with its convivial-sounding degree, the MPub) a great success. But I should also mention the remarkable Alan Twigg. He is best-known as the editor of *B.C. BookWorld*, the quarterly magazine he started in 1987.

That alone has proved to be a great contribution to the world of books. But Alan is so energetic that he has also been the man behind the B.C. Book Awards, and the author of several books documenting and celebrating local writers, among his many other activities . . . which, I'm happy to say, led to his becoming an honoured member of the Order of Canada in 2014, the same year bookselling Jim Munro made the list.

Best of all (I speak selfishly here) he has written a book for me about his great non-literary enthusiasm, playing soccer. *Full Time: A Soccer Story* (2008) recounts his adventures — as an old guy born in 1952 — with other keen Vancouver men no longer in the first flush of youth, who play for the sheer love of the sport. In the book the team heads off to Spain, and the tour is a great success everywhere except the official score sheet. (In the summer of 2013, however, Alan and his buddies on Vancouver United went to Italy and won the championship for their Over 50 age category in the World Masters Games, held every four years, like the Olympics, and open to teams from around the globe. They won seven games in seven days in Turin to do it. *World champions!* And off the pitch, in real life, they ranged from brain surgeons all the way down to simple literary magazine editors.)

I once watched one of their Sunday morning games (regretfully turning down the chance to take the place of the missing referee) and was impressed by how ubiquitous the youthful, curly-haired Alan seemed to be. It's the same in the book world. At my unzipped performance in Vancouver, my friend Alan was sitting quietly at the back of the audience, ready to play defence.

One of my greatest strokes of luck was to be given the chance to publish Jack Hodgins. In my chapter about Jack in *Stories About Storytellers* I talk about my pleasure in having Jack and Dianne as friends. I also talk about how wonderful it was to be introduced to the magical world of his island, Vancouver Island.

Over the years I have got to know the island well. I've described roaming around it as the equivalent of travelling through a dozen little European countries, each with their own geography, climate, and culture. From the bookshop-rich city of Victoria, with its sea view south across the Juan de Fuca Strait to the snow-capped

Jack Hodgins (1938–)

Olympic mountains, I've headed west to Sooke and taken the famous Sooke Harbour House Hotel chef's tour where you wander through the gardens *eating the flowers*. Beyond that, I've stayed at Point No Point, and watched the surfers at the very non-biblical Jordan River, on my way to Port Renfrew. Warnings of cougars in the parks lent a spice of danger to my solitary walks there.

Just north of Victoria, where I once spent a happy hour banding hummingbirds (yes!), lies Goldstream Park where my author Cam Finlay and I once saw a little bird, an American dipper, hitch a ride on the back of a salmon moving upstream. In turn, from the capital city I like to move upstream all the way north up the east coast of the island. That scenic route, with magical place names like Chemainus (say it aloud, then again), always provides surprise after surprise.

The Saanich Peninsula, for instance, contains not only rich farms and gardens (like the one Lorna Crozier and Patrick Lane used to own, and which Patrick showed me around with gruff pride) but also the Victoria Airport, with reliable skylarks on the perimeter, and, more surprisingly, clusters of lollygagging sea lions on the beach just to the west. When the road climbs over the Malahat, you're in high California-style country, full of arbutus trees. Eric Nicol, the superb Vancouver-based humourist I used to love to publish, once described the impact of a bright orange, peeling arbutus tree set against a line of sober green firs and cedars as "looking like a stripper in the Mormon Tabernacle Choir."

The road north takes us to Duncan, the scene of a superb logging museum, a reminder that the whole island was built on the backs of loggers, men who lived and died in that dangerous harvest of wood. You get a sense of what the early loggers faced, with their puny little axes and handsaws, if you head west to Port Alberni. Near Coombs (with its famous "goats on the roof" market — you'll see what I mean), you come on the Cathedral Grove of 800-year-old massive trees, preserved for us to ponder. West of Port Alberni, where the Gibson family once sailed on *The Lady Rose* to Ucluelet, is the road across the mountains of the Vancouver Island Ranges. In winter, I can attest, the snow lies deep beside the ploughed road — and then you hit the coast near Tofino, and people are surfing!

For some years I timed my trips west to allow me to walk the Pacific Rim beaches near Tofino in March, big storm season, so that

I could see the armies of waves crashing in from Japan. Once, near Wickaninnish, I crunched across a beach covered with giant hailstones and looked west. After a spell there, I almost came to believe that the giant Fuji-shaped waves on the horizon were a real range of mountains. Time to head home.

Logging and fishing were the staples of life everywhere on the Island. In Nanaimo there was something else. Robert Dunsmuir, a Scot from just outside Kilmarnock, was born in 1825, around the same time as my scary (*"It says here you broke your leg!"*) Kilmarnock great-grandfather, Robert. Who knows what they put in the water there in those days (although the town did produce Johnny Walker whisky). But we have fatherless Robert Gibson creating a tweed mill, and Robert Dunsmuir, a miner, coming to Vancouver Island, discovering a coal seam north of Nanaimo and creating a mining empire. He was another scary man. In the restrained words of *The Canadian Encyclopedia*: "His disregard for safety, and his employment of cheap Asian labour and disallowance of unions made him unpopular with labour." The coal tradition lingers in Nanaimo with colourful place names like "Jingle Pot Road."

North of the city of Nanaimo, the list of interesting coastal towns goes on past Jack Hodgins's boyhood home of Merville, all the way to Campbell River, with Quadra Island nearby. That was where a visit to my author Alan Fry in 1972 saw us launching a canoe amid (unbanded) hummingbirds; five minutes later we were gliding just beneath disdainful bald eagles.

In 2014, however, I skipped the constant pleasures of the drive through the coastal towns, which are expanding greatly as retirees across the country come to realize the joys of life in temperate B.C. I flew in to Comox, rented a car, and drove through town, remembering the visit I once paid to Alice Munro in the local emergency ward. Alice used to winter in Comox, which avoided the rigours of snowbelt Clinton and offered her husband, Gerry, the pleasures of skiing on nearby Mount Washington. Our dinner plans were prevented by Alice's trip to the hospital, but when the doctor arrived to interrupt our chat I was smart enough not to ask him to take special care of this special patient. That would have offended Alice's sturdy democratic values. So as she lay there, I clapped her on the ankle, and left.

Comox has an astonishing history. Way back in 1580, when Shakespeare was a sixteen-year-old boy in Stratford, Sir Francis Drake sailed around the world. He kept the details of his voyage a state secret (away from evil Spanish eyes) but the bold B.C. historian Samuel Bawlf in 2003 brought out *The Secret Voyage of Sir Francis Drake, 1577–1580*, revealing that Drake had sailed up the West Coast as far as modern Alaska, then turned south in search of the perfect spot to establish a Pacific base for England, a new centre to be called "Nova Albion."

Bawlf is satisfied that Drake's description makes it clear that the chosen location was on what we now call Vancouver Island just north of Denman Island, in "the bay of small ships," the canoe-filled harbour of what is now — ta-da! — Comox.

Of course, it took roughly 400 years for this English-speaking centre to spring up, in a small way. But locals proud of this early brush with heroic history may choose to overlook the fact that a sixteenth-century map reference to this point locates it on "the backside of Canada."

South of Comox, the summer of 2014, my first destination was Nanoose Bay, where I spent three idyllic days with my Dunlop-raised cousin Graeme Young (later of Avison-Young, at the start of our lives my tricycling companion) and his wife, Ann, gazing across the Strait of Georgia at the Sunshine Coast opposite. I planned to phone Andreas Schroeder out of the blue to tell him to look out of his window to see a giant cruise ship heading north to Alaska. Such a phone call from his Toronto-based friend would have caused considerable surprise, but the timing never quite worked. A good mischievous idea, though.

We were just south of Parksville, very near the superb Rathtrevor Beach. As a birder I was sorry we missed the annual spring Brant Festival, where the town celebrates the return of the little duck-sized geese. (Once, in Connecticut, with my binoculars fixed to my face I was rejoicing in the arrival of the first Brants with my irreverent friend, James Houston. The old Arctic hand dismissed my romantic enthusiasm with the laconic words, "Very good eating.") But we were able to see the annual Canadian Sand Sculpture Competition. Who knew? Professional sand artists (might the proper word be *carvers* or *sculptors*, rather than sandcastle makers?) come from all over, including countries like Holland and Mexico. Each of them is given equal area, on which a set amount of pre-sifted sand is dumped. They have a total of twenty-four hours to create a sand sculpture of their choice (this year's theme was music) *using all of the sand.*

The results, I can report, are astounding, with thin sand towers ascending taller than me, and elaborate shoulder-high sand bridges winding through ancient towns where every shutter and rooftile is detailed. The miniature worlds that result are almost beyond belief, and the rich prizes well deserved. It's appropriate to remember that this is happening in Jack Hodgins territory: The Invention of the World, indeed.

Ferries are central to B.C. coastal life. The pull of the last ferry ends parties and events as efficiently as any siren, and the internalized rhythm of ferry folk is as silent but as strong as the pull of the tides. Jack Hodgins knows this. That's one reason why *The Invention of the World* (1977) opens with the man "waving your car down the ramp onto the government ferry." Then we follow him home, after "the two-hour trip across the Strait of Georgia, while the long backbone ridge of the Island's mountains sharpens into blue and ragged shades of green, and the coastline shadows shape themselves into rocky cliffs and driftwood-cluttered bays."

The ferry across from Buckley Bay to Denman Island is a much smaller operation, and the trip takes only ten minutes. Then the whole heartbeat of the island quickens as the cars and bikes pour off the ferry and jostle their way uphill to the Denman village centre (the words "downtown Denman" resist my typing fingers since the island's population is just over 1,000). Roughly half the cars race off southeast across the island to reach the ferry to Hornby Island. The Hornby people, of course, I'm assured, are very different, practically a different species.

Somehow tiny Denman has created a nationally famous, very successful Readers & Writers Festival, which has been running for several years now. The range of major authors is astounding. In July 2014 I was brought in along with people like Angie Abdou, Caroline Adderson, Maude Barlow (whom I used to publish), Pauline Holdstock, the spoken-word poet Zaccheus Jackson, Derek Lundy (who told me fascinating stories about "the red hand of Ulster," where a Viking chief won the race to be the first to touch the coast by cutting off his left hand and throwing it ashore), the outspoken Chris Turner (not on Stephen Harper's Christmas card list), Rita Wong, and the novelist Richard Wagamese. We went to each other's readings, and gave workshops. My own workshop group of ten local would-be writers was remarkable. As we went around the group, hearing their introductions and hopes, we were all fascinated by the range of life stories assembled in that small room in the local school.

All the visiting authors wandered around the village centre, dropping into the post office, the general store (founded in 1908), and Abraxis Books (well-stocked with my book, and with charming tales like the quiet visit some winters ago by Alice Munro: when she was asked "Are you who I think you are?" she replied, "Well, I'm certainly not Margaret Atwood!"). We all dropped into some of the many studios, and the craft and pottery shops — and basically got swallowed up in the life of the village.

That's when we weren't giving our individual readings on the main stage (where there were nice meals in the Back Hall), or in the Seniors Hall (right beside the old museum, with its records of the earliest European settlers in the 1870s, some of them Orkney settlers with names like Isbister, who must have been abashed by the trees they found everywhere). My big moment came at the main stage on Friday night. The audience of Denmanites (and the odd Hornby visitor) provided a warm, lively response that was very kind, and we all had a good time.

A large part of the pleasure in all this comes from the kindness of the organizers, led by the delightful Debbie Frketich, who made everything run smoothly, and left us all feeling welcome at all times. One memory: I was sitting chatting in the sun outside the Activity Centre with Richard Wagamese and his friend when an older woman shyly asked us for advice about how best to absorb a little baby of Native heritage into her family. I shut up, while Richard, who can be a man of great eloquence, simply told this worried great-grandmother, "Love her. Just love her."

The Denman people who came to these events were an interesting cross-section: "I was at school in High River with W.O. Mitchell's kids." "I worked in Prince Rupert at the CBC station, and I remember the cloud of cigarette smoke when Peter Gzowski was in the studio." "We knew Jack Hodgins, who's still a friend, back in the days when he taught high school in Nanaimo, and, boy, he got so nervous before his class!" (And there were visitors, like Tina from Read Island, who asked me: "How's my sister doing, next door to you in Toronto?" This is a small country.)

I especially liked the door prize draws that were a feature of every night. One of the friendly volunteers who made all this work, Stewart Goodings, would get on stage with Del Phillips's pretty daughter in her cocktail dress made from a torn-up thesaurus ("Very nice to read you," I said), and she would draw the winning number. My favourite prize, which demonstrated that Denman was a real rural community, was the Free Septic Tank Pump-out donated by Able & Ready Septic Service. The winning ticket was greeted with a genuine whoop of joy. No sceptics there.

A final note about my Denman visit. The festival billets its visitors with friendly hosts, who often prove to be remarkable. That was the case with John and Marion Dillon, who looked after me. I learned that they had left the Prairies to go to Yellowknife, where soft-spoken John ran the prison service for the Northwest Territories, and Marion taught kindergarten. When I asked John to tell me something about today's North that I didn't know, he told me that over sixty percent of the convicted criminals there are in jail for serious sexual assault. He and his officials ditched the rule about segregating sex criminals from the general prison population because they made up the large majority. Astonishing.

John and Marion intended to go to the North for just a couple of years, but liked life in Yellowknife so much that they stayed for more than twenty.

The Dillons also gave me a glimpse of Denman's unique society, with PhDs apparently clustered along every quiet country road. One morning John left breakfast early "to look after his butterflies." I was due to take a walk through Boyle Point Provincial Park, right beside their house at the south end of the Island. I duly strolled through the silent trees until I reached the lookout to Chrome Island with its lighthouse. On the clifftop, as I studied the colony of cormorants clinging to the island's nearly vertical rocks, a bald eagle soared alongside me, within a Ping-Pong ball's throw.

But butterflies?

The final morning of my visit, still impressed by the ecstatic reception of Maude Barlow's talk (not to mention the fine talks by the seafaring Derek Lundy and the Harper-grilling Chris Turner), I set off to see "the butterflies." Apparently a little butterfly named the Taylor's checkerspot is threatened. It survives only in Oregon and Washington — and in two places in B.C., Denman and Hornby Island. A neighbour of John's, Peter Karsten, is the famous retired head of the Calgary Zoo, and he has set up a lab beside his house to breed the threatened butterflies. John joins him, as he told me, to help the little pupae "by changing their diapers." It's microscopic work. Just next door Peter is breeding a spectacular group of Pekin robins, and next to them he's breeding a range of hardy cacti, in unheated conditions. Some university labs are much less interesting.

You'll understand why I went off "to catch the ferry" stunned by what I had found on little Denman. At the wheel I was mindful of the visitor guide's polite warning: "Like many rural areas, the roads are winding and narrow; pedestrians, cyclists, horseback riders, and deer have to share them with cars, so please observe the speed limit and drive carefully." As we lined up for the ferry — the great equalizing island experience — I was not surprised to see a serious-minded great blue heron standing on the beach by the dock, apparently there to bid me farewell.

As I drove off the ferry I noticed the long, lanky figure of Zaccheus Jackson, walking ashore. His style of writing — as a spoken-word performer in poetry slams who drew on his tough times living on the street in Calgary and Vancouver as a crack cocaine addict — like his life, was very different from mine. But I had enjoyed meeting him, and admired how he was working with kids. His best Denman story was about his triumph in losing a big slam poetry final to a shy young woman he had persuaded to get into the game. We had hit it off. So I called over, "Hey, Zach. Can I give you a ride to Comox?"

"No thanks," he said, "I'm heading the other way. I'm fine, thanks."

The next month, visiting Toronto, Zach was struck and killed by a train. He was thirty-six.

In 1982, the Sunshine Coast Festival of the Written Arts held their first literary festival in Sechelt. For those outsiders who aren't sure exactly where it is, it's the part of B.C. that lies northwest of

Vancouver, cut off by mountains and sea running northeast, so that access is by ferry. Even people who haven't visited by ferry may know it. This is the scenic area popularized by Bruno Gerussi and *The Beachcombers* TV series. Readers may recognize it as the setting of the series of crime novels by L.R. ("Bunny") Wright, featuring the local policeman Karl Alberg. (As my earlier book records, Bunny was the Calgary author who was stunned by the live interviewer, all hair and teeth, who asked her off the bat why her novel "had no pictures?")

"The Sunshine Coast" may sound like the invention of a hotel-chain marketing whiz, but the area's exposure, facing the Georgia Strait to the south and the west, encourages a fine climate, and peaches and apricots grow there, and even palm trees. Certainly the weather was perfect as Jane and I skimmed up the coast, over islands and lighthouses and ferries, before landing at Sechelt. There we were met by Sally Quinn, a welcoming volunteer who identified herself brilliantly by displaying a copy of my book . . . always visible to an author's eye at 100 paces. A quick tour of Sechelt took us to the Festival site, where we met Jane Davidson, the festival director who had caught my unzipped show in Vancouver and invited me to her festival the next year. Really, that's the way this whole tour has developed: one event leads to another.

Jane Davidson was astonishingly relaxed, given that over the next three days she would be receiving more than twenty performing authors from across the country, including Michael Crummey from Newfoundland, and Linden MacIntyre, fresh from Edinburgh.

My own history with the festival, as a publisher, goes back to the very first year, when I was glad to send Jack Hodgins. If he had been able to come directly, as the raven flies, from his home in Lantzville, right across the Strait of Georgia, it would have taken no time at all. As one of the five authors attending that year, he enjoyed himself, and reported back with such enthusiasm that over the years I sent a steady stream of authors west, assuring them that they would "have a great time." They always did.

This year, in my new role as author, I got to see for myself. Jane Davidson took us to the hall where all of the readings/performances take place. It is an impressive, all-wood structure, the ceiling held up by tall pine poles, giving it the air of a West Coast longhouse ("crossed with a cathedral," as one admirer put it). Ten seconds on the empty stage were enough to show me that this was a very special theatre space, open yet intimate.

Since one of the strengths of this fine festival is that all events take place there, on the big-log stage, with no competing events at different venues, Jane and I were able to spend many happy hours in the audience at that theatre over the weekend, enjoying the varied readings, discussions, and performances. My own show was thoughtfully introduced by my old pal Andreas Schroeder, who was also our host at his local oceanside cottage.

Andreas and his wife, the author Sharon Brown, live beside the sea in nearby Roberts Creek. (Over time, we warned them, they may change from "Roberts Creekers" to "Roberts Creakies.") I have known Andreas forever, and admired his efforts as a crusading member of the Writers' Union to secure royalties for library use of an author's book. Incredibly, he stick-handled it all through, against the odds, so that the Public Lending Right is now the law of the land. As a result of that triumph I once saw him being carried shoulder-high out of a Writers' Union meeting. Given the physical condition of most of the cheering writers, I was relieved that Andreas is a small, trim figure. Also, as a keen motorcyclist, given to roaring around the high country, he was used to bumpy rides.

As a writer, Andreas has shown great range. He has written non-fiction, such as his prison memoir, *Shaking It Rough*, which came out in 1976, after I had left Doubleday. Andy was not the first or the last bright kid to fall afoul of the drug laws, and was able to write an "inside" account that showed, in his words, that "prison is simply *not* a face-off between long rows of malicious, sadistic uniformed gorillas on the one side, and an equal number of deranged, slavering mother-raping murderers on the other."

He has also written fiction about deeply eccentric characters such as the hero of *Dustship Glory* (1986), and has drawn on his own Mennonite background with novels such as *Renovating Heaven* (2008), a favourite of mine. His strict Mennonite parents discouraged the reading of books, so he had to steal them from the Agassiz Library. Then, since he was an honest little boy, he would *smuggle them back in*. It was an unusual twist on the usual pattern of parents nudging their kids to become readers. His crusading zeal to encourage reading shows up to this day on the road outside his house where he has created bookcases protected against the weather, but full of books open to people out there waiting for a bus, who could use a quick read.

He has also written journalism, poetry, and criticism, and is now the distinguished head of the Creative Non-Fiction Writing program at the University of British Columbia. There, he is such an inspiring teacher that a *Globe and Mail* article by Marsha Lederman in 2012 described him as "the godfather of B.C.'s non-fiction boom." The prize-winning writer Andrew Westoll was notably direct in his praise: "Andreas Schroeder is really single-handedly responsible for me going into creative non-fiction."

Much more important than all this trivia, however, is that in the 1990s he gained fame on CBC Radio's Arthur Black show, *Basic Black*, for his cheery series of reports on enterprising crooks. In the late 1990s I proudly went on to publish the series of books that resulted — *Scams, Scandals, and Skulduggery*; then *Cheats, Charlatans, and Chicanery*; and *Fakes, Frauds, and Flimflammery*. Alliteration always assists all authors — and the books bring bountiful benefits, too, since they are all great fun.

So is staying at Andreas and Sharon's place, where the path from the house down to the superb guest cabin right beside the saltchuck is so steep (at 116 steps, it leaves John Buchan's thirty-nine far behind) that he has devised a sort of funicular mechanical escalator to handle it. Over the years a parade of interesting authors has glided down those stairs to enjoy Andreas and Sharon's hospitality, Naomi Klein and her husband, Avi Lewis, among them. The list goes on to include my friends Myrna Kostash, Annabel Lyon (I published her father, Jim), Charlie Foran, Susan Swan, Newfoundland's Russell Wangersky, Zsuzsi Gartner, Robert Bringhurst, the dear departed Paul Quarrington (whom I once had to introduce at a musical event within a month of his death, which we all knew was coming), Susan Musgrave from Haida Gwaii, and Silver Donald Cameron and Marjorie Simmins all the way from Halifax, and another saltwater home.

An amazing list. And as for the blackberries! Words fail.

We had a fine time attending all of the sessions with Sharon and Andreas, who, for all his accomplishments is a typical laid-back, jeans-and-leather-vest West Coast guy. One of the festival's strong points is that at the end of each session the Great Hall is cleared, and everyone files out to drink, or buy a signed book, or chat, or — usually — line up for the next session. As a result, the placid queues along the rhododendron-lined paths are great places to meet old and new friends, and to chat about books and authors.

The local support for this annual festival is what you would hope for, and people are proud of what they've built up over the thirty years. One retired man who sought me out to get his copy of my book signed said it best. When I commented on what a great thing for the community this festival must be, he said, "This is why we moved here."

Haida Gwaii is the sort of place where unusual things happen sooner or later. I made my third visit to the island right after our Sunshine Coast events, flying from Vancouver to the magnificently named Sandspit Airport. The bus took us to the ferry, then on to Graham Island, and to Queen Charlotte City, where we were dropped off right at the door of the auto shop that was fixing the car Richard and Nancy Self told us we were free to use. No problem. Within minutes we had taken the island's main road north to Tlell, and settled in to James Houston's former home, Bridge Cottage, right beside the famous fishing river.

Courtesy of Richard and Nancy, the plan was to spend our days trying to outwit salmon, with the help of cunningly tied fishing flies and barbless hooks. Every morning our friend Noel Wotten would appear at the door (at 8 a.m., then 7:30, then 7:00) and lead us to places where we stood thigh-deep in water and cast our flies for fish. Our casting was highly satisfactory in every respect, except that of actually catching fish we could retain. Coho, our desired targets, were leaping around us, but we caught only cutthroat trout or sculpin. But Jane and I had mastered the key to fly fishing, which is the zen-like point that *catching fish doesn't really matter*. That's just an agreeable by-product of a wonderful time spent as part of the river, absorbing the sounds and sights. Twice a shadow on the water made me look up to see a giant bald eagle flying low overhead, almost ruffling my hair, using the river as a highway through the tall cedar, spruce, and hemlock trees that Emily Carr knew so well.

Thanks to smart work by some local friends, a show was arranged for me in Queen Charlotte City on Wednesday evening. We went with our friend Noel (who brought his mouth organ along for the drive back . . . "Four Strong Winds," "Summer Wages," and much else) and found the Legion Hall, which doubles as the Anglican church. Presumably "Onward, Christian Soldiers" is a popular hymn there.

The show drew forty-two interested people. The best moment came when I was walking around, greeting people as they came in and found a seat. I shook hands with one lady in her sixties and introduced myself. "Hello," she responded, "I'm Jane Austen."

"I'm very pleased to meet you, thank you very much for comin—" I said, then stopped and gaped at her. She confirmed that, yes, that was her name, and told me that an over-awed teenage girl once asked her to sign a copy of *Pride and Prejudice*.

Anyone who takes writers and writing seriously has the same thought when visiting a famous author's house. What would it be like to sit at the desk where the author did his or her work? How would it affect your own writing?

(This, by the way, is a central theme in the 2014 novel by Terry Fallis, *No Relation*, where a luckless author given the name Earnest Hemmingway tries to solve his writer's block by visiting every Hemingway site he can find. The results are unexpected, as you'd expect with Terry's work.)

I had the chance to experiment with this, in a minor way, when Jane and I were staying at Bridge Cottage, for many years the summer writing base of my friend James Houston. The conditions were scientifically perfect, since on Haida Gwaii Jim wrote in the early morning (check), by hand (check), and — above all — in the chair at the desk in the writing cabin that had been constructed for that very purpose (check, check, check).

Obviously, the piece of writing that you're reading now is no "Kubla Khan," but at this precise moment in its creation a Person from Porlock arrived to interrupt my writing. This Person had every right to do so, since it was our fishing friend Noel Wotten, the man who had built the writing cabin for Jim, in 1981, as the plaque outside "Hideaway Studio" reveals.

James Houston (1921–2005)

I resumed my experiment a full day later, after a fishing trip with Noel to Port Clements, farther up the island. Here I once visited the scene of the ecological crime so vividly described in John Vaillant's book *The Golden Spruce*. I'm sorry to report that the once golden icon is now a grey, shrunken, felled tree carcass, rotting away quietly in the water where it fell. Noel, I should note, is the man who chain-sawed the path to the tree that is now taken by mournful tourists.

As I've hinted earlier, the versatile Noel is a noted expert on fly fishing, having cast weightless flies great distances on salmon rivers around the world, landing the fly gently on the ripple most likely to provide shelter for a lurking fish. I've noticed, too, that after the fly has landed, Noel leans eagerly forward, artfully working the coils of line in his left hand, imagining the fish just beneath the tempting fly. Far from being just a skilful mechanical exercise — cast, float the fly, swing it back, cast again — it's an act of faith and imagination, making fleeting contact with that other world that lies beneath the surface.

These thoughts are, just possibly, channelled by the lingering spirit of the man who sat here writing. Often, as in the third volume of his memoirs, *Hideaway* (1999), written here, Jim deals with fishing. He openly admitted that it was his addiction to salmon fishing that brought him to the Queen Charlotte Islands, and to Bridge Cottage, and to the river Tlell in the first place. And, just as he did while writing *Hideaway*, I've just found myself getting up from my chair — *his* chair — to check up on the river.

The river Tlell dominates every moment you spend here, only an underhand stone's throw from its banks. Unless you are asleep, or deliberately turning your back and actively ignoring it, you always know which way the tide is running — upstream, or down the few kilometres to the salt water of Hecate Strait — and you know how high it has climbed against the bridge timbers, or how low it has fallen, to reveal sand beaches. The river dominates the view, decides our activities, and turns any thoughtful resident into a water creature.

Another interruption out there left me with an extraordinary river moment. When the salmon are running, as they are now, all eyes are on the surface of the river, looking for the circle in the water that may precede a silver leap. Standing up to watch them, I was like an eager dog on point as I saw five or six circles appear. *Five or six fish!* Then the entire surface of the water was pocked with hundreds of such circles, a miracle of teeming fish . . . until I realized that the storm clouds had just opened, and that these circles came courtesy of raindrops from above, not fish from below.

I wonder what the fish make of it all, when the ceiling of their world turns black, and full of noise, and of fresh, cold water.

Clearly, I had learned one of the great lessons of sitting at a writer's desk. When you are there, you are in the same surrounding world as he was. And if you are open to distraction, your distractions will be the same as his.

CHAPTER 6

ALICE MUNRO COUNTRY

Alice's Ancestors . . . Playing Host to Swedish Filmmakers . . .
The Novelist and the Tiger-Killer . . . Onto the Mennonite
World . . . 100 Years of Edna Staebler . . . Across the Maitland
River, and into Wingham . . . The Spirit of Blyth . . . I've
Never Been Proud of Coming from Clinton, Before This
. . . I Turn into Ingmar Bergman, En Route to Goderich . . .
Bayfield, and the Man Who Mapped the Great Lakes

You will find, ladies and gentlemen, that Alice Munro Country begins surprisingly close to Toronto. As you head west on the 401, approaching Milton, the horizon fills with the Niagara Escarpment, the long barrier of hills and cliffs that runs right across Ontario, all the way from the Falls to where Georgian Bay meets Lake Huron. But today, before you tackle the low gap through the barrier, you take the major decision to leave the 401. It has been a notable literary thoroughfare ever since Alistair MacLeod in *No Great Mischief* called it "Ontario's main highway" and assured us that "it will be true to you if you are true to it. And you will never, never, ever become lost."

But you, daringly, take exit 320 for Halton Hills, the area to which Alice Munro's ancestors, the Laidlaws, came in 1818, all the way from their home in the Ettrick Valley in the Scottish Borders.

"In those days they came usually by boat." That's the famous sentence that opens Donald Creighton's epic biography of Sir John A. Macdonald. The Macdonald family arrived in Canada in 1820, just two years after the Laidlaws. Both groups had endured the howling trials of the transatlantic voyage, then the trip up the St. Lawrence against the current, then the battle through the rapids west of Montreal, before the comparatively smooth waters of Lake Ontario allowed them to choose which part of "The Front" they wished to arrive at "by boat."

We know that the Laidlaws arrived at York (now Toronto), presumably tumbling gratefully off the boat to stretch their legs. We know, too, that they spent some time in the little port before heading west to the Halton Hills to take up their land in Esquising Township. This was a very Scottish area, with part of it actually called "The Scotch Block." In fact our destination (and from route 25 North we turn right on the James Snow Parkway, then right again until we find Boston Church Road) is named the Boston Presbyterian Church. This Boston, please note, has nothing to do with beans or Bruins or Cabots or cod. It's named after Thomas Boston, a famous Scot, the eighteenth-century minister in Ettrick who was so admired that the people who came to settle in this part of Canada named their pioneer church after him. Alice Munro has written sympathetically about him in a story, "Men of Ettrick," from *The View from Castle Rock*.

When you drive north along the quiet maple-shaded road, the houses fall away until the church appears on your right. As you walk up towards it, head for the front corner on the left. There, among the old gravestones, you will find many that remember generations of the Laidlaw family. Among them is James Laidlaw, the man who brought his family here, although he was almost sixty, a late time in life for a pioneer to start carving out a farm. His relative, the Scottish writer James Hogg, wrote about his decision to leave Ettrick for "America" (which in common speech included Canada): "For a number of years bygone he talked and read about America till he grew perfectly unhappy, and at last, when approaching his sixtieth year, actually set off to seek a temporary home and a grave in the new world."

Two fine, grim Scottish touches there. The phrase "perfectly unhappy" reverses the usual formula, while the words "and a grave" speak for themselves. The grave is right here, in the Boston Church graveyard, in memory of James Laidlaw, who died in 1829.

Alice Munro's great-great-great-grandfather.

I found myself back at the Boston Church in October 2013, acting as tour guide to a Swedish TV crew that was about to make a documentary film about new Nobel Laureate Alice Munro for SVT, the national broadcaster. In my new role as Assistant Director/ Transport Manager/Script Assistant/Actor/ Interviewee (and possibly even Best Boy) I spent a fascinating day with Lena Jordebo, the producer, and Sven-Ake Visen, the cameraman.

We stopped first at the Boston Church (built, by the way, on land given by Andrew Laidlaw, the son of old James), where I talked to the camera about the importance of these ordinary Scottish settlers for Alice and her work. Then it was back to the faithful 401, passing through the Escarpment gap with only a slight pressure on the accelerator, in contrast with the hard work and cracking whips that took the oxcarts up the hill to spread west into the thickly forested land beyond. It was said that the trees were so thick that an agile and ambitious squirrel could travel for hundreds of miles without ever descending to the ground.

The superb historian Desmond Morton, in *A Short History of Canada* (which I was proud to republish), has written about how

> for pioneers in a harsh and unfamiliar land, survival was a preoccupation, to be achieved only through relentless, back-breaking labour. The forest was the enemy. Huge first-growth trees resisted the puny axes and saws of settlers struggling to clear fields or merely to break through the overhanging gloom to the sun. The forest accentuated loneliness. Loneliness reduced pioneers to an unsmiling grimness. Women often faced life and even the terrors of childbirth without even a neighbour to help. A single careless blow with an axe could cripple a man or leave him to die in the stench and agony of gangrene.

Literature rules the world. If you find that truth hard to believe, consider this: the part of Canada now known as "Alice Munro Country" was founded by a novelist. John Galt was Scotland's most famous novelist after Sir Walter Scott, thanks to novels like *Annals of the Parish*. Yet he gave up the life of a successful, stay-at-home, pen-scratching creator of stories to run the Canada Company, and settle huge tracts of Upper Canada with mostly Scottish settlers. He and his explorer on the ground, "Tiger" Dunlop (in India he used to throw snuff in the faces of the tigers, he said, before shooting them), first founded Guelph, then cut a road to Waterloo, then on to Stratford, and then west into Huron County. There they established the county seat at Goderich, where Tiger's grave lies, overlooking the town. And they brought in many, many settlers, most of them Scots.

As John and Monica Ladell record in their 1979 book on century farms, *Inheritance*, they cut "a trail from Waterloo to Goderich, via what is now Stratford. . . . In the eleven years between 1829 and 1840 the Canada Company settled over six thousand people in the Huron Tract." All of the settlers lived hardscrabble lives, with survival among the trees the main aim; Galt's earlier literary life must have seemed almost unbelievable to them, since, as we'll see, books were not needed ("Nobody wants them"). Later, the Huron Tract settlers included the Laidlaw family.

But now on the 401 at Cambridge, incorporating Jane's hometown of, yes, Galt, it's time for you to take the turn off to Highway 8, leading to Kitchener and Waterloo. After you make the turn, ladies and gentlemen, please look to the right to see a ski hill. No, lower down . . . yes, that little bump is the Chicopee Ski Hill, which was big enough to hook the teenaged Jane on skiing. So firmly was this athletic girl from Galt hooked, in fact, that after her first university year at Western, she took a year off to become a ski bum in Switzerland! Morning and evening she worked as a cook/waitress. During the day, she skied. My respectable wife, "Nana" to our grandchildren! Clearly, it has all been downhill since then.

As you approach Kitchener and Waterloo, you have a choice of route. You can take the Tiger Dunlop southern route to Stratford via Shakespeare. (Don't miss the elderberry pie!) From Stratford you'd head northwest on the Old Huron Road, Highway 8. I know it so well from many visits to see Alice that I can happily reel off the names of the towns. Sebringville (one long main street, a thin snake of a town); Mitchell (once the home of my old friend Orlo Miller, who wrote *The Donnellys Must Die*, about the murders in nearby Lucan); Dublin (with its Liffey Drain, a triumph of realism over sentimentality); Seaforth (home of Lloyd Eisler, the skating star); then Clinton (home of a not-bad short story writer); and beyond that, on the lake, the county town of Goderich (named for the least memorable and least successful British prime minister of all time — a bold claim, I know, but *Chambers's Biographical Dictionary* records that after Goderich succeeded Canning "his weak leadership was soon exposed and he resigned willingly before meeting Parliament as Prime Minister [1827–28], the only premier to do so").

But with the Swedish film crew, instead I chose to take the northerly route along Highway 86, direct to Wingham, where Alice Laidlaw grew up. As we skirted Waterloo and headed west into the country towards Listowel, my Swedish friends were especially struck by three things. The richness of the very flat farmland. The large barns, designed on the two-storey principle, where the groaning haywagons came up a ramp to the upper level from which, all winter long, the hay could simply be forked down (call it the "gravity feed" principle) to the cattle housed in the lower storey. (If this detail seems excessive to you, I'm a country boy, and, hey, this is a book about stories!)

But what especially interested them was evidence that this was Old Order Mennonite country. I explained about the horse-drawn buggies that many traditional farmers still use, avoiding devilish machinery like cars. (Jane, a proud member of the Mennonite Brenneman family, had a grandfather who chose to break with the church in order to be a railroad engineer, in Stratford.) I was able to talk about the continuing marks of distinction in dress, with the women in kerchiefs and bonnets, and the men wearing black hats and choosing beard styles that reveal their marital status.

More important, I talked about how the Mennonites came north from Pennsylvania around 1800 and found the best land. They knew that black walnut trees grew only in rich, deep soil. So in their Conestoga wagons they followed "the trail of the black walnut," moving, almost literally, from tree to tree. As a result they found the very best land, and put down their own roots there, where they could produce the fine, hearty food for which they are renowned. Which brings us to Edna Staebler.

Edna was born in Berlin in 1906, the granddaughter of the very first Mennonite settler in Woolwich Township. She got a degree from the University of Toronto at a time when girls were not expected to turn into career women, and certainly not career writers. Edna's husband didn't support her writing ambitions, and in time they divorced. But magazines like *Chatelaine* and *Maclean's* and *Reader's Digest* were supportive. They admired Edna's system of immersing herself in the lives of her subjects, living for months in a Cape Breton fishing community, or with an Italian immigrant family adapting to life in Toronto, or with Old Order Mennonite friends and neighbours.

Her life changed in 1968 when she decided to write about the hearty traditional food that her Mennonite friends cooked. Her cookbook — daringly entitled *Food That Really Schmecks* — went on to become the bestselling hardcover cookbook in Canadian publishing history. In 1979, M&S brought out a second volume, *More Food That Really Schmecks* (the second title seemed much less daring), and again the sales went through the roof, making Edna rich and modestly famous. But to the alarm of her friends like Pierre Berton and Harold Horwood she went on living quietly by herself in a

Edna Staebler (1906–2006)

remote cottage beside Sunfish Lake near Waterloo. Her friends were appalled by this little old lady sometimes being visited by the paroled prisoners she was charitably assisting.

I was not on parole, but our paths crossed at some point, and I was charmed by this apple-cheeked old woman. I got to know her better when in 1986 M&S decided to bring out a third book in the "Schmecks" series. Because I then had an arm's-length relationship with the company, I felt able to enter the internal competition for a new title, and I won with *Schmecks Appeal.*

The prize was a home-cooked meal by Edna Staebler herself. Since my mother (the former Jenny Maitland) was visiting from Scotland (from tiger-free Dunlop, to be precise), and since she was the storyteller in our family, I thought that lunch with Edna at Sunfish Lake would be too good a treat for her to miss. And indeed the two ancient women got on well as we sat looking out at the lake and enjoying the delicious smell curling around us from the kitchen.

Edna invited us to the table, and excused herself to go into the kitchen. There were domestic sounds, and then a very un-Mennonite hissed, "Shit!"

"Is everything all right, Edna?" I called. "Can I help?"

She reluctantly agreed. When I walked into the sacred kitchen I found Edna trapped against the stove. Somehow, in removing a quiche from the oven, she had got the top of the quiche wedged vertically against the oven rack. She was crouched there, holding the fragile quiche in place with just enough pressure to stop it from collapsing in a yellow, eggy mess on the floor. I was able to slip a plate underneath, and the quiche was saved. It tasted wonderful. But the "celebrity chef" shows on television never seem to involve such high drama.

My next encounter with Edna was in business discussions when we and McGraw-Hill joined forces to bring out *all* of her recipes in a series of Schmecks books, on Soups, or Desserts, and so on — divided as a matter of course, you might say. And here Edna proved to be an apple-cheeked Granny from Hell, smilingly demanding outrageous terms for the contract. It almost worked, too. Everyone else in the room was scandalized as I rudely resisted the sweet requests made oh-so-gently by this little lady in her late eighties.

That side of Edna was on full display when in 1997 she delivered the prestigious Margaret Laurence Lecture at the Writers' Union Conference. At the end of a long publishing day I drove to Kingston to support good old Edna. She chose to take the audience through her career as an author, book by book. When she came to the first book published by M&S, she said: "Now I see Doug Gibson in the audience, and Doug, I have to say that when it came to promoting *More Food That Really Schmecks*, I was really disappointed by the job that M&S did. Really disappointed."

The audience of writers — not all of whom believed that their own publishers had promoted their own books ideally, successfully attracting every possible reader — was loudly delighted.

It got worse. Every book that we had published, it seemed, had been badly promoted, although each time Edna was "sorry to have to say this, Doug." Eventually I sat there in the middle of the audience (my neighbours drawing away from me) with my hands clasped protectively over my head. It was an admission that I was being publicly beaten up, from the stage, by a sweet little lady, now aged ninety-one, but still kicking.

Late in her life Edna instituted an award in her name for Creative Non-Fiction Writing, administered by Wilfrid Laurier University in Waterloo. In 1996 I was pleased to attend the ceremony honouring George Blackburn, a fine Second World War veteran who had written his memoirs of those days, *The Guns of Normandy*, in a continuous present tense in the second person ("You go along the trench," etc.) At the award ceremony, I was unexpectedly asked to "say a few words." With Edna and George on the platform I said: "I've attended hundreds of book award events over the years, but this is the first one when the combined ages of the donor, Edna (born in 1906), and the recipient, George (born in 1917), exceeds 170 years."

Edna shook her fist at me, but she did it playfully, and I think she was pleased; in my experience — and my mother died at ninety-nine — over ninety a lady doesn't mind her age being mentioned. At her 100th birthday party, organized by her friends at Wilfrid Laurier, Edna seemed glad to shake my hand and smile at me. She died a few months later.

When you leave Mennonite Country and get closer to Wingham, the country becomes less lush. Now the main feature is the Maitland River, which loops and meanders throughout Alice Munro country, all the way to where it pours into the lake at Goderich. Given that Maitland is my middle name (which, as a touch of home, was a comfort to Alice when we started to work together in the mid-'70s), I was interested to learn more about the man who gave the river his name.

Sir Peregrine Maitland (and there are no Peregrines in my mother's immediate family) was a British soldier who was lucky enough to serve with Wellington at Waterloo. That set him up for life, producing a string of appointments like becoming the Lieutenant-Governor of Upper Canada in 1818, a post he held for ten years before moving laterally to run Nova Scotia. One story about Maitland must have intrigued the romantic, young Alice Laidlaw, growing up beside the Maitland River. The stolid soldier *eloped* with the daughter of the Duke of Richmond. The father was not pleased. This proved to be a bad career move when the duke was made Governor in Chief of Canada, and thus Maitland's boss, but the all-powerful Duke of Wellington managed to patch things up between them.

The Duke of Richmond had a most dramatic end — stranger than fiction, and evidence that our history is full of amazing stories. He was inspecting the defences of his command, near Ottawa, when he was bitten by his pet fox. It had rabies. He developed hydrophobia and went raving mad. His troops, terrified of both his bark and his bite, tied him to a tree, and watched him die. Nobody had the good sense to have his musket go off by accident.

When you approach Wingham from the south, you cross the many-branched Maitland, and head up Josephine Street. As you drive up the slope you'll see a typical Ontario main street of two- or three-storey red- or yellow-brick buildings containing small stores or sales offices. After three blocks, on your right you'll see the grand old post office building. Stop there, because the tall building is now the local museum, with a corner devoted to Alice Munro, containing old photographs, an ancient typewriter, some books, and so on. Even better, you'll find a leaflet outlining an Alice Munro Tour of the town.

You don't have to go very far to start the tour. The Alice Munro Literary Garden is right next door to the museum. Its narrow lot is well designed to accommodate a bench where you can sit and think (or possibly just sit), along with an elegant metal archway proclaiming the garden, and a winding circular walkway where the paving stones on the right give the titles of Alice's books, while those on the left reflect some of the prizes she has won. Best of all, on the lawn at the front, fringed by flowers and shrubs, lies a metal statue of a young girl, chin in hand, lost in the book that she is reading, which is sweeping her off to another world.

Our Swedish cameraman spent a lot of time filming this evocative statue.

I was here in July 2001, when the Literary Garden was opened. In fact Jane and I interrupted our honeymoon to join in the celebration. In his excellent 2005 biography, *Alice Munro: Writing Her Lives*, Robert Thacker describes the event perfectly, including the part that took place in the old town hall theatre directly across the street:

> Almost five hundred people were there on a beautiful summer day. Munro was resplendent in a hat given by her daughter Jenny and her goddaughter Rebecca, and the press was out in force. Munro's picture was on the front page the next day of both the *Globe and Mail* and the

National Post, and the *Star* ran its story on the dedication under the witty, and apt, headline "Jubilation in Jubilee." Gibson and [agent Ginger] Barber spoke, as did David Staines, editor of the New Canadian Library [where Alice was on the editorial board], and Jane Urquhart, novelist and friend. At the local theatre [in the old town hall] each read from a favourite Munro story and talked about their associations with Alice, after which Munro read from one of her stories. A garden luncheon followed on the lawn. Among the contributors listed in the program was Munro's Books.

After a quick trip along Josephine, the Swedish filmmakers and I turned and headed back south. Before the river we turned right, and went on to the west, before winding around a sports field. An uphill left turn took us to the edge of town. On our left lay the very last house, the old Laidlaw farmhouse, where Alice grew up.

Built in the 1870s, it is a simple farmhouse. But it had ambitions, as is demonstrated by the artistic decorations in the "polychromatic" style, with patterns of yellow brick at the corners set off against the regular red-brick exterior, in a handsome display. The front of the house still faces west across the empty fields that Alice has described. In truth, any keen reader of Alice's work (especially *Lives of Girls and Women* and *Who Do You Think You Are?*) will feel, as they look at the house, that they know the inside very well, and may even sense her mother's presence.

To the east, towards the town, however, the field that used to supply hay has disappeared, and the rear of the house has new outbuildings that contain a hairdressing salon. Because I didn't want to disturb the owners — living in a literary house must be a pain, if tourists intrude — I asked our cameraman to be very discreet in his filming, and not to get too close to the house. *A discreet cameraman?* As Lena and I fidgeted by the car, Sven-Ake filmed the front of the house for ten endless minutes, then got even closer to the northwest corner for another ten, then got so close to the front window that he was only three steps away. "What the hell do you think you're doing?" was the roar that I expected to hear at any moment, but my urgent arm gestures ("Back! Back!") just seemed to make him more stubborn. It may be a Swedish thing.

When he did finally saunter back to the car he told me that

he'd once been arrested by the KGB in Moscow's Red Square, so a Wingham hairdressing salon held no terrors for him. Nevertheless, I had turned the car around, in case a quick getaway was needed. As I prepared to drive off I made a bad mistake. I said, making friendly conversation, "You know, this was Alice's favourite road to walk when she was young."

Four Swedish ears pricked up. Suddenly I had a new profession; while Sven-Ake sat in the front seat, I turned into a stunt driver. But this time the stunt was not to drive at Bullitt speed, but as slowly and as smoothly as possible. At first, from the passenger seat, he filmed my right ear — or at least filmed me driving. Then he unbuckled his safety belt, jammed his camera hard against the windshield and instructed me to drive "sloooowly . . . sloooowly," while I drove at walking pace, trying to avoid all the ruts in the dirt road without jerking the wheel. Try it some time. As we drove, and he filmed the road, we passed a field of dead, standing corn. This was a Munro-like lesson in finding the extraordinary in the everyday. My fascinated Swedish cameraman friend spent twenty minutes filming the empty October field of rustling cornstalks.

Finally, as we drove away from the house, I found myself looking at the neighbouring houses, trying to guess which one had been occupied by "Mrs. Netterfield," the crazy lady who prowled around baby Alice's house, while her mother clung to her for dear life.

On Highway 4 south to Blyth, then onto Clinton. Because of the damned cornstalks we were running late, so I wasn't able to take the side road east to the Wingham Golf and Curling Club, where I have happily attended two celebrations for Alice organized by local friends like her old schoolmate Ross Procter. These "AM in the PM" events are great fun, attended by Alice and people like Mary Swan, her bookseller friend in Bayfield, who once produced a thoughtful talk about Alice's writing that could have graced an academic conference. And the awards session showed that a crop of young writers was springing up, encouraged by Alice's example.

The sound of the local people was important, too, and something for visitors to concentrate on. The southwestern Ontario accent ("Straatford") is distinctive. Ken McGoogan quotes Carol Shields, an enormous fan of Alice's work, saying, "Her use of language is very sophisticated, but I can always hear, underlying the sentence and its rhythms, that rural Ontario sound." An obvious example I'd suggest is this: in the story "Home" we hear, "The cake's even a mix, I'm shamed to tell you. Next thing you know it'll be boughten."

Lying halfway between Wingham (where she was raised) and Clinton (where she came to live), Blyth is physically at the heart of Alice Munro Country. But it's central in another way. This was where Alice's ancestors came when they left Halton Hills to settle in Huron County. There were three Laidlaw boys in the party: John (twenty-one), Alice's great-grandfather Thomas (fifteen), and their cousin Robert (twenty-three). In 1907 Robert wrote his memories of their 1851 journey. His words are quoted in Robert Thacker's biography: "'We got a box of bedclothes and a few cooking utensils into a wagon and started from the County of Halton to try our fortunes in the wilds of Morris Township.' They got as far as Stratford, and thought to take the stage to Clinton but 'the stage had quit running, until the road froze up,' so the three young men 'got our axes on our shoulders and walked to Morris.'"

There, near Blyth, they found their land on the Ninth and Tenth concessions and started to build a shanty, and to fell the trees.

Now, just watch how Alice Munro uses this family material. In "A Wilderness Station," the second section of the story told in letters and other documents is a recollection by "Mr. George Herron." It begins:

> On the first day of September, 1851, my brother Simon and I got a box of bedclothes and household utensils together and I put them in a wagon with a horse to pull it, and set out from Halton County to try our fortunes in the wilds of Huron and Bruce, as wilds they were then thought to be.

Later, her story continues:

> The roads were always getting worse as we came west, so we thought it best to get our box sent on to Clinton by the stage. But the stage had quit running due to rains, and they were waiting till the roads froze up, so we told Archie Frame's boy to turn about and return with horse and

cart and goods back to Halton. Then we took our axes on our shoulders and walked to Carstairs.

Our wise historian friend, Desmond Morton, with his warnings about axe wounds (gangrene!) and the fatal accidents that befell so many people trying to clear their land of trees, could have predicted what happened next, both in real life, and in Alice's story. That death in the woods leads to the dead man's widow leaving her shanty near Carstairs (Blyth) to turn herself in at the local gaol in Walley (Goderich, where the historic gaol still stands). What makes "A Wilderness Station" such an important story is not only Alice Munro's clever use of different documents and letters that tell us a lot about pioneer times (a local minister's death prompts the landlord of the Carstairs Inn to complain about his effects: "There is some books here. Nobody wants them"). What amazes students of the short story form is that a final section in the story brings this tale of the 1850s right up to 1907, and the world of "steamer cars." A short story that deals with several generations? Who ever heard of such a thing?

The old pioneer farm northeast of Blyth was where Alice's father, Robert grew up. He walked into school each day, and was a good pupil. But Alice has written about his bashfulness as a farm boy in town, an outsider, and how he came to spend more and more time roaming around the countryside. Eventually, his hobby of trapping mink, muskrats, and foxes produced enough money that he began to think, like an angler turning to fish farming, that raising foxes for their pelts might be a fine way to make a living. And that is what he did, when he married and moved to Wingham. But Blyth remained the family centre, where young Alice would spend time with relatives when there was an emergency at home.

Alice's father, Robert Laidlaw, was just as fascinated by these pioneer times as his daughter. Late in his life he wrote about them in a novel, *The MacGregors*, which I published in 1979, at Alice's urging, after his death. I ran into some trouble with my bosses at Macmillan over this decision, but a) the book is a good, solid account of pioneer life in Ontario — as Jane Urquhart indicated when she read from it at the Alice Munro Tribute at Harbourfront in November 2012 — and b) publishing it strengthened our bonds with Alice. Case closed.

I know Blyth — another Huron County town with its main street running north-south — fairly well, because right in the heart of town is the Memorial Hall, which houses the Blyth Festival theatre. The festival has been running since 1975, and has an admirable policy of encouraging original plays, some of them based on work by local authors like Harry J. Boyle and, yes, Alice Munro. Indeed, on one occasion, when Alice was reluctant to cause a fuss by showing up in the audience, she used me as her undercover reviewer of a play based on one of her stories. I was able to report that it worked well.

Surprisingly, Alice has even acted in a couple of festival productions, which tend to enjoy strong local support. Once, she told me with a laugh, she played the part of a difficult, loud author. But how did this onstage stuff fit with the shy public person I knew? "Ah, it's easy when I'm just playing a role," said Alice.

Thanks to Val Ross in the *Globe and Mail*, the world now knows the story of how an American tourist once went to a chicken supper held in Blyth to raise funds for the local festival. As the grey-haired waitress cleared away the dirty dishes, the tourist indicated an elegant auburn-haired woman sitting off to the side. "I hear," he said to the waitress, "there's a famous lady writer who lives near here. Would that by any chance be her?"

The waitress paused in picking up the dishes. "I'm not sure," she said, peering closely. "Yes, I think that might be her." Then Alice Munro, the waitress, swept the pile of dirty dishes off the table and away to the noisy, steamy kitchen that was full of other volunteers.

It's a great story, and one that I'm always pleased to tell in my *Stories About Storytellers* show. In September 2012 I got to tell it in Blyth, at the theatre itself, to an audience containing many good people who had done their share of serving at chicken suppers. They liked the story. As for me, I loved all the behind-the-scenes stuff in the Green Room, knowing that Alice, too, had fretted there, and in the wings beside the backstage curtains, before striding onto the stage as a loud, bossy author.

A sad note. When Alice's husband, Gerry, died in April 2013, Alice decided that the family should return to its Blyth roots. He was buried in the graveyard there, where Alice will join him in due course.

Alice Munro (1931–)

In the spring of 2013 I gave my show in Stratford. To be precise, I gave two shows, for the SpringWorks Festival. The first, on a Friday afternoon, was for an audience largely made up of students from local schools — including a busload of grade twelve kids from Clinton.

From the stage I told them how lucky they were, and how for the rest of their lives they were going to run into people from all over the world who said, "Clinton, Ontario? You grew up in Clinton? Did you know Alice Munro? Did you know that she was writing world-famous stories around the corner from you, about people like your parents and their neighbours?" I told them how lucky they were to be in touch — even in a brief, glancing way — with world literature, in the form of a quiet neighbour they might pass in the supermarket or on the way to the post office.

Up on the stage I was not aware of any impact my words might be having, and anyway, these were grade twelve kids, being cool, and they were from the notably undemonstrative world of Huron County. So I got on with my show, talking about my authors, and working up to Alice Munro, whose place in literature I described in a way that must have left listeners wondering why she had never won the Nobel Prize.

Word filtered through to me from a teacher on the bus back to Clinton. Apparently, discussing what I had said, one young student said the words, "You know, I've never felt proud of coming from Clinton, before this."

My life has not been a total failure.

Alice's house is southwest of the town centre, near streets with names like Frederick and Dunlop (!). The nearby street names may ring bells with her readers. Not far from her house is Orange Street, with its links to her story "The Moon in the Orange Street Skating Rink." The street's name comes not from an artistic admiration for the warm colour in question. It goes back to old Ontario history when the fiercely anti-Catholic Orange Lodge was a power in the land. Once, driving in to see Alice from Bayfield, we passed a country road called the Roman Line. Alice confirmed my suspicion that this had nothing to do with gladiators or senators in togas, but with the Catholic religion of the people, usually from Ireland, who settled there in the nineteenth century.

The house is a neat, white two-storey wooden building. This is where she came to live with Gerry Fremlin, in what had been his mother's house, in August 1975. Gerry's mischievous influence can still be seen in the large garden, including irreverent pieces of outdoor art. There are no fairies at the bottom of this garden, but a railroad track where Alice and Gerry used to like to walk in summer, and use as a cross-country ski trail in winter, in their younger days.

These days are long gone. But when the Swedish film crew and I roamed around the garden of the unpretentious house, we were joined by Alice's great friend Rob Bundy (who later was part of the Munro group of celebrants in Stockholm). He told us how he made himself useful as a friend of the elderly couple, in this snow-belt area where walks have to be shovelled clear, and grass cut regularly in the growing season.

He had encouraging news for any car-bound tourist. Gerry, of course, was a geographer, and he loved to drive Alice around, explaining the ridges and moraines and drumlins to be seen. Later, Rob said, Alice's greatest pleasure (as a non-driver) was being driven around the rural roads in the scenery she has loved so well, the farms, and fields, and patches of hardwood bush that we call Alice Munro Country. All of us can catch the same feeling on these quiet, unchanged roads.

After a brief stop in Clinton, where they planned to return the next day, I rushed the film crew west towards Goderich. Why? Because, I told them, the great natural feature here was Lake Huron, and if we timed it right we could film the sun setting into the lake. This was my Bergman moment, and I think I was right, although it was cut from the final film, dammit.

Before that, however, Lena decided to film an interview with me in "typical Alice Munro Country." We drove past miles of really typical flat farm country, with me preparing to stop at any moment. Then we turned north of the road to Goderich and found the least typical spot in the entire county — a steep drop into a gorge where the Maitland River surged over rapids between tall, forested hills. It was such an alarming drop that as I posed for the camera at the edge of the cliff, looking wise, a carload of locals stopped to warn me that the edge often gave way. It would have made a very dramatic, Pythonesque end to the interview. But I survived, and we drove on to Goderich.

Although Stratford (or the more distant London) is the main shopping centre — and the main medical centre — for this area, Goderich is the county town. The octagonal central square is based around the courthouse planned from the early days of John Galt and Tiger Dunlop. Until a tornado swept in off the lake in the summer of 2012, the square housed a fine restaurant called Bailey's, which Alice used to enjoy as a place to meet visiting journalists, while her house in Clinton remained private.

I took my Swedish colleagues down to the lakefront, near the salt mine, where a ship was being loaded in a constant funnelled stream of falling whitish salt. While Sven-Ake filmed the sun setting on "Ontario's West Coast" I walked out along the pier. Here I had once surprised Alice and Gerry enjoying the same walk, Alice's hair blowing in the lake breeze.

The salt mines are Goderich's great local industry. Their discovery might have inspired an Alice Munro story. Do you remember how in "Hateship, Friendship, Loveship, Marriage," a prank played by two teenage girls sends a woman out West to join a man who is not expecting her? And how it all turns out well? In 1866, impressed by the value of oil strikes in Ontario, a local entrepreneur named Samuel Pratt tried drilling for oil in Goderich. Local legend has it that he had drilled so deep, with no success, that he was on the point of giving up. Then some local pranksters secretly dropped some oil in the bottom of his dry well. Encouraged, he kept drilling — and proceeded to find the largest salt mine in the world.

Goderich is the setting of one of Alice's greatest stories, "Meneseteung" (the Native name for the Maitland River). It's a fascinating look at a town in the post-pioneer stage, where the local paper, the *Vedette*, is hard at work keeping its readers up to the civilized urban mark. The "Poetess," Almeda, for example, comes close to romance with a neighbour, Jarvis Poulter, a man in the salt business. When he intervenes to roust a drunk woman that Almeda fears may be dead, the *Vedette* lectures its 1879 readers: "Incidents of this sort, unseemly, troublesome, and disgraceful to our town, have of late become all too common."

Then, having convinced us of the reality of the world of this woman, revealed in excerpts of her writing — not to mention finding Almeda's tombstone in the graveyard — the modern narrator steps into the final paragraph to say, "I may have got it wrong." Another short story rule broken. Another great Alice Munro tale created.

In the absence of Bailey's, people in search of a place to eat that has links with Alice Munro can now visit the Park House Hotel, at the top of the slope leading down to the harbour. One corner of the dining room preserves "Alice Munro's table." It was there that I had my last meal with Alice and Gerry. I had driven down to see if I could persuade Alice to do some publicity, but she and Gerry were firm in their rejection of the idea, so I simply enjoyed the company and the lunch.

As we left, in the doorway there was an elegiac moment. Alice held me at arm's-length and said, "Well, you and I have had many interesting adventures."

I mumbled something inadequate, and we hugged farewell.

The holiday town of Bayfield has long been one of Alice's favourite places around Clinton. The town on the lake is named after a great Canadian hero, a man who has saved thousands of lives over the years. But Henry Wolsey Bayfield is almost unknown, compared to the other two great British map-makers who charted our coasts, Captain James Cook and Captain George Vancouver. Yet perhaps he did more for Canada, and those who sail its waters, than both of them put together.

Bayfield joined the British navy at the age of eleven, and was a twenty-year-old midshipman at Quebec when he was persuaded to give up a dashing naval career (think Horatio Hornblower) for what Don W. Thomson in *Men and Meridians* calls "the vagaries, hardships, and low pay of hydrographic survey work."

Think about it. In naval surveying you're mapping in three dimensions, with lives to be lost on every unmarked reef. And unlike land surveyors, you can't ever spread your surveyor's chain on the surface of the water to measure distance. Every measurement involves compasses, sextants, lead lines, and other instruments. Endless calculations are involved, and most of the facts are gathered while bobbing about in small boats, at the mercy of winds and waves. Yet from 1817 until 1826, Henry Wolsey Bayfield quietly mapped the Canadian coasts of *all of the Great Lakes*.

A plaque in Charlottetown's central square tells the world that after his Great Lakes marathon (which involved chopping through the ice on Lake Superior in order to, literally, plumb the depths) Admiral Bayfield "conducted a thorough survey of the Gulf and River St. Lawrence, the coasts of Anticosti, Magdalen Islands, Prince Edward Island, Cape Breton, Sable Island, and parts of Nova Scotia and Labrador."

Whew! And he gave his name — for his long-forgotten services to ensure safety on the water — not to a city like Vancouver, but to a little town just south of Goderich.

In the past I've met Alice and Gerry for dinner in Bayfield at The Red Pump. In August 2014 she met Jane and me for an affectionate lunch in that favourite restaurant, and life went on with a Nobel Prize winner calmly eating mussels at one of their tables. I know that she has kindly agreed to do promotional events at the little bookshop there in the past. She once did a favour for her pal Margaret Atwood by staging a LongPen signing session at the store then run by her friend Mary Swan.

The bookshop has now moved to the village main street (on a summer weekend the sidewalks are so crowded with visitors that Yonge Street seems quiet in comparison), very close to the historic Little Inn. The new owner, Mary Brown, invited me in the summer of 2013 to do my show, and we stayed at the Little Inn — admiring the bookish Alice Munro reminders in the upstairs corridors.

My evening event was held in the historic clapboard 1882 town hall, on Clan Gregor Square, and it was a fine experience for me. As usual, I mingled with the audience beforehand, introducing myself and chatting. I came across several old friends, and, equally pleasing, a number of Alice's friends, who had fond stories to tell about her. There was a distinctly Huron County moment when I met a friendly lady, who said, "I came tonight because my friend saw your show in Stratford, and she told me that it was . . ." and I beamed modestly, awaiting the superlative adjective that was to come (although she was a little old for "awesome") "that it was . . . quite interesting."

Alice enjoyed that story when I told her about it the next day at home in Clinton, on the couch beneath the famous eighteenth-century print of a Scottish minister skating primly on an Edinburgh loch. She also liked the story about another town in the area where I attended a family funeral. I was pleased to be recognized by the lunch lady as the man who had given the show in Blyth, which was worth some extra sandwiches. When I was greeted at the reception by the local bookseller, I was emboldened by the belief that my deceased relative had bought some copies of my book.

"So," I said, smiling at my bookseller friend, "I guess you sold a few copies of my book last fall?" (It was, as language textbooks say, "A question expecting the answer Yes.")

"No, not really," she answered.

As Alice said, laughing delightedly, "That's Huron County — honesty over politeness every time!"

CHAPTER 7

HUGH MacLENNAN'S COUNTRY

Cape Breton Beginnings . . . Dickens Would Have Liked Halifax . . . A Thousand Miles to the Sea . . . Recalling How Trudeau Almost Killed Me . . . Brave Deeds on the Niagara Frontier . . . Hugh MacLennan's Secret . . . In the Treasure Trove . . . A Montreal Coincidence with James Houston . . . Quebec, the City that Was Never Young . . . Mothers and Mad Dogs . . . North Hatley's Piggery Might Fly . . . The Man with Two Tongues, Graham Fraser . . . To Sherbrooke and Lennoxville . . . Wolf Stories . . . The Colour of Canada

"The MacLennans originally came from near here." The speaker was Alistair MacLeod, at his summer home in Dunvegan on the west coast of Cape Breton Island, and he was talking about his friend Hugh MacLennan's family. Grandfather Neil MacLennan had left Kintail in the northwest of Scotland in 1832 to settle near what is now Alistair's place. Just north of Dunvegan lies the lovely valley of the Margaree River. In his wide-ranging 1974 book, *Rivers of Canada*, Hugh called it "the noblest stream of all Nova Scotia." Book-lovers will note that one branch flows out of Lake Ainslie, an unusual name that Hugh was to borrow for a major character in both *Each Man's Son* and *Return of the Sphinx*.

Both in his novels and his essays (and he won three Governor General's Awards for his novels, and two for his non-fiction essay collections) Hugh loved to write about the geography of Canada, starting very near to the traditional homestead. Just south and west of the Margaree lay "the valley of the Middle River, broad well-farmed meadows with many wine-glass elms, and it was here that my forebears on my father's side settled after their escape or deportation (it was never discussed what it was) from Kintail."

"I love these Nova Scotian streams because they are so intimate," Hugh wrote. "The air about nearly all of them is delicious with the fragrance of alders and wild flowers, especially clover, in some times and places so strong it is overpowering."

Glace Bay, where he grew up, was very different. In the words of his biographer, Elspeth Cameron (in her 1981 book, *Hugh MacLennan: A Writer's Life*), in the middle of the nineteenth century it was "a primitive place, a stark and lonely outpost on the northeastern edge of Cape Breton Island. On top of the black cliffs overlooking the sea, a single path had gradually become a road along which the coal miners had built their crude wooden cabins, surrounded by long, dry grasses flattened by the winds."

Here Hugh was raised, just outside the mining town, as the son

of Dr. Sam MacLennan, the colliery doctor. *Each Man's Son* gives
a vivid, unflattering portrait of that community, where the doctor
spent his time patching up men maimed in the mine, or injured in
the Saturday night fights.

In 1915, when Hugh was eight, his father moved the family to
Halifax, which was to be Hugh's home until he left Dalhousie for
Oxford. A distinct picture of old Halifax comes through Hugh's
essays. It was a city of the Atlantic Ocean. One of Hugh's earliest
memories is of being aboard a large ocean liner while wreaths were
thrown onto the sullen face of the sea, and the ship's band played
"Nearer, My God, to Thee." He later learned that they had just
sailed across the spot where the *Titanic* had gone down, exactly one
year earlier.

Less formally, he remembered messing about in boats in the
Halifax harbour, and how he and Tommy Waterfield almost lost
their lives because of his friend's misplaced faith that British naval
vessels were ready, aye ready, to give way to boats under sail, even
when the contest was between *Olympus*, the second largest ship in
the Navy, and Tommy's twelve-foot red dinghy. He recalled going
with his father aboard a visiting naval ship, where the officer of the
watch, in full Gilbert and Sullivan headgear, entered the wardroom,
sat down, drank a little tea, and asked the small boy if he lived in
Halifax. When Hugh politely said yes, the naval hero drawled:
"Beastly place."

But Hugh admired Halifax. There, he wrote, he "grew up believing
that eccentricity was a social asset." In another essay he wrote, "If
Dickens had been given a choice of a Canadian town in which to
spend Christmas, that's where I think he would have gone. . . . He
liked places where accidents were apt to happen." For most readers,
Halifax comes alive in Hugh's first novel, 1941's *Barometer Rising*.
Alistair MacLeod provided the Afterword to the New Canadian
Library edition (which came out under my aegis at M&S in 1989).
He writes that his family recalled the 1917 explosion being heard
in Cape Breton, although "Halifax was some 250 miles away, at the
end of winding and often muddy roads and across the waters of the
Strait of Canso." He goes on to say, shrewdly, "The city of Halifax
is one of the novel's major characters. . . . Dominated by an older
English aristocracy, it has become comfortably, if unimaginatively,

well-to-do, but still it suffers from a certain static listlessness and the feeling that it is being largely ignored by the larger world. It is not in the mainstream of either European or North American life."

In the novel, Angus Murray, who often expresses what we know to be Hugh's own opinion, muses about the city, thinking that "it was her birthright to serve the English in time of war and to sleep neglected when there was peace."

As I have travelled across the country with my show I have scandalized cautious souls by reading aloud a passage from early in the novel and describing it as the most important paragraph in Canadian literature. Let me repeat it here: "The sun had rolled on beyond Nova Scotia into the west. Now it was setting over Montreal and sending the shadow of the mountain deep into the valleys of Sherbrooke Street and Peel. It was turning the frozen banks of the St. Lawrence crimson."

And so on, across the Great Lakes, and across the Prairies, and over the Rockies, until we end with a sentence about the vital railway line that "lay with one end in the darkness of Nova Scotia and the other in the flush of a British Columbian noon."

You can see what Hugh was up to there, deliberately creating a national literature, a sense of Canada as a unit. This book of mine, I hope, will give you some sense of the importance, and the literary magic, of our geography. And Hugh MacLennan ("the cartographer of our dreams," as Robert Kroetsch called him) is a man who weaves his dreams from coast to coast.

To this day, whenever I visit Montreal, I see it through Hugh MacLennan's eyes. This is especially true when I come by car or train from Toronto, crossing the Ottawa River to reach the island of Montreal, and remembering the superb opening of *Two Solitudes* (1945), starting with the words:

> Northwest of Montreal, through a valley always in sight of the low mountains of the Laurentian shield, the Ottawa River flows out of Protestant Ontario into Catholic Quebec. It comes down broad and ale-coloured and joins the St. Lawrence, the two streams embrace the pan of Montreal Island, the Ottawa merges and loses itself, and the mainstream moves northeastward a thousand miles to the sea.

Hugh MacLennan (1907–1990)

Hugh moved to Montreal in 1935, first to teach at Lower Canada College, then, from 1951, at McGill. The city was his home, apart from summer breaks in North Hatley, until he died in 1990. It was there that I used to visit him, at his Summerhill Avenue apartment. This lay west along Sherbrooke from McGill, a walk that he made famous in some of his essays — and in *The Watch That Ends the Night*

(1958), where his narrator, George Stewart, also lived west of his McGill office, along Sherbrooke.

That office is well described in Silver Donald Cameron's 1973 book, *Conversations with Canadian Novelists*. His chapter on Hugh MacLennan begins: "The Arts Building at McGill exudes that slightly dignified shabbiness characteristic of old Canadian halls of learning. The door off the staircase landing would seem to lead to a closet, but behind it is a room less like an office than a rather gracious study in a private home."

A story about that office came my way in the fall of 2013. At the end of one of my shows a bright woman from the audience came to talk to me about her affectionate memories of Hugh MacLennan. She had been one of his students at McGill in the 1960s. In those innocent times university authorities were not alarmed that part of the course could involve female students (like her) going alone to the office of a male professor (like Hugh) for individual tutorials, where the student read an essay aloud and then they discussed it.

On this occasion, she told me, she had been ill, but felt well enough to go to Professor MacLennan's office to read her essay. In mid-reading, however, the sickness came back. Hugh noticed it, and kindly interrupted.

"Look," he said, "You're obviously not well. I have a bed in my inner office, and you should come and lie down." (Modern Deans would be pulling emergency switches at this point, setting alarm bells ringing.) She gladly agreed, and he ushered her into the inner room, saw her arranged comfortably on the little cot, and tiptoed out while she fell asleep.

About an hour later, he gently checked on her, and found that she was feeling a little better. So he helped her up, escorted her out of the office, an arm at her elbow, and ushered her down to Sherbrooke Street. There he hailed a cab, put her in it, gave the driver the money for the fare, and sent her home.

She was still grateful, all these years later, for his kindness, and she remembered the inner room, and the little bed. Keep it in your mind.

In my new role as an author I was delighted to come for the first time to Montreal to promote my book in the fall of 2011. This was at a very fine regular event, the brunch organized by Paragraphe

Books on regular Sundays at the Sheraton Hotel on René Lévesque Boulevard. When my turn to speak came I was able to surprise the crowd with the news that Pierre Trudeau had come very close to killing me on the street right outside our hotel. Although he was then a retired man well into his seventies, he had insisted on crossing the six-lane boulevard in the middle of the block. When the lights changed we were stranded in mid-stream. He cheerfully barked "Run!" and I, fresh from a back operation, did my limping best to follow him through the screeching, honking traffic. I lived to tell the tale, and never became the Trivial Pursuit question: "What was the name of the man killed alongside Pierre Elliott Trudeau in the tragic traffic accident on the Montreal street named after Trudeau's greatest rival?"

It was a very pleasant, well-attended brunch event, with lots of books signed and sold at the end. I was touched to find that several former authors like Dick Irvin ("He writes! He publishes!") and Bill Weintraub (who had passed along Mavis Gallant's famous quote about me, "I'll kill him!") had showed up to cheer me on.

Among the other authors speaking at that breakfast was David Gilmour, who mysteriously chose to sit outside the event, with his publicist, to the surprise of the rest of us. By way of contrast, David Wilson, the author of a fine book about D'Arcy McGee, did join the other authors and the book-loving crowd, and indeed sat at the same table as me, and we became good friends. I knew David Wilson slightly already, since he was then the head of Celtic Studies at St. Michael's College in Toronto, and I, as the president of the St. Andrews Society of Toronto, was involved in supporting his students with grants each year. But our table talk that day in Montreal revealed what a fascinating, witty man he was, and our friendship was sealed when he brought his D'Arcy McGee speech to a close by whipping out a tin whistle and playing a plaintive Celtic tune on it. I hope that his new job as the head of the *Dictionary of Canadian Biography* allows him the same musical opportunities.

David was soon to whistle up a brave tale about the Niagara Frontier, which I always associate with Hugh MacLennan. One of Hugh's most exciting passages in *Rivers of Canada* deals with the Niagara River. In his words,

Given a stupendous momentum by the steady pressure of the continental reservoir behind it, abetted by the 325-foot drop over a distance of only thirty-four miles from Erie to Lake Ontario, the Niagara River proved itself one of the world's most spectacular geological agents. . . . So the Falls of Niagara wear steadily backwards. If they continue to erode at this rate, they will disappear all the way back to Lake Erie within another 25,000 years and disappear into a rapid.

Near that Lake Erie shore, and just west of Fort Erie, lies Ridgeway, a little town so attractive that it might prove to be a southern bookend matching Niagara-on-the-Lake at the north end of the Niagara Parkway. For its very first Ridgeway Reads Literary Festival in June 2012, Mary Friesen and her team had put together a sparkling series of authors, including Charles Foran (*Mordecai: The Life and Times*), Andrew Westoll (of Taylor Prize–winning fame), Olive Senior (*Dancing Lessons*), Richard Wright (*Clara Callan*, etc.), Phil Hall, whose book *Killdeer* was up for that year's Griffin Poetry Prize, and our friend David (D'Arcy McGee) Wilson.

I had the pleasure of giving my show on the opening Friday night, introduced by Rhyming Barb, who concluded her vote of thanks by asking me for another "chapter," because to provide it, ahem, no one would be "apter." (Ogden Nash did not live in vain).

We had to leave after Charlie Foran's marvellous Saturday morning talk on my old sparring partner, Mordecai (his letters to me would continue our duel more in sorrow than in anger, wearily beginning, "Gibson, Gibson"). Mordecai, of course, was a man with a very keen ear for stories. He once reported meeting a woman who admitted that she, too, had a gift for writing: "The only thing I struggle with is putting my ideas into words." That afternoon Jane had a high school reunion to attend in Cambridge. High school reunions wait for no man, or woman, so this meant that we missed the following wonderful event in Ridgeway, bravely described by an anonymous observer very close to David Wilson.

On Saturday afternoon there was a formal unveiling of a mural celebrating the 1866 Battle of Ridgeway against villainous Fenian invaders from Buffalo, which lies just across the border to the south. A high point of the official speech (shouted into a high wind by the local MP, then the minister of justice, en route to becoming the minister of foreign affairs, Rob Nicholson) was when he praised the literary festival: "This is a wonderful event, with some of Canada's best-known writers. One of them, who gave a most enjoyable talk last night on stories about storytellers, was [*short pause*] none other than [*slightly longer pause*] Doug Wilson."

Several people in the crowd shouted out, "No, no, Doug *Gibson*." But my triumphant amorphous role (as in Trudeau's "Fred Gibson") was established once again.

Montreal's own Stephen Leacock was apparently directing the events around the formal unveiling of the mural. First, the procession to the mural was delayed because the two regiments involved in the original battle (or, more correctly, the original headlong retreat) were unable to agree on which of them should lead the way. The gallant men of the Queen's Own Rifles stood firm against the equally determined, jut-jawed heroes from the 13th Hamilton Regiment. After a long stand-off (possibly longer than their appearance in the actual battle, before both regiments ran away) the Hamilton men picked up their rifles and flounced off home.

My anonymous observer's account continues:

Second, the Town Crier immediately led the parade through the back alleys of Ridgeway, without waiting for the dignitaries to arrive, and without paying any attention to the prescribed route along the main street; deaf to all cries to wait, he pressed on fearlessly and relentlessly.

Third, when the Queen's Own and the dignitaries finally made it to the mural, it turned out that the cover over the mural had been tied down so tightly that it couldn't be removed. Eventually, the ropes were cut, and someone leaned out from the window above the mural to catch the cover as it billowed in the wind, and to haul it in like a ship's sail.

Where, I want to know, were Leacock's Knights of Pythias in all this?

At Ridgeway Charles Foran told me that for a good event in Montreal (and as the author of the prizewinning book about Mordecai you can imagine how much he knew about good literary venues in Montreal) I should approach the people at the Atwater Library. I followed up this good idea, and, bingo, some months later found myself being shown around the library before my lunchtime show. The cheerful librarian, Lynn Verge, has an interesting history; in a previous life she was the leader of the Conservative Party in Newfoundland, the province's first female leader. And the library itself has an interesting history. It's in the old Mechanics' Institute Building, which has done good work from pre-Victorian times on, spreading the joys of reading and education far beyond the higher classes that traditionally enjoyed formal schooling. To this day the library still houses worthy but impecunious literary groups.

After Lynn's enjoyable tour of these offices, I started to meet and mingle with the audience assembling for my show, including publishers, authors, and translators, as well as civilians who were not yet friends.

A pleasant, open-faced woman of about sixty approached and asked if she could have a private word with me. I glanced, not too obviously, at my watch and warned her that I could only spare five minutes before the show had to start. She agreed, and we went off to an empty office. After the usual polite preliminaries she said, "Apparently, I am Hugh MacLennan's daughter."

I was speechless. I knew that Hugh had been married twice, to Dorothy Duncan and then to Frances "Tota" Walker. Both marriages had been childless. So how could this be?

She told me calmly that Hugh and her mother, a married woman, had for many years been secret lovers, and she was the love child that resulted. She had, she said, a fair number of letters in her possession. Could we stay in touch to explore this further?

I agreed, then staggered off to give my performance. And we did indeed stay in touch by email, and when I came back to Montreal many months later to give a show at McGill, we arranged to meet. At the meeting, in a coffee shop on St. Catherine Street, Jane and I chatted with her — let's call her Emily — and she told us her story before trustingly turning over to me several heavy bags of documents.

Let me be clear about this: I'm no expert in this area (and no DNA tests are available). But the most convincing evidence of her family link with Hugh was her face. She had brought along a smiling photograph of Hugh where he might have posed deliberately to look as much like her as possible — the same wide features, the same nose and eyes. I happened to know, although the photo was in black and white, that they shared the same colouring. Jane, a wise and neutral judge in such matters, later said simply, "She certainly looks like him."

But people often look like both parents. The documents, which included photographs of Emily's mother, show that she inherited absolutely none of her looks from that side of the family — her mother was a slim-faced, narrow-nosed, dark-haired woman. As for her mother's husband, Emily's official father, I cannot comment, since I have seen no photographs, and he passed away a long time ago.

Emily is comfortable with — in fact very proud of — her claimed link with Hugh MacLennan, which her mother spelled out to her very clearly after her husband's death. But there are other family members for whom this revealed parentage would be a shock, so I must leave her mother's identity secret, for now. Let's call her Joanna.

Joanna was a musician and a teacher of music. I must admit that when I heard this, I reacted unscientifically, thinking, "A musician, of course!" Music meant so much to Hugh that he wrote about it, and, indeed, often *to it*. In *The Watch That Ends the Night*, written to the music of Bach, he pays a remarkable tribute to music. On the subject of death he writes:

> Here at last is the nature of the final human struggle. Within, not without. Without there is nothing to be done. But within. Nobody has ever described such a struggle truly in words. Nobody can. But others have described it and I can tell you who they are.
>
> Go to the musicians. In the work of a few musicians you can hear every aspect of this conflict between light and dark within the soul . . .

Hugh's appreciation of musicians also appears in his less formal writings, such as this July 1975 letter to Joanna:

> After Handel had been working night and day for fifteen days on the *Messiah*, his servant downstairs, hearing him tramping around, shouting snatches of melodies, never speaking when he brought in sandwiches and tea — then suddenly there was total silence and it lasted. The servant ran upstairs, afraid his master had dropped dead (he had a heart condition) and saw him sitting with liquid pouring out of his eyes.
>
> "I have just seen the Great God in all his glory," Handel said. Then shrugged his shoulders and went back to his desk.

He had just completed the Halleljah Chorus.

Joanna and her husband lived in Montreal and were friends of the MacLennans. In Emily's words:

According to my mother, they all met in the late 1930s or very early '40s. They were part of the same circle of friends, artists, writers, musicians, doctors, etc. I have a vague memory of my mother telling me that they met at a party at Norman Bethune's place and all dipped their hands in cans of paint, put their palm prints on the bathroom wall and signed their names inside their palm prints alongside the many others who had been asked to do the same thing.

Both were married at the time. As she said, "We soon realized we were both married to the wrong people, but there was nothing to be done about that." At that point in history, divorce was pretty well out of the question, but I am told that both were extremely attracted to each other from the get-go, both physically and intellectually. They were, however, very discreet, thank goodness. The two couples would only run into each other at social gatherings or concerts, where they would be cordial, but were definitely not friends who dined and spent evenings together. I asked my mother what she thought of Dorothy and she shrugged her shoulders slightly and said, "I liked her. She was a nice woman."

Emily later notes that when Hugh called her house, if Joanna's husband answered Hugh would hang up: if Emily or her brother answered he would ask to speak to "your mother." "We recognized his voice and would mouth *Hughie-Mac* and then say, 'For you' out loud."

It is relevant here to note that Hugh, born in 1907, married Dorothy Duncan (born in 1903) in June 1936. It is also relevant to note that from March 1947 Dorothy's health started to decline, and she was stricken by an embolism in early 1948, and was almost an invalid thereafter. Let me also note that Hugh, the former tennis champion, was a physically active man who enjoyed muscular activities like chopping down trees in North Hatley. He revealed this in his essay praising the Eastern Townships, "my part of the country," entitled "Confessions of a Wood-chopping Man." There he speaks of the English politician William Gladstone and the significance of his wood-chopping: "Humbler men without the need to sublimate a libido must have stacked and burned Mr. Gladstone's slash."

Emily was born in 1950.

What do these carefully preserved documents — clippings and letters — tell us? That Emily has been a diligent collector of articles by or about Hugh MacLennan. That his letters to her mother are always affectionate, and often ask about Emily. And although there are frequent references to Emily's health, there is never one that uses the word "child" or "daughter." One letter does, however, begin with the word, "Darlings."

Two other dates are important here. Dorothy died in April 1957, after many years of long decline, mirrored by the decline of George Stewart's wife Catherine in *The Watch That Ends the Night*. In May 1959, Hugh married "Tota" Walker.

The correspondence shown to me covers many years. There is no "smoking gun" where he speaks of his fatherhood, or of his passion for Emily's mother. A student of secret affairs might, however, be impressed by how often this married man encourages his equally married female correspondent to use "the mail drop at McGill," or tells her precisely when he expects to be at the office there, and thus available for a visit. (Here, our knowledge about the little bed there assumes some importance.) There is the card made out "For a very precious person." And there is the extraordinary love poem, unsigned, but clearly from his typewriter, that gives every sign of moonstruck infatuation. The second verse reads:

> I would love you in the long night
> be in you sleep in you
> to wake in you to the wells of time.

And among the letters that end "Blessings" or "Always" there is one that finishes with the words: "So much I'd like to say and so much I can't, but perhaps it's not necessary. Love, Hugh."

So where does this leave us? I think it leaves us with the extremely strong likelihood that for a number of years Hugh MacLennan (a very recognizable public figure) led a secret life, with a secret lover and a secret daughter. If Emily chooses to come forward publicly I will be glad to help her to do so. As she wrote to me, "Probably now that *you* know and are writing about it, I can put it all to bed and let sleeping ghosts lie still, and I can occasionally wave at the whole thing from far off in the distance."

One of Emily's letters, dated September 2, 1985, contained a bombshell that marked an explosion in Hugh's life. He had taught at McGill since 1951, and even after his official retirement from teaching had continued to be a major, revered figure on the campus.

> Joanna,
>
> I've tried, without success, to reach you by phone. Meanwhile, since mid-June, I have felt as though the roof had fallen in on me and stayed there.
>
> I was abruptly told by my department chief and the Dean that I must vacate my office. That over-stuffed English Dept., by this time nearly entirely American, the majority of them there because of the Viet Nam War, had for once nobody on sabbatical, and therefore my office was required. This meant going through several thousand papers accumulated (along with mss and copies of addresses I'd made) for nearly fifty years. The papers began in 1936. Calgary University Library had wanted them, and I had put off sorting them. Finally they were despatched by courier and weighed, all told, about forty-five lbs.
>
> Then the books had to be packed, and after them the furniture. The only place for them was the North Hatley cottage and I got them down about a week ago. They still have to be sorted . . .
>
> However, it now seems that I'll get another office in Concordia. Graham Fraser, Blair's son, is now *The Globe and Mail* correspondent in Quebec and he knew what had happened to the office. He was outraged, and knows the new Rector of Concordia, and apparently an office will be available for me there.

I had learned about this fiasco too late to intervene, although I tried, offering to rouse public opinion on Hugh's behalf, but he chose not to make a fuss. Word got out, however, and the university took a well-earned hammering. The *Ottawa Citizen* ran an editorial that stated, "Any university that can't find room for Hugh MacLennan has lost its mind. Has McGill lost its soul as well?" After this ugly business, as you can imagine, relations between the MacLennans and

McGill were very frosty and stayed that way for the rest of Hugh's life. Yet his 1990 funeral was held in the McGill Chapel. What happened?

After I took my show around, including my description of Hugh's funeral, I received an explanation from Tota's nephew, Michael Ogilvie, a friend of mine from North Hatley. When Hugh died, Michael realized that his aged aunt was in no condition to organize a funeral for her late husband. He himself was flying off to the Maritimes, but he knew that this was a crisis. So although he had never met David Johnston, the principal of McGill (and later Canada's very popular Governor General), he looked up his home phone number while at the airport and called him *at 6:30 in the morning*, introducing himself as "Hugh MacLennan's nephew."

David Johnston came to the phone (think pyjamas, and a bathrobe) and cut short a possibly complicated conversation with the breathtakingly wise and generous words "I assume you're calling, Michael, to give us a chance to bring Hugh home . . ."

Michael was very grateful, and McGill proceeded to organize, on Tota's behalf, the whole fine event the following Wednesday in the McGill Chapel, with a string quartet playing Hugh's favourite music and four speakers honoured to be asked to talk about his life, including the most grateful of all, his publisher.

We were lucky to have a Governor General like David Johnston.

In July 2013 I gave my show at a Westmount residence for seniors, named Place Kensington. It's a fine, lively place and the residents include two authors of mine, the charming crime novelist Ted Phillips and my friend William Weintraub, the author of *City Unique* (1996). Bill Weintraub is also famous for the classic novel *Why Rock the Boat?* (1961) and I proudly edited his last novel, 2005's *Crazy About Lili*, providing it with a very funny cover illustration by the wonderful Anthony Jenkins, whose path was later to cross mine, as my readers know.

As always, I adapted my show for the local audience, and I decided to spend extra time on James Houston and his Montreal-based Arctic adventures. I told them that once, on the train to Montreal, I happened to look up at the spring skies above. I noticed a skein of geese heading north to Jim Houston's Arctic. Then I noticed another giant V, then another, then another. Soon the skies above our train were filled with hundreds, then thousands, then many thousands of geese. But as the train rattled on beyond Cornwall the other passengers were all seemingly oblivious to the seasonal miracle that was filling the skies above us.

In the show I talked about Jim Houston and Montreal, where he had met his wife, Alma Bardon, when she interviewed him for a Montreal newspaper — and one thing led to another, including John and Sam Houston. And I recalled the huge role that the Montreal-based Canadian Guild of Crafts played in encouraging Jim to collect and display early Inuit art, and his own superb Arctic sketches.

In the course of my show, when I was talking about Jim bringing that early art out of the North, an older man in the audience spoke up, "When was this?"

"In 1948," I replied.

"Yes, that sounds about right."

He went on to explain that he had been setting up his medical practice around then, and had wandered into the Canadian Guild shop and come across a very fine portrait of a young Inuit woman in a full sealskin traditional outfit. He stood there admiring this piece of finely drawn art that revealed another world, far from Montreal. Then another customer, a young dark-haired man, came and stood beside him, looking over his shoulder at the drawing.

"Do you like it?" the stranger asked.

"Yes, I do," said the young doctor, "but I'm just setting up my medical practice, and I'm sure I can't afford it."

"Can you afford fifty bucks?" asked the man.

"Yes," said the surprised doctor, and James Houston made the deal with him right there and then, remarking that this was the first of his Northern drawings that he had ever sold.

Hugh wrote in *Rivers of Canada*, which has, at its heart, a chapter all about the St. Lawrence above and below Quebec City,

> Quebec, to me at least, has the air of a city that never was young. No city in America, few in Europe, give out such a feeling of antiquity as does Quebec's Lower Town. A little like Calais perhaps, but far nobler with its rock and wilderness behind it and the great river at its foot. These stern grey walls with their Norman or Mediterranean roofs two centu-

ries ago sheltered an embattled, isolated people who lived as long and as hard in a decade as most communities live in a century.

He reminds us of just how old this old city is. "At the core of the modern capital lie the stones of Champlain's fortress, founded a dozen years before the Pilgrim Fathers saw Plymouth Rock."

I know Quebec City a little, and I like it a lot, so I had been pleased to learn about the Quebec City ImagiNation Writers Festival, an English-language event that takes place in the heart of the old city every spring. I was delighted when, thanks to local friends like Neil Bissoondath, I was invited to bring my show there.

The organizer, Elizabeth Perreault, is so calm and efficient on email that I was expecting a much older person than the fresh-faced young woman who greeted Jane and me. She runs a top-class festival, too, with authors like Charles Foran, Emma Donoghue, and Guy Vanderhaeghe in attendance. We saw readings in two remarkable rooms in the Morrin Centre, in the heart of old Scottish Quebec. If you think I exaggerate there (old Scottish Quebec?), the Morrin Centre is named after a Scottish doctor from the early nineteenth century, and stands on the Chaussée des Écossais, right opposite the old Scottish church, St. Andrew's, and the "Kirk Hall."

Inside, the great hall of the centre (housing the Literary and Historical Society) is constructed on nineteenth-century Scottish traditional lines, so that the electric light bulbs seem almost like an intrusion on the chandeliers. The library is equally famous, with its wooden statue of Wolfe casting a dramatic arm out from a corner of the two-storey ranks of shelves. Louise Penny fans will be familiar with the setting, and after seeing Peter Dube talking about his books there, I learned that authors from Charles Dickens to Mark Twain had given readings in the ancient building.

Jane and I were housed in the grand old Clarendon Hotel, in the heart of the ancient upper town, just north of the Château Frontenac. Almost next door stood the Anglican cathedral, a traditional Wren-style building modelled after St. Martin-in-the-Fields. We were not far from the former St. Matthew's Anglican Church, where Canon Frederick Scott officiated before heading off to the First World War as the First Division's padre, leaving his son, my friend the poet F.R. Scott, at home.

Three stories there, the first two from Sandra Djwa's biography of the poet son: Reverend Scott once plunged off the Quebec to Levis ferry on a cold night to save a man from drowning. This heroic act prompted "one of the reigning Anglican ecclesiastics" to marvel, "And to think that you did it for a French Canadian." Scott swiftly replied, "My lord, I did it for a fellow Canadian."

At the front, Canon Scott was also heroic. Sandra Djwa, in *The Politics of the Imagination: A Life of F.R. Scott* (1987), tells of how the canon's son Harry was killed by a sniper, and buried hastily in no man's land. In the shell-ploughed landscape, in mud both slippery and sticky, lit by the flash of exploding shells, Canon Scott and the soldier helping him searched for twenty-four hours, digging here and there, until it seemed hopeless. Eventually they dug beside a little white cross, and in the canon's words, after the soldier "had taken off a few shovelfuls of earth something white was laid bare and there was darling Harry's left hand with the signet ring on his little finger. It was like a miracle . . ." With the sound of shells whistling overhead, Canon Scott conducted the burial service for his son.

The final story is appropriate, given St. Matthew's long association with the literary Scott family. When falling numbers in the congregation caused the church to close in the 1970s, it was transformed into a notably beautiful library.

Right below our hotel room window, to the west, huddled the Ursulines Convent. This is so ancient that the nuns famously performed acts of Christian charity to assist the invading Scottish soldiers who occupied the city after the battle in 1759. During the fierce winter that fell on the shell-shocked town, the kilted Scottish soldiers were at great risk of suffering frostbite and other painful indignities. The maidenly Ursulines (many of them farm-raised, among herds of brothers) were all too aware of the Highlanders' manly predicament, so they very kindly knitted woolen underwear for them, to protect their privates — although, of course, their corporals and sergeants and other ranks were equally grateful.

The Ursulines, of course, continued for generations to provide Quebec's best finishing school for the daughters of the province's landed gentry. Their culture was so strong, apparently, that it was fashionable for well-bred young ladies on seigneuries across the province to speak with "an Ursuline lisp."

But at the ImagiNation Writers Festival we were immersed in more recent history. After Guy Vanderhaeghe entertained us with tales of western history in this eastern city, I recalled for him that it was exactly thirty years earlier that he and I had celebrated his Governor General's Award win for *Man Descending* in Quebec City. This year, on the Sunday afternoon, I gave my show in the grand old hall, and the crowd responded very kindly with a standing ovation. (Jane, I must report, far from leading this excellent development, said to Elizabeth Perreault, "Do I have to stand up, too?" If anyone wonders about my being a grounded sort of fellow, look no further than this story for a reason.) But a standing ovation in Quebec City is something worth recording, if I can find a suitably capacious tombstone.

Time for a family story. Not a boring one, but a matter of life and death. By this time you may be wondering how I became a story-teller, or at least a man who loves stories. It's always sensible to blame the parents. Specifically, I blame my tiny mother (only five feet tall) who was the great storyteller in our family, and loomed large in my life, and perhaps in my choice of career.

I grew up in the small village of Dunlop in southwest Scotland. It was so small that it held only about 700 people, even when all the dairy farmers were in town. In fact it was so small that it couldn't even muster a real crossroads. The centre of the village was indeed called "the Cross," but I was in my teens before I realized that it was really just a Y junction. Around it clustered the news agent's shop (which sold important bottles of fizzy "lemonade"), the post office (with mysterious tailors' dummies that let Mr. Hamilton keep his stitching hand in, between weighing letters), the bank, and the five general stores where the local housewives like my mother did their daily shopping, with their wicker baskets in hand.

These shopping expeditions were the 1950s Scottish equivalent of a giant, floating cocktail party. Every housewife (and my mother wore that description like a badge of honour, like all of her friends) met and chatted with every other housewife, returning home with exciting stories.

I grew up, then, in a house where every shopping expedition — even if the walk took less than a minute — was expected to produce interesting stories well worth repeating. In this concentrated world, this moveable stage setting, everyone was expected to play his or her part as "a character." It was important to be "a character" (or, even better, "a real character") and it was much better to be an eccentric — even an unpleasant one — than to be so dull that no stories resulted from your behaviour or conversation. Alice Munro's small towns know all about this. And Hugh MacLennan, you'll recall, grew up believing that "eccentricity was a social asset."

As a result, I remember the village of my youth (what W.O. Mitchell called "the litmus years") as being populated by accomplished eccentrics, who seemed to work at it. For example, there was Miss McKnight, who would pause in the laneway beside our house after every shopping trip. To my mother's delight she would shelter beside the hawthorn hedge *in order to count her change, penny by penny,* to be sure that she had not been unfairly treated in any of the village shops. My mother was so thrilled by this performance that she would beckon me to the window to peek out at Miss McKnight and the ritual checking of the purse.

As a storyteller, my mother was voluble and tireless, and gained local fame as "wee Mrs. Gibson," a reliable source of great stories. But one story she told only with great reluctance, and it concerned me. Family legend tells us that I was gurgling happily in my baby carriage one fine day at "the Cross." My pram was parked right outside Mrs. Bull's, the best shop for fruit and vegetables, where my mother was perhaps discussing the merits of the new Ayrshire potatoes, when a mad dog jumped up on my baby carriage and confronted me.

I assume that they knew the dog was mad because it was foaming at the mouth, and growling menacingly. I assume, too, that my mother (a brave woman) was either unaware of this drama outside, or physically prevented from intervening, while the manager of the Clydesdale Bank across the street was summoned, and appeared in this emergency *carrying a shotgun.*

The mad dog was swept off my baby carriage, and shot.

My reaction is not recorded, since my mother did not enjoy recalling details of The Incident of the Dog in the Daytime. But I think we can take it that I didn't like the shotgun blast going off so close to my baby ears. (And who would ever have thought that the banker in our sleepy little village would be *armed,* since there was no local Bonnie and Clyde tradition, even in the bonny Clydesdale Bank?) And it is certainly true that all of my conscious life, my enthusiasm for barking dogs has been noticeably restrained.

"Find North Hatley on the map. Go there." That's the advice given by one tourist guide, for people looking for the ideal place to visit in the Eastern Townships. It's a place that I know well. In *Rivers of Canada* Hugh writes of the rivers "of the Eastern Townships with their deep volcanic lakes and rolling hills like the Scottish Lowlands." Perhaps that's why I felt at home in this part of Quebec, when I married into a family that summered there, with Hugh MacLennan a cottaging neighbour and friend. Everything was perfect, and Lake Massawippi was ideal for long swims or canoe expeditions, although the roads were not perfect for jogging because of barking farm dogs — aha! — especially near the Piggery Theatre.

In recent years we've been lucky enough to visit the little town as friends of Norman and Pat Webster. Norman, a superb journalist, was the editor of both the *Globe and Mail* and the *Montreal Gazette*. Pat is a woman of many talents, who leads gardening tours around Europe, not to mention of her own lakeside garden. They are such good friends that in Montreal, after my bruising encounter with Mavis Gallant ("*I'll kill him!*"), Pat took me home and fed me dinner and sympathy.

In 2013, Pat suggested that I contact the people at the Piggery, a little theatre converted from its original use raising pigs, to give my show. I was delighted. After a few phone conversations with Ruth McKinven, we were all set. Or almost all set. I had stupidly failed to specify the sort of equipment that my show would require, but this is a rural community where everyone helps out in an emergency, even just before a show. Miraculously, a screen came from here, a projector was picked up from there, and we started just twenty minutes late. The Piggery held about 100 people, in comfortable seats, and the show seemed to go well, with Alison Pick commenting that the contents had really changed since she had seen it in Moose Jaw.

I had made special local changes to deal with Hugh MacLennan and the 2004 North Hatley book *I'll Tell You a Secret* by Anne Coleman, about her teenage infatuation with "Mr. MacLennan." It's a fascinating book, about what was clearly a strong attraction between

Hugh and her, although nothing physical ever occurred. I even suggested that Hugh, immersed through all these years in writing *The Watch That Ends the Night* (where the fourth most important character is young Sally, the daughter of Catherine and Jerome Martell), might have had literary reasons for spending so much time with this teenaged girl, the same age and background as his character. After all, I said, he had no daughter of his own . . .

One of the best things about my Piggery performance was that I was introduced by Graham Fraser, a friend for more than forty years. I've learned that he wasn't given much time to prepare his introduction that night, but he certainly used it well. He clearly relished the fact that after many publishing events where I had introduced him as the author, he was able to turn the tables.

He was very, very funny. He spoke about the lonely life of the author, submerged for weeks, or months, or even years, in the depths of his writing, always with the gnawing doubt at the back of the mind that this is all a waste of time, it's no good, nobody will be interested in this stuff. Then comes a call from the publisher, thrilled by what he has just read. Apparently, if the publisher was me, the enthusiasm was so extreme, for the writer it was like a shot of adrenaline to the heart, as I talked about how the writing was splendid, very close to perfect.

The long-jawed face that Graham inherited from his father, Blair, softened in delight as my friend warmed to his task, re-enacting my inspiring conversations. As the phone call about this superb manuscript developed it seemed that I would mention that perhaps there might be a useful little nip here, and just possibly a beneficial tuck there — and by now the North Hatley audience was rocking with mirth — and had he considered the possibility of a tiny new insertion there, a matter of a few minutes' work. I emerged as a cross between a cheerleader and Macchiavelli. It was a bravura performance, warm, affectionate, and very funny.

Of course, Graham knew about the challenges of an author's life from an early age. His eminent father, for many years the Ottawa correspondent for *Maclean's* (before becoming the editor), wrote the fine history *The Search For Identity: Canada, 1945–1967* for Doubleday Canada, the company that hired me. I note that he dedicated it to my predecessor with the words "To George Nelson — a man of saintly patience." This speaks for itself.

Blair brought his family to North Hatley every year, which meant that Graham grew up there among literary greats like Hugh MacLennan and F.R. Scott. I've told the story of the tall, stork-like poet falling splashingly out of his canoe at a picnic farther up the lake, to the delight of four-year-old Graham, who clapped his hands and requested, "Do it again, Mr. Scott, do it again!"

Canoes were not always a source of merriment. Blair died in a canoeing accident, going down the Petawawa River with some Ottawa friends, at the age of fifty-nine. I remember the shroud of sorrow that hung over the Doubleday Canada office the day in 1968 that young Graham came in to look after some final business. In the summer of 2013, Graham led three generations of Frasers on a memorial trip on the Petawawa, sympathetically reported by Roy MacGregor in the *Globe*.

Graham's own career in publications like the *Globe*, the *Star*, and *Maclean's* took him to many important foreign postings. But it was his move to Quebec City in 1979 for the *Montreal Gazette* that changed his life. Quebec was in the headlines, its future in Canada uncertain, and Graham (an Ottawa-raised anglophone who had decided to really work at becoming bilingual) had put himself on the front lines. I was proud to publish his important book *PQ: René Lévesque and the Parti Quebecois in Power* in 1984 (mischievously launched at the Literary and Historical Society building in Quebec, to remind Lévesque and his cabinet members of its existence), and was pleased when it was nominated for the Governor General's Award that year.

That Rideau Hall reference reminds me that since 1968 Graham has been married to the remarkable Barbara Uteck, with two sons, two grandchildren, and many friends to applaud their marriage. Barbara's distinguished career in the public service reached its zenith when she ran Rideau Hall for the Governor General, as the chief of staff to Adrienne Clarkson. This meant that she and Graham had to slum it in "Rideau Cottage," a mansion on the Rideau Hall grounds that I, like many of their friends, stayed in overnight. It was wonderful, although I resented the absence of a butler at breakfast.

In 1989 Graham brought out a comprehensive, nationwide look at a Canadian election, entitled *Playing for Keeps: The Making of the*

Prime Minister, 1988. It began with a MacLennan-inspired swoop across the country, as the helicopter-borne camera seemed to pan across the leaders' constituencies, from Baie Comeau to Oshawa all the way to John Turner's Vancouver. The book on the election was a fine, prompt, thoughtful piece of work, but it didn't succeed as well as it deserved. The market had moved on beyond reflective books on political events, in favour of fast, up-to-the-minute reporting . . . and hold the reflection.

The acknowledgements shed some light on how books begin:

> This book had its origin in a chat with Doug Gibson and [*Globe* reporter] Hugh Winsor in the fall of 1986, when I expounded at some length on the degree of insanity that was involved in writing a book, and how I felt cured of that particular disease. Almost from that moment forward, I was infected, once again, with the bacteria. My wife began finding scribbled ideas and odd notes, like the hints of an illicit affair . . .

In 2006, with my truly enthusiastic backing, Graham wrote the book that he had been intended by the God of Authors to write: *Sorry, I Don't Speak French: Confronting the Canadian Crisis that Won't Go Away*. I edited it in a state of jubilation, aware that it was answering every question that observers on all sides might ask. It was hugely successful, and very influential, not least in Graham's own life. The position of Commissioner of Official Languages came open in the same year. When Graham and I discussed his idea of applying for the job I joked that he had already completed a 90,000-word application.

He got the job. And he's done well in it ever since, confronting "the Canadian crisis that won't go away," but doing his best, anyway.

The centre of the Eastern Townships is Sherbrooke, the third largest city in Quebec. In 1967's *The Colour of Canada* Hugh wrote that "Sherbrooke, once centred on an English garrison (when Lord Palmerston became Colonial Secretary his first order was to strengthen it against American invasion), is now largely French-speaking." A much more interesting fact about "Old Pam," who went on to become prime minister, is that he "died in his eighty-second year of a heart attack while engaged in a sex act with a young parlour maid on his billiard table" (as Karl Shaw records in *Five People Who Died During Sex*). He was a much-loved leader. And our Canadian history books are much too dull.

The town was named after Sir John Coape Sherbrooke, yet another military man who served with Wellington. It sprang up where the Magog River runs down to join the St. Francis. Roaming around, Jane and I found that King Street (surely the steepest main street in Canada) runs parallel to the falling river, which powered the many textile mills that attracted Quebec workers. Inevitably, the main downtown cross street is named Wellington.

It was on historic Wellington Street that our friend Linda Morra, a professor at Bishop's University in nearby Lennoxville, took us for a celebration dinner after I gave my show in the small, distinctive English-speaking university. Lennoxville (named to honour the family of the unfortunate Duke of Richmond, bitten, you'll recall, by his pet fox) is the centre of English culture in the region, with Bishop's front and centre. In literary terms, it's renowned for its association with teachers such as Ralph Gustafson, and students such as Michael Ondaatje, who met his first wife, the multi-talented Kim, while he was a young student there, and she was a professor's wife.

Michael always was a handsome devil. Although he has been happily partnered with Linda Spalding for many years, ten years or so ago, when we were both well into our sixties (he's a couple of months older than I am), I saw the almost magnetic attraction that he has for women. In my publisher role, I once attended a summer reading that he gave outdoors in the courtyard at Hart House in the University of Toronto. I listened to the cadence of his low, softly accented voice and saw the hair, the colour of wood-smoke, rising above his tanned, striking face. Surveying the women around me, who were leaning forward, with parted lips, it was clear that they fell into two groups — those who had fallen in love with him, and those who were heading that way.

Bishop's has always enjoyed an enviable reputation as a very convivial university, where the undergraduates have a very good time "on the mighty Massawippi shore," as the school fight song has it. Special pride is taken in the brave deeds of the small school's mighty football team. To this day my old newspaper friends Norman Webster and Michael Goldbloom, the current principal, live or die on fall weekends according to the fortunes of the gallant "Gaiters."

I worked with Michael Goldbloom, when he headed the *Montreal Gazette*, to bring out *The Ice Storm* by Mark Abley in 1998. Now, many years later, Michael recalls a much earlier literary incident in which his father, Victor, as a student at Lower Canada College, published something written by one of his teachers in his school magazine, thus becoming "Hugh MacLennan's first publisher." Michael kindly turned out to join the audience for my show, a model for university leaders across the country.

But then, Bishop's, founded by Bishop Jehoshaphat Mountain (*Jehoshaphat!*), has tended to have interesting leaders. It was once headed by my friend C.L.O. ("Oggie") Glass, who as a young Navy officer fighting U-boats during the war got so plastered that when he was formally introduced to the Admiral at a dinner in Londonderry — a major moment in a young officer's career — he leered winningly

Michael Ondaatje (1943–)

at him and asked, "May I have the pleashure of thish dansh?" before being hustled away.

Ah, Bishop's.

Moving west from his beloved Eastern Townships, in *Rivers of Canada* Hugh discussed the Ottawa River, and the wolves that prowled the Quebec bank, in the Laurentians. Close to Ottawa! He even interviewed a guide who was hunted, with his fishing party, by a hungry pack, in August "within a hundred and twenty-five miles of Ottawa."

He went on, "It was like being hunted in a war, the way they came seemed so organized. I don't mind saying I took them more seriously than my party did. How many there were I don't know, but there were enough to have torn us to pieces. They were closing in."

He and his group of hunters kept their tractor going down the trail as fast as it could go. The wolves "were getting confident when we came around a bend in the trail and there was a light in an Indian's cabin. I figure that light saved us, for they faded out."

"If I hadn't had my rifle," the man said after another such wolf encounter beside the Ottawa, "I wouldn't be talking to you now."

Impossible, you say. Well-read wolves know that academics agree that they never attack people. I discussed this recently with Harold Johnson, my Cree friend from Moose Jaw, who was raised and now lives much farther north, near La Ronge. Harold is one of the few people raised on a trapline who got a law degree from Harvard. He now works as a Crown prosecutor, when he's not writing novels. And he knows about dogs. Growing up with them in the bush he knew that it was risky even to work with dogs when you were sick, and thus less of an alpha male. And he knows about wolves.

Once, as a young man, he was walking alone in the bush in the early morning. The hair rose on the back of his neck, and he turned quickly and looked around. Nothing. He walked on, but the extra sense continued to prickle his neck. He whirled around and saw a wolf, flattened to the ground, stalking him. It was very big, and very close, and this was not an accidental encounter.

Harold found himself engaged in a fight with the wolf, which made many darting attacks. Because of his work with dogs, he knew that fear was his greatest enemy, and anger the weapon he had to channel. So he raged and threw things and leaped at the wolf, but without effect. He tells me that it was only when he got so angry that he really decided that he was going to kill this damned wolf, and hurled a rock designed to do it, that the wolf got the message, magically, and abandoned its attack, and disappeared.

I once wrote that every successful Canadian non-fiction book must involve stories about bears, wolves, hockey players, and bush pilots. I enjoyed helping Bobby Orr sign books for his fans, with full, friendly eye contact. And the national mourning for Jean Béliveau sent me back to the copy of his autobiography signed to me, and reminded me how he once interrupted a Montreal Salon du Livre signing session to get up from his desk and cross the aisle to greet his delighted and honoured friend Doug.

Three out of four so far. Watch this space.

I've called this chapter "Hugh MacLennan's Country" because Hugh wanted to take the country as his canvas. He loved to write about the whole country, and many Canadians enjoyed his essayist's blend of history and geography and landscape and people. Naturally, enterprising publishers took advantage of that fact. For Centennial Year he was asked to write the text for the heavily illustrated (with superb photographs by John de Visser) *The Colour of Canada*. It sold so well that it was reprinted many times. Hundreds of thousands of copies of this classic book stand on Canadian bookshelves, possibly in yours.

The same impulse produced a request for Hugh to write *Rivers of Canada*, which I've dipped into so often here. Hugh took its national scope so seriously that he travelled far and wide. In B.C., for example, he wandered beside the fearsome Fraser, its "furious frothing water scandalously yellow against the green," on its lush banks. "It roars like an ocean storm, but ocean storms blow themselves out, while the Fraser's roar is forever." He stands on the bridge at Lytton, where the very large Thompson River meets the Fraser. "The Fraser," he notes in amazement, "swallows the Thompson in less than a hundred yards."

To cover the country from sea to sea to sea he took a trip down the Mackenzie to the Beaufort Sea, conscious always of his great advance man, Alexander Mackenzie, the Nor'Wester who found his way to two great oceans. Hugh spent many days sailing on the Mackenzie, a river system so huge that "in flow it ranks seventh in the world.

And in the western hemisphere is exceeded only by those mighty waterways, the Amazon and the Mississippi." He recalls seeing the phenomenon of the Liard joining the main Mackenzie stream. He could see "the Liard's brown water flowing alongside the left bank while the clean water keeps to the right. The two streams are distinguishable side by side for nearly two hundred miles below Fort Simpson."

This is the land where the bush pilot is important, but where the winter is king. And here, as promised, is a bush pilot story, one you will not soon forget. In Hugh's words:

> When winter comes to this region, it does not come slowly, it strikes with a crack. I met a veteran of many years on the Mackenzie who told me that he once escaped having to spend an entire long winter in Aklavik by a matter of a minute. His was the last plane out, and as he stood on one of its pontoons filling his tank with gas, he suddenly noticed ice forming on the water. He threw the can away, jumped into the pilot's seat without even taking the time to screw on the cap of the gas tank, gunned the plane, and took off. The thin ice was crackling about the pontoons before he became airborne, and as he made his circle to head south he saw the pack ice thrusting in, and the lagoon from which he had risen turn opaque as though the frost had cast a wand over it.

CHAPTER 8

IN THE MIDDLE OF CANADA

Finding Ontario . . . Underground to Windsor . . . Alistair MacLeod's City . . . A Sad Winter . . . Paul Martin on the Border . . . Nino Ricci's Leamington . . . As Far South as California, a Little Chat . . . Sarnia Surprises . . . Dudley George and the Dark Legacy of Ipperwash . . . London, Our London . . . John Galt's Guelph . . . The Convenient Tom King . . . The Niagara Frontier . . . St. Catharines and Richard B. Wright . . . Port Colborne Offers Canada's Best

"As a publisher, what makes you decide to publish a manuscript that you read?" "Where is Canadian publishing heading?" "What's it like, being married to Margaret Atwood?" And even, "What is your philosophy of life?"

These are just a few of the questions that have been fired at me as I've roamed around Ontario promoting my book, and my travels have given me a rare chance to really get to know Ontario. The first lesson, of course, is that you can't really get to know it. The province is so big, physically (with more than a million square kilometres of land, and countless shorelines, one of them fronting salt water), and its population (at over thirteen million) is so huge, that it's best to regard it as more like a country than a province, and perhaps more like a continent than a country.

The people in the province (few of whom use the word "Ontarian" with any real enthusiasm, unlike, for example, their "Albertan" cousins) are so varied in every way, including their lifestyle and living conditions, that nothing can safely be described as typical. It's like trying to find something typical about Europe, where the variety in geography, in architecture, in language, and in lifestyle makes typical a needle hard to find in a haystack that includes the fiords of Norway, the boulevards of Paris, and the beaches of Crete.

In earlier chapters I've dealt with downtown Toronto (and how typical is that of Ontario?), Northwestern Ontario, as represented by Thunder Bay and the Lake of the Woods country (where the same question applies), and Alice Munro Country, and its approaches. Now, in the next two chapters, in my tour of what I'll call Central Ontario, I think you'll find lots of fascinating people and places, some surprising history and geography, and some great books, authors, and stories. But typical?

Consider this. How typical is Windsor, with its view across the Detroit River to the American towers to the north? How typical is Lakefield, with its ice-cream-licking tourists and cottagers swelling

the little lakeside town every summer weekend? Or London, with
its sober yellow-brick houses lining well-treed streets that contain a
major university, in an old business centre with half a million people?
Or, by way of contrast, how about the very modern Brock University,
perched high on the Niagara Escarpment, above St. Catharines? Or
Eganville, close to Foymount, the highest community in Eastern
Ontario, with its amazing view up the Ottawa Valley and across the
river into Quebec? Or low-lying but wealthy Burlington, placed
right beside Lake Ontario at a point that makes it a suburb of
Hamilton, or of Toronto, according to taste and commuter choices.
Or Ottawa, or Uxbridge, or Kingston, or Barrie, or Flesherton, or
Sarnia, or Thornbury, where the Beaver River flows into Georgian
Bay? Ontario, a country all its own. And anything but typical.

Jane and I drove on a fine fall day down Alistair MacLeod's 401 ("If
you are true to it, it will be true to you . . ."). We ticked off the literary references as we passed the turnoffs to Kitchener-Waterloo
(and Alice Munro Country), and to Dutton (the setting for John
Kenneth Galbraith's farm memoir, *The Scotch*, including the famous
line that dampened his teenage ardour, "Well, it's your cow"), or to
Thamesville, the boyhood home of Robertson Davies, and the setting for the early scenes in *Fifth Business* (before the plot snowballs to
include the First World War and Dunstan Ramsay's teaching career
at Toronto's "Colborne College").

Beyond Chatham we drive through rich, placid farmlands that
might lead the lazy observer to think that nothing much happened
here. But the place name North Buxton reminds us that this peaceful
country was directly linked to a world of horror. For this was the end
of the Underground Railroad.

We all know that it wasn't a conventional railroad. To keep
everything secret they used a railroad code, although "the passengers" were actually runaway slaves. They were running away from
the American Southern states where slavery was legal. "The passengers" were helped along their way by "conductors," who were men
or women, black or white (often Quakers or Methodists), but were
united in the belief that slavery was evil, and were willing to take
great risks to help people run away to freedom.

It was a very risky business. The runaways spent every second of every hour under threat, hiding by day and stumbling through dark woods by night, avoiding farms and towns (dogs!), sheltering only in the safe barns and houses that were pointed out to them. All this, for hundreds of miles, crossing rivers and swamps and hills and mountains, avoiding well-travelled roads all the way.

To modern minds, it seems almost unbelievable that their travels had to be so secret, and were so dangerous. But to the Southern slave-owners it was an outrage that these valuable pieces of property took it into their heads to run away — in effect, *to steal themselves* — and this meant that the forces of law and order were on the owners' side.

So much money was involved — and the dangers to slave-owning plantations were so clear if slaves got away with running away — that the slave-owners set their whip-cracking overseers, or bounty hunters (and their bloodhounds), to pursue the runaways and bring them back. Not gently. And these rough men with whips and guns who were busy reclaiming "stolen property" were unlikely to be gentle with anyone they encountered by night assisting in this "theft."

Between 1840 and 1860 roughly 30,000 slaves — men, women, and children — took "the railroad" north to Canada, the Promised Land, where they would be free. In 1967 Martin Luther King Jr. in his Massey Lectures told his Canadian audience that slaves

> knew that far to the north a land existed where a fugitive slave, if he survived the horrors of the journey, could find freedom. The legendary underground railroad started in the south and ended in Canada. The freedom road links us together. Our spirituals, now so widely admired around the world, were often codes. We sang of "heaven" that awaited us and the slave masters listened in innocence, not realizing that we were not speaking of the hereafter. Heaven was the word for Canada and the Negro sang of the hope that his escape on the underground railroad would carry him there. One of our spirituals, "Follow the Drinking Gourd," in its disguised lyrics contained directions for escape. The gourd was the big dipper, and the North Star to which its handle pointed gave the celestial map that directed the flight to the Canadian border.

"Heaven was the word for Canada." It's hard to read these words without pride.

The runaways followed the Drinking Gourd, and knew that they had made it when they crossed "the River Jordan," that is, the Detroit River. That was the destination for most of the fugitives, although the whole Niagara frontier or the north shore of Lake Erie, anywhere, were also desperately sought. In 1850 a law was passed in the United States to deal with the runaway "problem." This made it legal to kidnap and take back south any slave who had made it to safety in the "free" states of the North. You won't be surprised to learn that from then on the flow of slaves going all the way to truly free Canada swelled to a flood, and it took a civil war to stop it.

The drama of every single runaway's story speaks for itself. Escape by night, with every stranger a potential enemy who can betray you. Wading through swamps, or tearing through thickets of thorn, pursued by lawmen and bounty hunters with horses and guns, and, in the background, the constant sound of bloodhounds baying. If you're interested in great stories — and if you're immersed in this book, the chances that you're keen on stories are pretty good — there are thousands of such stories to discover. And if you're a writer, you might find inspiration in the general theme — as Linda Spalding did with her novel of slavery in western Virginia around 1800, *The Purchase*, which won the Governor General's Award in 2012.

There have been many fine books about the subject. One that I can strongly recommend is an old classic, *Underground to Canada* (1977), by Barbara Smucker (now deceased, and a woman whom I met only briefly). This is for young adults, but is a fine work for readers of all ages. It bravely uses ugly language, realistically, just as it was used by slave-owners. As Lawrence Hill, author of *The Book of Negroes*, puts it in his introduction to the 2013 edition:

> The "N" word is offensive to the extreme by modern standards — as was the institution of slavery, and as was the Holocaust. But writers, teachers and parents do no one a favour by pretending that such things didn't exist. Much better to acknowledge them, to understand them, and to ensure that our children and grandchildren are even better equipped than we are to learn from the monstrous mistakes in our past.

Lawrence goes on to tackle the fact that life in Canada was not a bed of roses for the slaves who made it here. "Barbara Smucker is to be credited for acknowledging that life in this country was fraught with difficulties for Black people." He concludes with the words: "In the meantime, Barbara Smucker has created a sensitive and dramatic story about a young girl's flight from slavery, and — some three decades after it first appeared in print — *Underground to Canada* still serves as a wonderful introduction to a vital and fascinating element of Canadian history."

And Lawrence, as the author of *The Book of Negroes*, which has won many prizes and enthralled a million readers (not to mention TV viewers), knows a thing or two about writing compelling books about race. And anyone who wishes to get close to the Underground Railroad experience can always turn off the 401 and head to North Buxton, where a museum and a realistic settler's cabin records the African American community that settled here, at the end of the railroad.

Or, as it happens, not quite the end. When Jane and I gave our show in May 2014 much farther north — in Flesherton, way up in Grey County, on "the roof of Ontario" — we were amazed when our hosts, Barry Penhale and Jane (no relation) Gibson, took us to a little burial ground commemorating local African American settlers from these early days.

A French officer named Antoine de la Mothe Cadillac founded Detroit in 1701, bringing French settlers to the area, and giving a great name to a luxury car when the auto industry emerged more than two centuries later. In 1749, the first land grants were given in what is now Windsor, and attracted French settlers from the Lower St. Lawrence . . . which, when you think of the journey involved, is an amazing story in itself. As in Hugh MacLennan's Quebec, the land grants ran — in traditional French style — in long, thin strips back from the river. Ever since then (and Windsor boasts of being the oldest European settlement in Ontario) there has been a strong French presence in the area (Belle River!), and Windsor is an officially bilingual area.

As the auto industry grew, and Detroit came to stand for the car-making industry, Windsor gloried in the colonial title "Auto Capital of the British Empire." The population accelerated from 21,000 in 1908 to 105,000 in 1928, as the new assembly lines seemed to turn

Alistair MacLeod (1936–2014)

out people as well as cars. Today Windsor is a city of over 200,000, with its own university and art gallery. And midway between them lies Alistair MacLeod's house.

I've often told the story of my piratical trip to Windsor in 1999 to pry the manuscript of *No Great Mischief* out of Alistair's hands. He, in turn, retaliated by describing my entirely helpful and well-intentioned visit as "a home invasion." But since it all worked out not too badly, I've been a welcome visitor at Alistair and Anita's house since then.

A word about the family, and the house. It's a fine, comfortable house (with no distinguishing plaque outside it — yet). But one of the key reasons why Alistair wasn't free to turn out dozens of books is that he and Anita were kept very busy raising six children there — Alexander, Lewis, Kenneth, Marion, Daniel, and Andrew. And since they are all fine, healthy specimens — with young Andrew the biggest of them all — there must have been times when the house on Curry Avenue was bursting at the seams. Andrew, in fact, recently referred to the inevitable squabbles that came from sharing your space with people you thought you despised, until you realized they mattered more to you than anyone in the world. Now the seams are threatened only at times like Christmas, when returning grandchildren swell the merry throng, or in October 2014, when the Windsor Book Festival's tribute to the author I called "a great writer and a great man" drew the family together. You'll be glad to know that I knocked on the door, saying, "I'm Doug Gibson, and I've come for a manuscript."

I've often told the story of my horror when, in the course of my original manuscript-grabbing visit, I saw the blood-chilling MacLeod clan motto, "Hold Fast," framed above the piano. In a subsequent visit I've joined the crowd around that piano, as Marion (now a distinguished academic with a string of degrees in the field of music) played traditional songs that we all roared out with the greatest enthusiasm. A MacLeod family *ceilidh* in Windsor is a wonderful thing.

Outside the house, in the wider world of Windsor, Alistair was very popular, like a walking, smiling civic monument that everyone knew and admired. I've seen this at public events in his honour, and I've seen it on the street, where his many years of teaching at the university, and his decades as an involved parent at sporting and school events, made him a very popular man in the community. Add to this the fact that Windsor is proud to have this internationally famous author as *their* best-known writer, and you see why to be in Alistair's company was a great thing.

In 2011 I was a guest at the annual Book Fest Windsor event, held at the art gallery. Two things stand out from that show. First, I found myself talking about my list of distinguished Canadian authors in the Canadian gallery, which meant that I was flanked by superb Group of Seven paintings showing Ontario's North Country. Now, if only I could take them with me, as part of the travelling show's backdrop . . .

Second, as I neared the end, Alistair slipped in, having fulfilled a conflicting appointment. It was a very pleasing experience to adapt my talk ("Here's what I've been saying about you behind your back!") and speak affectionately about Alistair in his presence.

Alistair's life in Windsor slowed dramatically in the sad winter of 2014. I was in constant touch, so I knew about the hard stroke that felled him and left him bedridden in January. (And many people in the Windsor media knew about it, too, but because the family wanted it kept private, they maintained a respectful silence — which I find wonderful.) We talked by phone, although talking became harder for him. At the end of February Jane and I went down to see a University of Windsor presentation of the play *No Great Mischief*. But we really went to see Alistair.

Anita said that he was pleased to hear that we were coming. And, sure enough, although his right side was paralyzed, and speaking was hard, he had prepared a joke for us in greeting. Had we, he wanted to know, "been dancing in Scotsville recently?" This was a good private joke, a reminder of the time eighteen months earlier when a summer visit to Cape Breton had led to him and Anita inviting us to join in a square dancing evening in Scotsville. A fine evening, with wonderful memories.

That whole final visit — and we all suspected that it would be the final one — was cheerful, fond, and full of good memories. When the time came, my friend and I shook hands left-handed, and his handshake was significantly long and strong, and his brown-eyed gaze direct and meaningful. At this moment of dumbstruck high emotion, I remembered the MacLeod family motto above the piano at his home. "Hold fast," I blurted out.

Alistair made a farewell gesture between a wave and a thumbs-up sign. "All right," he said, and nodded. I like to think that it was more than a casual response. I like to believe that in fact it was the considered view of a fond husband and a father of six fine children who knew that all things considered, including a few million admiring readers, his life, now drawing to a close, had gone all right.

After his death I went by train to the first visitation in Windsor. It began at the funeral home at 7 p.m., and I was there right on time to avoid the crowd. Not a chance. By 7 there were already fifty or sixty people in the line to sign the book, file past the coffin and greet Anita and the children. As we inched forward I muttered to the man ahead of me, "You never know what to say." But when I reached Anita, and we hugged, and she held me out at arm's-length, no doubt remembering our regular calls over the past weeks, miraculously, I found that I did know what to say. I said, "Aren't we lucky?"

She instantly understood the unspoken words "lucky to have had this wonderful man play a part in our lives," and we hugged again.

Three weeks later Jane drove us down to Windsor for the funeral mass that was held in Our Lady of the Assumption Church. It lies near the river, literally in the shadow of the Ambassador Bridge, on the University of Windsor campus where Alistair taught. Hundreds of people turned out to pay their respects. When Alistair's old friend Rev. Joseph Quinn was delayed in his homily by a technical mix-up, he noted that he was certain that Alistair was looking down and laughing at him. It was a good touch.

Perhaps the best part of the reception afterwards was when Lewis remembered his father. As a Windsor student, at the end of the day Lewis would sometimes come to his father's English department office, in the hope of a ride that would save him the twenty-minute walk home. Lewis found that usually no time was saved, as his father's walk along the department corridor involved constant office drop-ins, with friendly greetings and little stories. He remembered that even a janitor changing the light bulbs in the hall would be greeted with the affectionate joke: "You are the light of my life." And I remembered that in his role as silly grandpa, Alistair would bid his grandchildren goodbye, saying, outrageously, "See you later . . . crocodile."

A lovely man. I'm very lucky.

At the end of his long and distinguished political career, Paul Martin Sr. (for many years the MP for Windsor's Essex East constituents) was Canada's High Commissioner in London. He became famous for asking any group of visiting Canadians, "Is there anybody here from Windsor?" Once a politician, always . . .

His son Paul Martin, our former prime minister, published his memoirs, *Hell or High Water*, with me in 2008. It gives a memorable picture of the Windsor he knew as a boy growing up there and in Ottawa.

Windsor was a multi-ethnic boomtown in the shadow of the United States. . . . A border town that was proud of its racy legacy from the era of Prohibition. I remember my mother pointing out a house near the cottage that had once been a "blind pig" — or speakeasy — and I remember the implication that she had been an occasional customer. According to legend, freighters would show up at the Hiram Walker distillery on Monday to be loaded for Cuba only to be back two days later to reload.

Young Paul also remembered attending the opening of a new post office at Belle River. As the local MP who had made this happen, his father was the subject of much oratorical praise, and there were many speeches "about how important the building was — the greatest human achievement since St. Peter's in Rome, it was generally agreed." A day or two later he attended a session of the United Nations in New York. "I sat with the Canadian delegation and heard my father praised by country after country in speeches from the podium. When it was all over, someone asked me what I thought of all these people saying what a great man Dad was, to which I was heard to reply: 'Well, it wasn't bad, but the speeches were better in Belle River!'"

As you can see, Paul Martin tells a very good story, and I greatly enjoyed working with him. Here's a final Windsor story that will be familiar to readers of my earlier book, but is worth repeating. On the very day in 1993 that Paul was sworn in as Jean Chrétien's minister of finance (traditionally a career-limiting post for potential prime ministers), his mother was rushed to Hotel-Dieu Grace Hospital in Windsor. He flew from Ottawa to join his sister Mary Anne and a family group huddled beside her bed. She looked up at the faces around her, and asked, "Why?"

Thinking she was wondering why we were all at her bedside, Mary Anne told her we had come because she was ill, and then she slipped back to sleep. A few minutes later, she woke up and asked again, "Why?"

I told her, "Mother, we've explained to you. You've been sick, and we're all here to make sure you get better." And then she said, "No, no. I don't mean that. I mean, why Finance? Why would you want to be minister of finance?"

We didn't drive out of Windsor via Belle River, to see the famous post office, but took the southern route. To be precise, we headed for "Canada's South Coast." The shore of Lake Erie just east of Leamington is indeed shown on the map as "Canada's South Coast."

Leamington may be known to most of us as the town that gave us canned tomatoes and ketchup. But Leamington is famous in the Canadian literary world for having something unique — a superb novel about what it was like to grow up in an Italian-Canadian community. Toronto, with its huge Italian population — including its fair share of interesting writers — has yet to produce such a book.

The author, of course, is Nino Ricci, who was born there in 1959, and lived in the town while growing up. Leamington, however, played absolutely no part in the setting of his first novel, which catapulted the young man to instant fame in 1990. *Lives of the Saints* won the Governor General's Award, the W.H. Smith/*Books in Canada* First Novel prize, and several other distinguished prizes. The book, entirely set in Italy, tells the story of young Vittorio Innocente and his mother, Cristina, in the Valle del Sole in the Apeninnes. It made waves in many places, was shortlisted for awards in Quebec and Los Angeles, and was published all over the world.

The book was well-launched in Canada by its risk-taking publisher, Cormorant, a small Ontario house. Then I, in the shameless role of Big, Rich Publisher, proceeded to elbow them aside (literary agents tend to favour the Big and the Rich) and acquired for M&S the next two books in Nino's trilogy, *In a Glass House* (1993) and *Where She Has Gone* (1997). In a case of cosmic justice, neither of these books had the sensational success of his *Lives of the Saints*.

Which was too bad, because *In a Glass House* was a superb picture of Leamington, or, as the opening words have it, "the town of Mersea." With its many greenhouses (that's where the title comes from, and that's where so many Italian families settle and work, and socialize — "*Como stai, paesano?*"), the countryside outside town is distinctive. To a young immigrant from Italy, it seemed split by concession roads that "came off Highway 76 with a Euclidean regularity, as if some giant had merely taken a great pencil and ruler in hand and divided the wilderness into a tidy grid. In Italy the roads had snaked and curved to the rhythm of the land like a part of it, but here

Nino Ricci (1959–)

it seemed as if the battle against nature had been fiercer, the stakes higher, the need to dominate more complete."

Nino's book is a fine portrait of hard labour, in the fields and the glass houses, and one Leamington friend tells me that he even got the smells right, from the downtown canning plant aroma to the close-up distinctive smell of peat as the plantings begin. And as Vittorio (now Victor) survives bullying on the bus to school, grows up, starts dating, and goes off to university in Toronto (Nino himself went to York), and has pool-room scuffles, and smokes pot (Nino himself, surely, had no contact with any such illegal activity), most of us will recognize the stages in his life.

I was very pleased to publish the book (and then the third in the trilogy) because it introduced me to Nino, a fine writer who was clearly going places. In the years since (after he moved on without any hard feelings to another publisher), he has roamed around as a professional writer and teacher, and is now based in tomato-free Toronto, where he lives with his wife, the writer Erika de Vasconcelos. I've been delighted to follow the subsequent career of this charming, gentle, big man as he won many prizes (including another Governor General's Award). It's instructive that even such a successful fiction writer as Nino has had to patch together a career of university teacher here, writer-in-residence there, and performer at this festival or that library. That's the life of a Canadian writer.

In his Leamington novel Nino refers to "Point Chippewa National Park," but we all know he means Point Pelee. For a birder like me, driving south of Leamington to Point Pelee is a religious experience, because this is sacred territory; even its shape seems to represent the beak of a gannet diving south into Lake Erie. *A Bird-Finding Guide to Canada* (and I republished Cam Finlay's book with great enthusiasm) speaks glowingly of Point Pelee, with its "Carolinian Forests" (meaning lush, as in the Carolinas far to the south), and its "spectacular spring migration of warblers and other land birds peaking in the second week of May." Unfortunately, in the book publishing world, May is such a busy month that, year after year, I missed visiting Point Pelee, although in the book's words it is "widely regarded as one of the best places to experience bird migration in all of North America." (I'm happy to report that in Spring 2014 we finally made it, and saw our first eastern bluebird, eastern grosbeak, and prothonotary warbler, and a shabby common nighthawk that seemed to be sleeping off a hangover.)

The book's detailed description of all the many birds (almost 370 different species have been recorded in the provincial park) that are to be seen, and heard, reaches heights of lyricism that may surprise innocent outsiders who stray into this fanatical world. "In both spring and fall, the woods can be alive with the sounds of scratching feet as hundreds of migrating white-throated sparrow actively forage in the leaf litter." As for the yellow-breasted chat, "on occasion, it even sings at night!"

In November, however, Point Pelee was silent and bare, with not even a hint of "scratching feet," and for us its main attraction was its southernmost point. In search of Ontario's limits, I scrambled down to the very tip and dipped a toe in the water. As every school child knows, this is the southernmost point on the Canadian mainland. It lies farther south than parts of Northern California, although this is so widely known that few bar bets can be won by this particular piece of Ontario lore.

Independent booksellers — like some Point Pelee birds — tend to be colourful, but thin on the ground, and very welcome when spotted. As a species, however, they tend to be rare, and under threat. I'm always glad to help local booksellers whenever I can (especially when helping them helps my book sales), so when my old M&S colleague Susan Chamberlain invited me to come to Sarnia with my show, I jumped at the chance.

Susan runs a first-class independent bookstore, the Book Keeper. Susan was a sales rep at M&S for some years. Undeterred by her knowledge of just how tough the bookselling life is, she got into the game in Sarnia, and is doing a wonderful job there.

Dropping in to the store beforehand, I encountered a man coming in off the street, clutching a newspaper clipping about me. I was happy to sign a book for him, and ended up unexpectedly signing copies for two other friendly customers who also happened to be on the scene. It's that kind of place.

We stayed with our friends Sue and Chris at their place on the spectacular, sandy shore of Lake Huron and were pleased to find that at that time their near neighbour was the mother of our friend Susan Swan, the novelist. The literary links go on forever: Susan's great-grandfather, who bought the cottage for the family, in his youth had played cards with Walt Whitman when the American poet came to Ontario to visit Richard Bucke, the famous London psychiatrist, author, Whitman biographer — and, of course, former Sarnia resident.

Sarnia was named by the early governor Sir John Colborne (whose own name was borrowed by Robertson Davies for his fictional Toronto school, Colborne College). "Sarnia" is the Latin name for the island of Guernsey, where Sir John had practised being a governor, before a promotion in that line of work brought him to Canada.

The grandly named town (its resemblance to a small Channel Island lost in the mists of time) got an early start in the oil-refining business because it was the nearest port to Oil Springs. That is where the very first commercial oil well in North America went into production, way back in 1858. *The Canadian Encyclopedia* tells us that "in 1898 Imperial Oil Co. moved to Sarnia from Petrolia, and built a refinery." Since then it has remained a petro-chemical centre, and the southern end of an oil pipeline from Alberta.

Despite what you have just read (and the jeering description "Chemical Valley"), if you go to Lakeshore Road, on the northeast side of Sarnia, you'll find that the shoreline of Lake Huron is spectacularly beautiful. The Michigan shore lies off to the west, while waves crash in from Lake Huron to the north. The vast possibilities of the great lake leave you feeling that Alice Munro Country places like Goderich are almost in sight, just off to the northeast.

Sarnia is the hometown of Paul Wells, the shrewdly acerbic political columnist for *Maclean's*. I persuaded Paul to extend his journalistic talents to writing books about our politics, which he did for me with *Right Side Up: The Fall of Paul Martin and the Rise of Stephen Harper's New Conservatism*, published in 2006. In 2013 I was pleased to see him bring out another fine, stylish book, this one entitled *The Longer I'm Prime Minister*, which takes Stephen Harper's success very seriously. It deservedly won the Shaughnessy Cohen Prize as the best political book of the year. The boy from Sarnia is doing very well.

The next day we drove straight to London, and did not swerve north to Ipperwash Park on the Lake Huron shore, where Dudley George was killed. As with the story of the Underground Railroad, I've chosen to discuss it here, because it adds texture to the Ontario we think we know. This story, however, does not have a good ending, and is not a source of pride.

I know a fair amount about Ipperwash because after the Stoddart Publishing company went under, I was glad to be able to pick up the fine book by Peter Edwards, *One Dead Indian: The Premier, the Police, and the Ipperwash Crisis*. I republished it in an updated edition in 2003.

To summarize Peter's well-researched book, a land claim dispute arose between the local Native band and the province over the ownership of Ipperwash Provincial Park. Native protesters occupied the park, and the protest turned violent. It became such a major problem that a meeting was held at Queen's Park that included the premier, Mike Harris. The official notes of the meeting concluded: "The Province will take steps to remove the occupiers."

Encouraged by this official instruction, the Ontario Provincial Police moved in, and an unarmed protester, Dudley George, was shot and killed.

For years the outraged members of Dudley George's family fought for justice, both in the courts, where the OPP officer who shot the fatal bullet was tried and sentenced, and in the court of public opinion, where through an official inquiry the government's role might be revealed, providing an explanation of how this could have happened. Finally, in 2003, a provincial inquiry was set up by the incoming Liberal government of Dalton McGuinty, under the respected former Ontario chief justice, Sidney Linden.

The inquiry's hearings were hugely important, and very closely followed, because of the underlying possibility that instructions by a premier might have started the trail that led to the death of an unarmed citizen at the hands of the OPP. At one point, under oath, a former member of Mike Harris's Cabinet (the former provincial Attorney General), Charles Harnick, testified that at the key Queen's Park meeting, Harris shouted, "I want the fucking Indians out of my park."

Former Harris aide Deb Hutton was also at that meeting. Also under oath, she failed to corroborate this testimony from the province's former leading legal officer, because she could not recollect any specific conversations. This led one cross-examiner to note that she had used phrases such as "I don't recall" and "I don't specifically recall" on 134 separate occasions.

On February 14, 2006, former premier Mike Harris appeared before the inquiry. He testified that he had never made the statements attributed to him by his former Attorney General. However, in his final report, in 2007, Justice Linden "found the statements were made." He went on to note "and they were racist, whether intended or not."

So where are they all now?

Dudley George is dead.

Charles Harnick has found that his testimony under oath did not advance his political career.

Mike Harris has retired from politics, but continues his life as a member of many boards, including his role on the board of Magna, which attracted much criticism when under him the board awarded many millions to Magna's former owner, Frank Stronach.

And the forgetful Deb Hutton is now married to Tim Hudak, who led the Conservative Party in Ontario to defeat in the 2014 election.

I spent my first Christmas in Canada in London. And I got to sleep in a bed!

Let me explain. When I arrived in Toronto in September 1967, I had very little money, so my sleeping bag went on friends' floors or couches. As I looked for a job, my money drained away, and on some days it was a choice between getting a TTC bus fare or a newspaper, for the want ads. Yet for reasons of pride I avoided writing home for money, and wrote regular letters to my parents (cheaper than phone calls to Scotland) assuring them that all was well.

When I got a job in November, it was with the impressive title of "Administrative Assistant to the Registrar" at McMaster University. I had just enough money to spend a week at the downtown Hamilton YMCA.

Then some kind friends who also worked at McMaster invited me to stay with them at their apartment, in "Camelot Towers." The deal was that I would sleep on the orange couch (the term "couch-surfing" had not yet been invented), and pay each of them five dollars a week for the privilege. The price was right, so I made the deal with Messrs. Stokes, Lou, and Van Hoeckel. Unfortunately the orange couch's central location in the living room left me with an abiding distaste for late-night TV.

So it was a great thing when a kind London family, cousins of an old girlfriend in the other London, invited me to spend Christmas with them, in a bedroom of my own, *with a bed and everything*! I had a very happy Christmas with the Browns, and it left me with a great affection for London, and with dazzling memories of walking through Victoria Park in the snow to the sound of carols.

My other great London memory is of my first meeting with Alice Munro. This was in fall 1974, when Alice had returned from the West

Coast, and was settling back into Alice Munro Country, initially as the writer-in-residence at the University of Western Ontario. I was a young editor, still close to penniless, and I took the bus down to London to meet this promising writer whose work I liked so much. We met, I recall, for dinner at the Holiday Inn downtown.

My memories of the meeting are vivid. I liked Alice from the start, but I was stunned by what she told me. I was there to worship at the feet of this accomplished author whose career was so promising. But the reality, it turned out, was different. She confessed that everyone in the publishing world was pressing her to stop wasting her time on this short story stuff — it was time to get serious, and write a novel. The pressure was so constant, and so unanimous, that she was trying to write a novel, and finding it so hard that she was now unable to write at all. She was "blocked."

Here are her own words about the situation, in a letter written about me (without my knowledge) that's quoted in Robert Thacker's biography, *Alice Munro: Writing Her Lives*: "No one in Canada had shown the least interest in taking on a writer who was going to turn out book after book of short stories. The result of this was that I wasted much time and effort trying to turn myself into a novelist, and had become so depressed that I was unable to write at all."

This was the moment when I was lucky enough to come on the scene, right there at the London Holiday Inn. I told her, "Alice, they're all wrong! You're a great short story writer, and that's what you should keep on doing. I believe this so strongly that I can promise you that if you come and publish with me, I will never, ever, ask you for a novel."

It seems so obvious now, but at the time this assurance was important and helpful to Alice. Her secret letter about me continued with these words: "Doug changed that. He was absolutely the first person in Canadian publishing who made me feel that there was no need to apologize for being a short story writer, and that a book of short stories could be published and promoted as major fiction. This was a fairly revolutionary idea at the time."

I never did ask Alice to write a novel, and things seem to have worked out all right with the eleven books of short stories we've brought out since then. Not bad.

London plays a role in a number of Alice's stories, especially those suggested by her own days as a student there. In "The Beggar

Maid," for example, we have Rose going to sell her blood, as Alice did, at Victoria Hospital. Discussing the year she spent as writer in residence, Robert Thacker's book records, "One party Rose attends in *Who Do You Think You Are?*, for instance, was derived from some Munro attended and one she herself gave during her time in London. Much of Simon's personal history in 'Simon's Luck,' for instance, came to Munro from a faculty member recounting his own history at one of these parties." In "Carried Away," the last section of the story, headed "Tolpuddle Martyrs," is set near Victoria Park in high summer, and speaks of a temporary bus station among "tall yellow-gray brick houses," which I think catches London perfectly.

Also, in the title story of the 2014 collection of selected stories, *Family Furnishings*, the student narrator, on her reluctant way to meet an unfashionable aunt named Alfrida, walks through

> parts of the city that were entirely strange to me. The shade trees along the northern streets had just come out in leaf, and the lilacs, the ornamental crab apple trees, the beds of tulips were all in flower, the lawns like fresh carpets. But after a while I found myself walking along streets where there were no shade trees, streets where the houses were hardly an arm's reach from the sidewalk, and where such lilacs as there were — lilacs will grow anywhere — were pale, as if sun-bleached, and their fragrance did not carry. On these streets, as well as houses there were narrow apartment buildings, only two or three stories high — some with the utilitarian decoration of a rim of bricks around their doors, and some with raised windows and limp curtains falling out over their sills.

Alice Munro is always the shrewd observer of the details of class differences, even in the suburbs of London. "Limp curtains."

More alarmingly, however, we find that creepy Mr. Purvis's house in "Wenlock Edge" ("'Here is where you leave your clothes,' Mrs. Winner said") is kept carefully anonymous, in terms of the outside face it presents to the world. That leaves a visitor to London wondering what goes on inside these houses, just as a reader of that story in *Too Much Happiness* (2009) will wonder just what mischief the mailed address in the final paragraph will produce. After all, as the final words show, this is Alice Munro's world, where people are capable of "deeds they didn't yet know they had in them."

Which brings us to Doug Gibson, the editor in the shadows, now the Shameless Touring Performer. I gave my show at Wolf Hall, the central auditorium attached to the London Central Library downtown. The stage was as big as a badminton court, with the screen located uncomfortably close to the front, but by this point the old pro could adapt to almost anything. With an introduction by Sheila Lui, of the library, and a Q&A at the end, the evening seemed to go well. Mark, of the Oxford Book Shop, the sponsoring local bookseller, sold lots of copies, many of them signed by me with a legible signature. Later, Mary Lake and Robert Collins, a couple of good friends who live in "The Oldest Brick House In London," bought *ten copies* of my book. Now, if all of our friends . . .

Even later, in October 2014, I returned to London, staying with Mary and Robert, to give a show on campus at Western, in order to spread the word about the university's creation of an Alice Munro Chair in Creativity. It was a creative use of my show (we drew more than 200 people!) and I was honoured to be able to help the very worthy fundraising campaign, across Canada, with my next stop in Victoria.

The day after our Wolf Hall library gig, we drove to Guelph, the last stop in this one-show-a-day, Windsor-Sarnia-London vaudeville tour. Guelph celebrates John McCrae, whose 1915 poem, "In Flanders Fields," scribbled on the field of battle, is known to every Canadian. The McCrae House (its garden graced by notably ancient hollyhocks) is carefully preserved for visitors beside the Speed River, near downtown Guelph. That downtown is dominated by The Church That Wants To Be A Cathedral. It's the massive Roman Catholic Church of Our Lady Immaculate, and it really does loom over the town, and in 2015 it was graced outside with a brand-new statue to John McCrae.

I once went there to check on some details for an Alice Munro story that is partly set within it ("Child's Play"), and found that although Alice had changed the church's name to "Our Lady of Perpetual Help Cathedral," she got all the atmospheric details right in describing her character's visit to a priest.

But Guelph's Presbyterian founders, our old friends John Galt and Tiger Dunlop, would have been more at ease in two other ancient downtown churches, St. Andrew's Presbyterian, on Norfolk

Street, or even Royal City Church, on Quebec Street. Right across Quebec Street lies the Bookshelf, one of Canada's best bookstores, which Doug Minett and his trusty team have turned into a cultural hub by offering not only books but a café upstairs, which also stages a number of events, such as — *ta-da* — my show!

It was fun for us to be so well received by Doug and his staff, especially the lively Dan, who runs the shows there. Returning from a trip to the car I was delighted to hear Jane's voice intoning, "One, two, three, testing, testing . . ." I could see that she really had got into the full "techie" or even "roadie" role. Watch for tattoos next!

The stage in the café is about two paces wide, but the show went on in front of an audience of about fifty, including my old comrade-in-arms Jonathan Webb, who was M&S's managing editor in my day (and who once watched with suppressed delight as I resisted the requests of an aged Mexican author who had, supposedly, found the key to eternal youth, and in my office was tensing his thigh muscles while urging me to test their immortal strength by squeezing them: "Feeeel! Feeeel!").

Jonathan, still an editor much in demand, later posted kind things about my show, especially the interesting shrewdly paradoxical description that I am "a self-deprecating, self-assured Scot." I blush to repeat his compliments. Almost. The audience, he wrote, "came away with a bit of insight into how books are made. They heard a number of good stories. And they were treated to a masterful performance, a life turned into art."

The University of Guelph now has 22,000 students, and is famous for its superb Scottish Studies department. I have given a version of my show there on campus — concentrating on my authors with a connection to Scotland — in the course of an academic symposium. I'm proud to relate that I sold a copy to a visiting Scottish professor because he had been so thrilled to find his hero, Hugh MacLennan (whom he saw as a major international figure), finally being properly recognized at home in Canada.

I was well cosseted during my Guelph evening at the Bookshelf, and at dinner in the café with Doug after the show, but the kindness of the staff there extends far beyond the booklined walls of the store. The Eden Mills Writers' Festival is held every fall in that little community nearby. The Bookshelf is the official bookseller there, setting up its booth right on the main street, which is crowded all weekend long (given good September weather) with eager book-buyers from all over the Greater Toronto Area. In 2012 I was featured alongside Alistair MacLeod, and his presence attracted so many visitors that the little church where we performed was full to bursting, the pews almost creaking with the strain. I'm told that the crowds outside were so large that some MacLeod fans even tried pressing their ears against the Gothic church windows, but no divine intervention magnified the joyful sound, and they heard nothing.

After our double act — where we gave individual readings, then I drew out great stories from Alistair, including the epic tale of the midnight ride with W.O. from Calgary to Banff in a blizzard — the bookstore had set up a signing session for the authors. I sat beside Alistair while two eccentric people lined up (can two people constitute a lineup?) in front of me and my modest pile of books. By contrast, Alistair's lineup stretched right across the street, and almost into the woods. As I sat there idly, watching Alistair sign copy after copy of *No Great Mischief* or *Island* (or sometimes both), I whispered to him, "Would you sign the next one with the words *"Please buy my friend Doug Gibson's book, too"*? but my suggestion went unheeded.

Meanwhile, the kind people from the bookstore worked hard to prevent me from feeling ignored by making bright, cheerful conversation with me. In my publisher role, I've found myself making precisely that sort of conversation, many times, to shield neglected authors from hurt. It was very kind of them, and they spoke the language of the situation well, but I really didn't need their help. After all, I'm the man who wrote the rules that say that autographing sessions should never be seen as competitive events. And this was *Alistair MacLeod!*

I'm sorry that I didn't run into my friend Tom King, another Guelph resident. I've known Tom ever since he edited a collection of Native writing called *All My Relations* for us at M&S in 1990. His own background is very interesting. He is a Cherokee from California, with Greek and German roots also in his family tree. He has all of the usual academic credentials, plus the unique fact that he spent some years in Australia, working as a photojournalist. (We need more of them in the CanLit world!) He also spent some time being an involved, radical protester for Native rights.

Along the way in his academic career he spent time at the University of Lethbridge, where he met his long-time partner, Helen Hoy, now an English professor at the University of Guelph, and a huge influence on his writing, as we shall see.

As a writer, Tom has done it all. An anthologist (see above); a novelist (*Medicine River* in 1989, *Green Grass, Running Water* in 1993, and, most recently, *The Back of the Turtle*, the G.G. award-winner in 2014); a short story writer (*One Good Story, That One* in 1993); a children's book author (*A Coyote Columbus Story* in 1992 — when did the man sleep?); a CBC Radio series called *The Dead Dog Café Comedy Hour* (as ironic a look at cultural stereotypes as you will ever see, or rather hear); and a series of non-fiction books, notably his 2003 Massey Lectures book, *The Truth About Stories*.

But for me, his crowning achievement (and of course he has won his share of prizes) is his angry 2012 book, *The Inconvenient Indian: A Curious Account of Native People in North America*. It's a powerful, shaming story that he has to tell, and he's such a shrewd writer that he uses humour to tell it, making it all the more powerful. Very early in the book, for instance, he writes: "When I announced to my family that I was going to write a book about Indians in North America, Helen said, 'Just don't start with Columbus.' She always gives me good advice. And I always give it my full consideration.

"In October of 1492, Christopher Columbus . . ."

But don't let the fact that this is very funny fool you. This is a very fine book, telling a terrible history. Smiling Tom King hits very hard.

In person, Tom, a big, husky fellow, is very good, laconic company, full of sly jokes. It was a tragedy for Canada that when he ran for the NDP in the 2008 election — and Jack Layton was there to hold his hand aloft in triumph at the nomination meeting — the political gods decided that his witty oratory was too much for Parliament, which might have never recovered from the shock.

The Niagara Frontier was, of course, the frontier that beckoned the Loyalists escaping from New York State. The American Revolution had turned them into hated Tories, targets for tarring and feathering (and did you know that tarring and feathering, with boiling tar, was usually fatal, not just humiliating, and that being "ridden out of town on a rail" often produced serious injuries, especially to a man?), and on the run to a new life in Canada. In *Murther and Walking Spirits* (1991) Robertson Davies has given a vivid account of just such an escape, as we follow the Gage Vermeulen family as they run north. It's a very sympathetic account of their escape by canoe up the Mohawk River towards Canada — as you'd expect, because R.D. based it on his own family's journey. As his narrator/observer/ stand-in, Gil Gilmartin, puts it:

> August Vermeulen is sitting on the step of his very decent house at a small settlement called Stoney Creek. He is smoking a long pipe, and resting from a long day at his profession, which is that of a land surveyor. He is very busy, for new lands are being apportioned to new settlers, refugees from the American States. He is a contented, prosperous man.
>
> Who are these tatterdemalions who have opened his gate and are coming towards him? A woman, brown as an Indian and in rags, with a dirty boy who holds his head very high, and a girl carrying what might be a monkey, but which from its wails he judges to be a child.
>
> The woman is weeping. "Gus," she calls; "Gus, it's Anna."

Gilmartin is weeping, too, because he has recognized the Anna figure as his great-great-great-great-grandmother. And possibly R.D.'s eyes were damp as he wrote this account of his own ancestors, a story that had been bred in the bone.

You'll notice that "Uncle Gus" was a surveyor, which is interesting. Even a brief look at a map of the Niagara region shows that these early surveyors did their work differently here. To accommodate the flood of refugees they made the lots smaller, which means that a modern visitor finds concession roads criss-crossing the country every two minutes. A fascinating 1790 map ("For the use of His Majesty's Governor and Council, Compiled in the Surveyor General's Office") makes this very clear, showing the plans "for the District of Nassau," dividing the area all along the Lake Ontario coastline, and the area fronting the Niagara River, into tiny, quilt-like patches. The map is signed by an assistant named John Collins, and by the surveyor general himself, Samuel Holland.

We'll meet Holland again in another chapter, when we cross the Holland Marsh, but for now let's take the time for an amazing story about a famous Canadian duel. His son Samuel, a lieutenant in the 60th Regiment, stationed in Montreal, became embroiled in a bitter feud with a brother officer, a Captain Shoedde. Eventually, a duel was arranged, at Point St. Charles. In the words of Don W. Thomson in *Men and Meridians* (1966),

> Hearing of the insulting behaviour of Captain Shoedde towards the Holland family, the father sent Samuel a brace of engraved duelling pistols which he claimed had been given to him by a famous commander. "Samuel, my boy," wrote the Surveyor General, "here are the weapons which my beloved friend, General Wolfe, presented to me on the day of his death. Use them to keep the old family without stain."

The dazzling history of the pistols in his opponent's hand did not affect Captain Shoedde's aim. Young Samuel Holland was shot and killed. His duelling pistols are still to be seen at the McCord Museum in Montreal.

For Holland, and every other surveyor, the great challenge in the Niagara area is the abrupt, craggy Escarpment. This is where Brock University — named after the genuinely gallant general who died in 1812 defending this very frontier — is located, high above St. Catharines. Brock U. will always be admired in our house, because it was the very first Ontario university to invite me to present my show, which I did to a mixed group of students and visiting faculty attending a conference on Canadian themes. I presented the show in what is maybe the only room in an Ontario university with an Arctic name — Pond Inlet — and my re-enacted polar bear attack on James Houston's dogs seemed to benefit from it. And I was very glad to descend from Brock's academic heights to the Garden City, St. Catharines, the home for many years of Richard B. Wright.

Richard was born and raised in Midland, Ontario, but came south from Georgian Bay to work in Canadian publishing. He worked first for Macmillan, the company I was soon to join, and legends lingered of long, liquid lunches among the lads. He rose, in due course, to become a sales manager, but his main claim to fame is that he secretly wrote a book for young people, and submitted it anonymously to his colleagues. Against all the odds, it worked! (Although the first meeting with the *nom-de-plumed* new author must have been interesting.)

He had moved to work at Oxford University Press, in the suburbs, when his first adult novel, *The Weekend Man*, came out in 1970, followed by *In the Middle of a Life* in 1973. Both were realistic, ironic looks at typical middle-class, suburban life. The first, for example, includes an office Christmas party scene in which Wes Wakeham finds himself alone with Mrs. Bruner, requesting her Christmas kiss:

> And a fine hot open-mouthed kiss it is too, full of searching tongues and wild warm air a-mingling in our throats! Really we find ourselves locked together in the most stormy embrace, groping into each other's mouths like teenagers. She pushes her long groin into mine while I clutch her corseted bottom and hang on for dear life. . . . And so in this quick flagrant ardour we muzzle each other for the longest time, pressed against my steel-top desk. An amazing turn of events!

Both books attracted admiring attention. Mordecai Richler, for instance, described him as "a very talented man, the best novelist to emerge out of Canada in recent years," and the *New York Times* said that he "writes with the apparent ease of breathing, and he is both touching and very, very funny."

Richard is a small, neat, undemonstrative man, with a dry voice and a dryly sceptical view of the world (In *The Weekend Man*, a relative exhibits family affection: "'Well now. And here we are again. Our own little family happily reunited. Isn't it delightful!' She immediately linked arms with Landon and Ginny and pulled them towards her. This show of feeling was unlike her. She must have been into the sauce.") This unsentimental realism must have come in handy when he became a teacher at Ridley College to bolster his income from fiction writing. But he kept on writing novels, and hit the jackpot (a modest, Canadian jackpot) with *Clara Callan* in 2001, which won the Giller Prize, the Governor General's Award, and Ontario's Trillium Book Award. It's a fine example of the epistolary novel, where everything unfolds in letters. I hope that the many readers who enjoyed it will explore his earlier novels, some of which I was lucky enough to edit.

The best of these (although Brian Moore warned that it is "as brutal as a mailed fist") is *Final Things* (1980), a taut story of what happens to a divorced Toronto man when his twelve-year-old son doesn't come back from the corner store. Very powerful and very bleak. *The Teacher's Daughter* (1982) has the courage to deal directly with the forbidden subject of class, as a middle-class girl gets involved with a guy who loves muscle shirts and muscle cars. (I recall that we put a Camaro's flaming hood decoration on the cover of the hardcover book, to make our point.)

Above all, I'd recommend *Farthing's Fortunes* (1976) because it's almost unique in Canadian writing, a big sprawling novel that covers many decades as our young hero leaves small-town Ontario, survives life as a young thief on the Toronto streets, works for a society family, follows a music-hall star to New York in the not-so-gay nineties (where a friend wins a brothel competition with the help of eight impressed ladies in a few, short hours), is swept up in the Klondike gold rush, and fights in the First World War, where his experience on the Somme, on July 1, 1916, "the blackest day in the history of the British army," shakes him — and the reader — and sets him off to try to assassinate the man responsible, General Douglas Haig.

The later chapters deal with riding the rails in Canada's West in the Depression, or surviving in hard times by managing a young black prize-fighter, until fate brings him back home, and to the Craven Falls retirement home, Sunset Manor, where he encounters the solemn, humourless publisher who introduces this surprising volume of "memoirs." Although the stolid publisher is (to me) an unconvincing figure, Richard's novel is a fascinating look at the development of a country, as well as one man. I'm surprised that more people don't try their hand at writing plot-driven, picaresque novels that move around. I'm even surprised that more people don't try their hand at writing picaresque *non-fiction* books, full of stories. Come to think of it . . .

The other great physical feature of the Niagara Frontier is the Welland Canal. Built in 1829 to smooth out the drop from Lake Erie to Lake Ontario (few cargo-bearing ships adapted well to the 100-metre drop over Niagara Falls) it is an engineering feat that apparently excites canal fans everywhere. According to the breathless words of *The Canadian Encyclopedia*, "Locks 4, 5, and 6 comprise the world-famous series of twinned flight locks, with a length of almost 1249.7 m and a rise of 42.5 m." Bird-watching seems restrained in comparison.

The canal created Port Colborne, at the south end where Lake Erie flows into it. And somehow, the little town of roughly 20,000 has created the Best Reading Series In Canada. Let me explain. Every year, from September to May, with a break for Christmas, there are monthly "Readings at the Roselawn," the theatre where all 300 seats are sold out for an evening with a selected author. And this has been going on for eighteen years!

As always, there is a moving spirit here, one person driving it all forward. In this case it's a writer, William Thomas of nearby Sunset Beach. You may know some of William's popular funny books, such as 2003's *The Dog Rules (Damn Near Everything!)*, or 2002's *Never Hitchhike on the Road Less Travelled*, or his humorous newspaper columns. You certainly will know many of the authors he has persuaded over the years to come, have dinner with him in an Italian family restaurant, then head off to the Roselawn theatre to be greeted by sold-out crowds eager to hear them and then buy their books. William persuades them to come, even if (perhaps especially if) they don't know where the hell Port Colborne is. One Toronto author, who shall remain nameless, assured him that there would be no trouble getting there, since she'd had a cottage in Muskoka for many years . . .

So who are the people who come, and who sit for their photographic portrait so that they can join the astonishing Roselawn photo gallery? Well, they're all what we might call "surname-only authors" like Atwood, Berton, Richler, Mowat, MacLeod, Hill, Fotheringham, Vassanji, Quarrington, Lam, Rooke, Ferguson, Johnston, and on and on and on. And even Gibson.

My turn came on a harsh night in February, yet, as promised, every seat was sold. With Jane high in the projectionist box overhead, changing the slides for me, it went off well. So well that William later wrote of my show as "CanLit to the power of one," and claimed that he had never seen his audience "leap from their seats so fast and stay on their feet so long." Warming to his work, he even called me "the editor who is outshining his stable of stars."

Not quite. But it's a nice way to end a chapter.

CHAPTER 9

THE ON-TO-OTTAWA TREK

Linwood Barclay, the Suburban Storyteller . . . Marching
to a Different Drummer . . . A Short Drive East of Toronto
. . . Tuxbridge . . . A Detour to the Land of Leacock . . .
Peterborough, Lakefield, and the Mafia . . . Along the Front
. . . The Loyalist Al Purdy . . . Amherst Island . . . Hissed at in
Kingston . . . Ottawa . . . Politics and the Pen in the Nation's
Capital . . . The Deserted Bookstore . . . Arnprior and the
Robertson Davies Trail . . . Good Cheer at Bonnechere . . .
Muskoka Cottage Country

In 1998, at my publisher's office at McClelland & Stewart, I received the following letter:

Dear Mr. Gibson,

So I came home from the Writers' Development Trust dinner back in November and told my wife Neetha a very friendly guy said hello and told me about how his daughter often feels embarrassed when he drops in to the restaurant where she works, just like in the column I wrote about our daughter Paige not wanting to be seen with me in the mall. And he said he really liked my takeoff on Bre-X books, particularly the Pierre Berton coffee table book *The Bre-X Quest*, seeing as how his company had just published the first of the Bre-X books. And I said:

"And what did you say your name was?"

"Doug Gibson, with McClelland and Stewart."

"And what do you do there?"

"I'm the publisher."

And Neetha said, and I believe these were her exact words: "You twit."

So maybe I don't know the names of Canada's top publishers the way I should, but I hope that doesn't mean you won't take a look at the enclosed proposal, about my teen years, which I spent living at and running a cottage resort in Ontario.

The letter was signed "Linwood Barclay."

The new book idea turned into *Last Resort* (2000), a fine memoir of the summer when young Linwood helped his mother run the family business, keeping it going after his father's untimely death. One of the most affecting themes in this gentle reminiscence is how much help the struggling Linwood got from many of the regular dads on holiday. Instead of demanding the perfect vacation, when things like the plumbing went wrong, they were there to fix them, with plungers, wrenches, and rolled-up sleeves. It was a lovely book, and we published it in 2000 with great pride. And that, in turn, gave me not only a friendship with Linwood, but also a front-row seat as Linwood Barclay became one of Canada's most successful authors.

Most Canadians don't know what a world figure we have in Oakville's own Linwood Barclay. He's a middle-aged, middle-height, middle-weight dad, with lots of wavy grey hair. After Trent University he had a fine career in newspapers, rising to become the man in the hot seat who laid out the front pages of the *Toronto Star*. Then he astonished the *Star*'s John Honderich with the jaw-dropping news (and John has the jaw for it) that he'd like to become the new Gary Lautens, the beloved veteran who wrote funny columns about family life (including the details of the visit to a fancy bathroom store where a four-year-old Lautens boy happily used one of the sleek, dry toilets in the floor display).

Linwood made the change with ease. It's always tricky to write for the public about your family, yet Neetha (a teacher) and their son, Spencer, and their daughter, Paige, seemed to have survived just fine. His first book of collected columns had the title *Father Knows Zilch* (1996), which catches the general tone very well. Equally significant, when the new premier of Ontario, Kathleen Wynne, first met him — long after the columns had ended — what she urgently wanted to know was, "How is Paige?"

Yet in the wider world, his crime novels now sell in the millions. They rack up hundreds of thousands of sales in North America, and they routinely shoot to the very top of the bestseller lists in Britain. In 2007 the *Guardian* newspaper listed *No Time for Goodbye* as the bestselling book of the year in that country. What's surprising about that last point is that his novels are always set in the USA — more specifically in the suburbs of some anonymous town in New England or near New York.

The anonymity, I think, is a key point ("Well, it sounds just like our town! This could be happening right here!"). But I'd suggest that the suburban setting is equally important, because Linwood has come up with the obvious truth that (pause to allow head-slap) *most readers live in the suburbs.* If you want to engage your readers with a story about dramatic things happening to someone just like them, it's a great start if that someone lives in a place very like their own.

Linwood Barclay (1955–)

So Linwood's stories involve ordinary guys who spend a lot of time in the car (and the make of car is pretty important, too), and who know their way around the local malls, and the streets and the sports fields where their kids play. But that really doesn't help them much when dirty Fate steps in, to turn their ordinary, suburban lives upside down.

Even the titles are compressed works of genius: *Bad Move* (2004, and the first of the wildly successful string of books that, by the way, I did not publish), *Bad Guys* (2005), *Lone Wolf* (2006), *Stone Rain* (2007), *No Time for Goodbye* (2007 — and you can see how his training as a *Star* newspaper columnist affected his amazing output), *Too Close to Home* (2008 — no comment), *Fear the Worst* (2009), *Never Look Away* (2010), *The Accident* (2011), *Never Saw It Coming* (2012), *Trust Your Eyes* (2012), *A Tap on the Window* (2013), and *No Safe House* (2014).

If you think the word genius is too generous when it comes to his undoubtedly clever titles, take a look at his opening paragraphs. Any writers who are reading this book in search of tips should get a pen at once and make a note to study how Linwood grabs his reader in the opening sentence. For example, here's the start of *Fear the Worst*: "The morning of the day I lost her, my daughter asked me to scramble her some eggs."

There you go, hooked by the first eight words in the book. No wonder the *National Post* praised the book's "throat-grabbing premise." Note, too, the domestic simplicity of good old Dad scrambling eggs.

As for *Trust Your Eyes*, Stephen King, who knows something about storytelling, wrote about it in these words: "Riveting, frequently scary, occasionally funny, and surprisingly, wonderfully tender. I could believe this might happen to people living two streets over from me. Great entertainment from a suspense master."

Aha! "Living two streets over."

Let me give one more example of a perfect start, even if it takes more than eight words to set the hook. Here's how Linwood begins *A Tap on the Window*: "A middle-aged guy would have to be a total fool to pick up a teenage girl standing outside a bar with her thumb sticking out. Not that bright on her part, either, when you think about it. But we're talking about my stupidity, not hers."

And soon there comes the titular tap on the window, and before he can get rid of her she recognizes him as "Scott Weaver's dad."

"'Yeah,' I said. I had been."

And we're off, in Scott's dad's trusty Accord, on a scary ride you'll enjoy as much as Stephen King did.

When I roam around the country, I'm often cornered by apprentice writers asking, "What is your advice on the best way to get published?" People of all ages are visibly disappointed when I tell them that the trick is to write a first sentence that draws the reader on to the second sentence, and so on, and so on. That's why reading

— and studying — the hard-working Linwood Barclay can be so useful. You don't have to mimic all of his habits; constructing a huge model train layout in the basement (complete with a sleazy bar on the wrong side of the tracks) is one of his habits that may not be necessary for every fiction writer keen to create a new world. But you never know.

Certainly, if you follow his writing lessons, it will help. And if it leads to fame and fortune, you can always modestly say that you never saw it coming.

Linwood lived for many years in Burlington, home to A Different Drummer bookstore, which hosted my last show of 2011, which was in several ways the biggest. Ian Elliot at the store had bravely booked the new Burlington Performing Arts Centre (recently opened by Prime Minister Stephen Harper, and then christened by a performance from the more generally popular Sarah McLachlan). Even more bravely, he had asked me to — damn the torpedoes — do the full ninety-minute version of the show.

The hall (the smaller of the two) was so new that the sound guys were still finding out which switch did what. This delayed the start, meaning that the crowd was kept in the lobby, milling outside the closed theatre doors. I took the chance to go out (no tortured artist squirming in the Green Room here!) and walk around, explaining that this was just a brief technical hitch, and we'd be starting soon. The best part was that I was able to meet lots of old friends, and to make some new ones, so that when the show started, I felt at home.

In the end, 125 people showed up to fill the place, paying ten dollars for the privilege and stretching their legs in appreciation at the end. Best of all, Ian reported that an usher on duty, who had been disgruntled at not being assigned to work the (very expensive) Sarah McLachlan show, felt compensated — at least partly.

In the bookselling world (and, boy, we really need these people) everyone admires Ian and his predecessor, the rabbinically bearded Richard Bachmann. He was such a notable book-lover that he kept the store afloat, despite the fact that successive chain bookstores set up shop in the neighbourhood, with the apparent aim of driving him out of business. They came, and they went. A Different Drummer marches on.

I should mention that my old friend Richard was an insistent voice in the friendly campaign to persuade me to write my first book. When I, aware of his frequent very witty letters to newspapers, in turn suggested that he might try his hand at writing, perhaps a novel, he was quick to reject the idea. He said, decisively, "I don't know other people well enough to be a good novelist." So then we talked about Alice Munro, and about my reaction after reading each of her stories for the first time: "How does she know so much?"

On a fine Saturday in May I travelled east to Whitby to speak at a well-attended local Ontario Writers' Conference. The sun-dappled setting was the Deer Creek Golf Course. I was there to give a lunch-time talk to the 175 people at the conference, and was wearing my "publisher's uniform." As a publisher I always instructed my authors that on the promotion trail they should plan to look like their book cover photo, wearing the same clothes, hairstyle/beard, and so on. Obedient to my own advice, when I'm appearing as "author," I routinely wear the blue blazer, grey flannels, white or blue button-down shirt, and the striped orange-and-blue Brooks Brothers tie that the unflattering Tony Jenkins caught so well on the book cover.

As you'd expect, this was a much more formal outfit than the ones being worn by the dozens of golfers who were enjoying the Deer Creek sunshine, warming up by dreamily swinging the clubs that were soon going to break their hearts. When I left the conference to stroll around the tees before lunch, my outfit led to a misunderstanding. I was silently standing there, watching people teeing off (always an interesting experience for an old golfer — a slice of life, you might say), when — on two occasions — golfers keen to start their round mistook me for the Official Starter. They were polite Asian Canadians, and they came up to me, bowed low, and presented me with their official Starter's card.

I explained that I was just a spectator, and withdrew before there were any more Authority Figure misunderstandings. (The best of which was when a French tour guide in Cambodia assumed that I was running a Cambodian circus, which is another story for another day — although after running a Canadian publishing company, a Cambodian circus sounds pretty easy.) But the possibilities for golf course mischief ("Sure, go ahead and drive, I'm sure you won't hit the players just in front . . . they're farther off than they look") have stayed with me. There may even be a murder mystery plot there. And a title, *Drive, He Said.* I must pass it on to Linwood Barclay.

Uxbridge (or as Terry Fallis called it, since the event was a formal dinner, "Tuxbridge") staged a fine Book Lover's Ball in April 2012, in aid of the local library. The setting was the local Wooden Sticks Golf Club, a name that spoke to the ancient tradition of golf clubs with handles of hickory or some other strong, whippy wood. In my talk I was able to boast that in my ancient Scottish village I actually grew up playing golf with wooden stick clubs, which at the time seemed normal to me. But then, true to my "make things last" Scottish roots, I confessed that I was wearing the tux that my parents had given me in 1964 as a twenty-first birthday present. Dinner jacket styles hadn't really changed much over forty-eight years, and nor had my lean shape — nor had my respect for my mother's sage advice that if I looked after my tux properly I "should get many years of wear out of it."

After our salad course, the excellent Terry spoke wittily about his three books (and he really is an example of the Nice Guy Who Finished First in the Author Stakes). I did my stuff after the chicken course, talking about some of the authors featured in my book, and telling stories about them.

But the best speaker of the evening — and by far the best story-teller — was Michael, a local dentist. He told us about his family's experience escaping from Vietnam as "boat people" who were sponsored by kind people in Uxbridge. The local librarian, he said, always made a point of asking him what he was reading. Like dental patients flossing before an appointment (an interesting professional analogy that sprang to his mind) he read constantly to be able, always, to answer her question.

When the family moved away from Uxbridge to downtown Toronto, things were hard for them. Although his parents worked at two jobs, the young family could afford only to live in a tough area. Then their old Uxbridge friends contacted them, offering to bring them back, with a down payment on a house provided by an anonymous benefactor. The family accepted eagerly, with one condition: that they learn the name of the benefactor, in order to pay him back.

It was the librarian.

Now here was Michael (like his brothers and sisters, a successful professional) giving back to the Uxbridge community northeast of Toronto by providing major sponsorship for this fundraiser for the Uxbridge Library.

Stories really matter, don't they?

Loyal followers know that Orillia (or Mariposa, if you like butterfly kisses) has been hugely important in my life. Not only did it lure me to Canada, thanks to Leacock's *Sunshine Sketches*, it then provided me with the classic 1977 war book *The Corvette Navy* by James Lamb (editor of the *Packet and Times*). In the summer of 2012 I went to Orillia for the thrilling announcement about the winners of the Canadian Authors Association prizes. I and Jonathan Vance and Richard Gwyn had been nominated (from among, they told us, countless authors of Canadian non-fiction books) for the Lela Common Award for Canadian History.

I was, of course, very pleased to have my book nominated for an award, and in such good company. But the "history" designation worried me. So when the local TV station asked me what I planned to do if I won, I said, "Demand a recount!" My objection was that while Richard and Jonathan are real historians (who wear white gloves in archives, and get ancient dust up their noses as they research Sir John A., or Canadians in Britain during the First World War) my book was a cheerful personal memoir of working with twenty famous Canadian authors, some of whom are still with us. I argued in fact that while I am certainly a "mature" individual, I am not yet "history," and I want no part of it. Yet.

As the day wore on, however, and I and Jonathan (a very tall, very friendly historian from Western) read aloud from our books, smiled continuously, and were relentlessly charming, my objections to receiving the award weakened. At the evening dinner I was the keynote speaker, and the stars seemed to be aligned for a triumph for *Stories About Storytellers*. It was not to be. The absent Richard Gwyn received the award, and Jonathan and I consoled ourselves by confiding that this was the result that we'd expected.

And as the announcement was made, sitting with my game face on I had just enough of a whiff of the smell of success to realize that while it's very pleasing to be nominated for a book prize, it must be much more pleasing to win one. Is anyone listening?

July 2013 brought me to the Lakefield Festival, where the organizers remembered me affectionately from a few years earlier, as host/ interviewer at an evening celebrating Michael Crummey's *Galore* (now there's a title!) and Linden MacIntyre's *The Bishop's Man*. This time they presented me with an offer I could not refuse. I would give my solo *Stories About Storytellers* show at 2:30 on Saturday afternoon, then act as host/interviewer for the evening session at 8:00 with three authors — count them, three. Then, presumably, I would collapse offstage, but the show would be over by then. No problem.

Ruthless people, these folks who live in idyllic Lakefield.

On the Friday evening we had dinner with Orm and Barb Mitchell (W.O.'s son and daughter-in-law) and Norman Jewison and his wife, Lynne. Norman, the distinguished Hollywood film director from Ontario, enlivened our dinner with tales of his Caledon neighbour, Robertson Davies, and also about his friend Sean Connery, whom I can imitate shupremely well. (Once, Norman was worried about casting an aged Italian actor, and called his friend Sean, who had acted with him recently, for an honest report. "He can't shee," said Sean indignantly, "and he can't hear . . . and he'll shteal every fuckin' sheen!" Norman hired him.)

Saturday was spent roaming around downtown Lakefield, with more ice creams per square foot than any other community in cottage country. We found Margaret Laurence's old house, before we went on to the superb encircling theatre at Lakefield School. There, I was introduced by Alistair's son Lewis, an English professor at nearby Trent University. At a previous show at Trent's Catharine Parr Traill College he had also introduced me, speaking of growing up aware of the name "Doug Gibson." Its owner was a mysterious someone who distributed good things "like a sort of Tooth Fairy," but who over time developed a more threatening side, "like a Mafioso."

At the end of my show so many books were sold, and signed, that the local bookseller ran out, and we were able to replenish her supplies with extra copies brought in from the hot car. Ah, the glamorous life of a touring author.

The evening session featured three very fine novelists, reading from their recent books, then chatting about them with me. The final part of the evening allowed the audience to throw questions at any of the authors.

The books in question were very different: *Annabel* by Kathleen Winter tells the story of an intersex baby raised as a boy in Labrador in the 1970s; *The Empty Room* by Lauren B. Davis tells the modern story of a day in the life of a middle-aged Toronto woman when her alcoholism catches up with her; *The Purchase* by Linda Spalding is set on the violent Virginia frontier around 1800 when an abolitionist Quaker finds himself the owner of a slave.

All very different, all very good. I recommend each one of them whole-heartedly, and am proud that our discussion centred exclusively on the books, as opposed to the prizes won, or the brothers or husbands (including Ron Davis, an excellent photographer) who might have earned a mention. Our main problem was that we ran out of time before all of the audience's eager questions could be answered. But the books are there to be read.

And I didn't collapse, onstage or off, and even attended a post-show party before sleeping very soundly that night.

In the nineteenth century, before the trains carved up the land, immigrants from Europe to Upper Canada or Ontario always arrived by boat at one of the many Lake Ontario ports dotted along "The Front." In those days towns like Cobourg and Port Hope were busy with boats unloading white-faced settlers clinging anxiously to their children's hands — and later with schooners loading up with timber or wheat for sale across the lake.

Jane Urquhart's *Away* (1993) catches that scene beautifully, through the eyes of six-year-old Liam, arriving with his parents from Ireland. He is dazzled by the sight of the white house on the Port Hope shore, which "burst out at him from the collection of darker buildings in the new harbour; glass and carved verandahs and white-washed clapboard." Then Liam looked "beyond the house and the small harbour town for a moment, to a line of hills and heard his father say, 'That darkness there . . . that darkness would be the forest.'"

Indeed it is. And Liam and his family are soon swallowed up in it, in the wilds of Hastings County, north of Belleville. In Jane Urquhart's memorable words,

In a few years' time, Liam would know corduroy roads and rail fences and stumping machines, horses and cutters and banks of snow taller than a man, and the webbed shoes shaped like teardrops that one must wear to cross fields in winter. He would know the smell of wood in newly constructed buildings and the view through glass to graveyards only half filled with alert white stones. He would come to be familiar with cumbersome tools invented to cut through the flesh of trees or to tear at earth and rock.

This, of course, is the land described by Susanna Moodie and Catharine Parr Traill in their books about "the backwoods" and "the bush." Neither of these literary pioneers became acquainted with Liam.

Robertson Davies used to tell of going to see *The Cherry Orchard* in Cobourg in the early 1950s, when the old Upper Canada was being transformed almost daily. Yet the traditional audience of old local families stood around at intermission "in dinner jackets green with age" complaining that they didn't see what this fellow Chekhov was on about; all the while, the countryside was full of the metaphorical sound of cherry trees being felled, to make way for subdivisions. Today, each little historic town on what used to be "The Front" now has its share of writers.

Farther east, Prince Edward County brings us into Loyalist territory, as the little towns filled with old Georgian orange-brick houses indicates, while the expansive farmhouses show that this was rich land. Follow the road past the ancient aboriginal Carrying Place to Ameliasburgh. That's where the old Al Purdy A-frame is to be found, far from the spacious Loyalist mansions.

You may recall that I was part of a group that decided to save this old clubhouse that Al and Eurithe had banged together out of scrap lumber on the shores of Roblin Lake. It was visited by several generations of Canadian poets, providing epic tales of wild parties with homemade wine or beer, and legends of good discussion, not to mention indecorous peeing by the boys of all ages. And it really was on the point of crumbling away. We were just in time, and were able with local help to restore it, so that now lucky young poets can hole up there, to see what life will be like surrounded by trees that knew Al Purdy, and how it will affect their work. If they're really lucky,

Al Purdy (1918–2000)

they might even spot a man high in the air, repairing the lofty steeple across Roblin Lake.

Here I turn to our old friend from Thunder Bay, Charles Wilkins. One of his later books begins in that city, and you can guess where it ends from the title, *Walk to New York* (2004). He was such an Al Purdy fan that he angled his blistering walk to include a visit to Al's sacred Ameliasburgh, because, "in a sense it was Ameliasburgh that made him a poet. He moved there still in obscurity, in 1957, because it was close to his home town of Trenton. And there, in the earth fields and crumbling architecture, he discovered a sense of his own constitution and past and began immediately to redirect his own poetry."

Charles gives us alarming details about life in the A-frame. Al and Eurithe moved there in 1960, and "spent their first winter in the house without electricity or plumbing. They lit oil lamps to read and chopped through a metre of ice for water. During the coldest months, Purdy set the alarm to wake him every two hours to stoke the cast-iron stove that was the building's only source of heat."

Al wrote about these hard times for *Maclean's* in 1971: "While living there — trapped if you like — I was forced to explore my immediate surroundings. Wandering the roads on foot or driving when we had money for gas I got interested in old buildings — not as an expert, but with the idea that houses express the character of long-dead owners and builders." (An interesting link, perhaps, with Al's own rescued A-frame.) Certainly Charles Wilkins writes admiringly about Al's "insistence on the link between a person's verse-making and his or her landscape or scenery."

During their limping visit to Ameliasburgh, Charles and his friend George failed to find the A-frame (it's on Gibson Road, for Heaven's sake!) and had little success in rousing quotable memories of Al at the local store. At the cemetery, however, they "came to the riverside where a shiny black slab of granite in the shape of a book had been erected over Al's remains, 'The Voice of the Land.'"

Prince Edward County — "the County" — is rolling land full of varied farms, and even vineyards, where the combination of limestone and a warming climate has produced good wines for weak-minded souls (like Jane) who enjoy that sort of thing. Geoff Heinricks described the magic of the lure that turned him from a Toronto writer into a winemaker: his 2004 book is entitled *A Fool and Forty Acres*, and I was pleased to publish it. Now the County is full of other such fools, some of them friends of mine with names very similar to Michael MacMillan and Seaton McLean.

Meanwhile, not only does Sandbanks Provincial Park draw my grandchildren for happy camping weeks, it also has astonishing windsurfing, with conditions so good on occasion that keen surfers in on the secret are drawn all the way from Montreal. But we know of an even better secret: Amherst Island.

Amherst Island lies farther along the Loyalist shores that run all the way from Glenora to Kingston, and beyond. Christopher Moore's *The Loyalists* reminds us that, incredibly, the British army under Swiss-born Sir Frederick Haldimand moved so fast that they were able to take in, and settle, 10,000 Loyalists in Upper Canada right after the American Revolution. These, I'd remind you, were real refugees. They may have been rich lawyers in New York, or politicians in Boston, they might even have come with slaves, but they had to start afresh, clearing the land assigned to them, with the tools (and, in some cases, the food) handed out by Haldimand's men. Al Purdy's ancestors were among them. So were the ancestors of millions of Canadians today.

After driving east along the Loyalist shores beyond the Glenora ferry, past places like Adolphustown and Bath, when you reach the port of Millhaven you know that you're ready for the ferry across to Amherst. The name Millhaven, of course, reminds us that we're near Kingston, with its array of prisons. The touring singer Mary Lou Fallis (a relation, yes, of the man who wrote *No Relation*) once told me of appearing at the prison for women. As usual, her act contained the sentimental country-and-western song "Home on the Range" (you know, where the deer and antelope play). Big mistake. Tears and more tears. Sobbing everywhere.

Mary Lou had forgotten that the long balconies around the prison's central hall, encircled by individual cells, are known as "ranges." Her sweet song literally came too close to home.

The ferry ride across to Amherst Island is not a major voyage, like the trip from Digby to Saint John or Tsawwassen to Sidney. It's more like the shuttle across to Denman, or to the Toronto Islands. But like all islands, Amherst Island is different. It *feels* different from the mainland, and its residents will happily tell you that they are, well, different. Looked at objectively, the shortage of the grand, elegant, old Loyalist houses you'll find on the mainland would seem to indicate that the flat land of Amherst Island was never as rich for farming, although we visited friends who have the largest sheep farm in this part of Ontario. The sheep are safe from wolves except in very harsh winters, when the ice provides a safe passage over from the mainland for hungry, fairy-tale wolves — although the sheep are guarded by large dogs.

Another note. Like Wolfe Island just off Kingston, Amherst has hordes of little voles, such a delicacy that the two islands have attracted more snowy owls than any other place *on the continent*. Birders have taken note, and can be spotted gathering at the ferry on winter weekends, in full winter plumage.

The island is named after the British military officer Sir Jeffrey Amherst, who played a distinguished role in the capture of Quebec in 1760. Sadly, he was also a genocidal thug. In the long history of broken promises that marked the dealings between white invaders in Canada and the Native people they replaced, nothing was so terrible as the germ warfare that Amherst proposed to introduce around Fort Detroit in 1763 by giving local Indians a gift of smallpox-infected blankets, hoping, in his own words, to "extirpate" them.

Despite its namesake, Amherst Island is a fine place, home to almost 1,000 people in the summer, with pleasing roads that circle the island, or cut right across it, to make a rough figure eight. The centre spot is Stella, at the ferry dock, and the central spot there is the Lodge. This is the combined hotel and arts and community centre owned by Molly Stroyman, who invited Jane and me to stay and put on another show. When we gave the show on Saturday night, the turnout was amazing, so that by the end a surprisingly high percentage of Amherst Island residents were proud owners of a copy of *Stories About Storytellers*.

One female member of the audience, impressed by my introduction of Jane as "my lovely and talented assistant," asked her seriously if she had married me in the course of our tour. A very pleasing thought . . . lowly young techie succeeds in persuading the great star to marry her, and make an honest woman of her.

Kingston should be perfect territory for a book like mine. Its grey limestone buildings ring out the message that this is an old city (Canada's capital for some years) with a fine literary tradition. Robertson Davies grew up here after Renfrew, and made it the "Salterton" of his early novels. The filmmaker John McGreevy persuaded him to tour the streets in an ancient carriage, telling stories that sprang to mind, to John's camera. One that I recall is of an idealistic Queen's University professor who started a series of lectures for prisoners in one of Kingston's jails with the inspiring title "Literature as a Means of Escape" (and R.D. leans towards the camera and says, "And that story is *true!*").

I have a number of Kingston literary friends, and have attended several literary events there. I remember the Writers' Union conference held at Queen's when Hugh MacLennan gave the inaugural

Margaret Laurence Lecture. He reported with delight a recent conversation with a very frank small boy. "You're eighty years old, and
that's an awful thing," said the boy. "What does it feel like to know
that you'll soon be dead?"

I should have taken that as a warning. But here I was in bookish
Kingston, invited by the mighty Indigo chain to come and perform
in their main downtown store. What could possibly go wrong?

Well, despite the fact that Indigo had asked me to come there
from Toronto, and the fact that I'd chatted with the store organizer
by phone, it was clear when we got there that they had no idea what
to do with me. Um . . . what about sitting at a little table near the
door, in case someone wanted to get me to sign a copy of my book?
Not a good idea, I suggested.

In the end they put me, with a dozen chairs for a gigantic audience, upstairs beside the in-store coffee bar. And when I say "beside,"
I mean within spitting distance. I can tell you that a coffee bar with
customers shouting out their orders above the racket of hissing
espresso machines is not a silent place. "Yes, let me tell you how
Alistair Mac —" HISSSSS. Or "Well, Alice Munro once said —"
GRRRRRRIND. (Hold onto your chairs while everything shakes.)
It was so bad that one member of the audience, a brave female friend
of mine, actually went up to the coffee bar to shout a protest. It was
a noble idea, but it didn't work.

Eventually, I brought things to a dignified close ("I said A
DIGNIFIED CLOSE!") and signed a few copies and escaped. Since
then, Kingston has remained a Gibson-free zone.

I know Ottawa fairly well. I even know the history, of the Shiners
Wars in the 1830s when street fighting between gangs of French and
Irish over the lumber trade made it the most dangerous town in the
country. Just think, gangs fighting in Ottawa, without any formal
party affiliation!

In the late 1980s I was on the board of the Canadian Conference
of the Arts, an Ottawa-based group that lobbied for government
support of the arts in general. I vividly remember one day when our
elite attack squads were dispatched to a variety of government offices
to press our message home. I was with the group that included Karen

Kain, for ballet, Lotfi Mansouri, for opera, and R.H. Thompson, for theatre. We were making our case with the minister of communications, Flora MacDonald, and I had not yet spoken when Flora objected. "All your talk of ballet and opera is great, and is just fine for big cities. But I'm from a small town. What use is what you're doing to a young girl like me, growing up in a small town?"

Sometimes the gods are good to us. I spoke up as the publisher of W.O. Mitchell, and Margaret Laurence, and Alistair MacLeod, and Alice Munro, all of whom (can you hear my voice rising?) were giving young Canadian readers the most priceless gift of all: the belief that the lives that they, and their friends, and their parents, and their neighbours were living was material for great literature. Great literature was not about dead Englishmen or big-city Americans. It was about us, right here.

I think it is fair to say we won that one. And Flora has remained a friend.

For many years now the Writers' Trust has sponsored a very successful fundraising event in Ottawa. The Politics and the Pen dinner at the Château Laurier is now a fixture on the March Ottawa social scene, with guests promised that their table will feature both a politician and an author.

In the past I used to attend the dinner as a publisher. In fact, my first book tells how I first met Sheila and Paul Martin when I was placed at the prime minister's table because an organizer had said, "Oh, Doug can talk to anyone." And I always had a good time, especially when my authors (such as Max and Monique Nemni) were winning the evening's big award, the Shaughnessy Cohen Prize.

After my book came out, however, I was upgraded, and became an Author. This meant that I was invited to attend, free, and flown to Ottawa, and positively cossetted at the dinner, where all authors are issued a medal and a colourful ribbon (green one year, red the next) to hang around the neck like a proud Olympian. It's all very good fun, and for an excellent cause.

Before the dinner I visited Sean Wilson, who bravely took an early chance on me at his Ottawa International Writers Festival, then spent a fascinating half hour at the office of my old friend Jeffrey

Simpson, of the *Globe and Mail*. He's always full of interesting ideas (the man's a columnist, after all!) but he's also a fascinating witness to major changes in the Canadian book business. He has produced non-fiction bestsellers about Canadian public issues in the 1980s, the 1990s, the 2000s, and right up until 2012, when his book about our medical system hit the stands.

He told me that everything had changed from the "magic carpet" days when your publisher would whisk you around the country from city to city, from one book talk show to the next. Now it's up to the author to behave as his own publicist. He used the adjective "brazen," and estimated that of the forty or so public appearances/speeches he made to promote his new book, he personally arranged thirty of them. He and I found ourselves excitedly (although Jeff doesn't do "excited" very well) confirming each other's findings that the new world out there demands ever more active author involvement in promotion — although I can't promise a one-man stage show from Jeff Simpson in the near future. (I'd buy a ticket.)

My final stop was at the CBC building, where my wife's niece, Amy Castle (the producer of the daily TV show *Power and Politics* with my old author Evan Solomon as host), invited me to sit in the control room. Fascinating! Everyone knows about the number of screens up there in front of the room, and the constant directions to switch to this camera or this piece of film, but the instant typing of the links for the host on the teleprompter and the person at the front choosing which tweets to add as crawlers to the screen were new to me.

After that it was time to rush to the Château Laurier and don my forty-eight-year-old dinner jacket, plus medal, and then mingle. Luckily my Ottawa links go back to the civilized days of inter-party contact. I suspect that few guests were able to range as widely on the political spectrum as I did, chatting with old friends from Ed Broadbent to Preston Manning. Later, at the bar I was able to tell Justin Trudeau stories about his father that he had never heard, including my "Trivial Pursuit" moment, when he almost killed me.

At our table I had a very good time, enjoying the evening that was MC'd by John Baird and Mark Carney, but I did not shine. In my role as author, I politely went around the table to meet my companions. I found myself sitting beside a very pleasant woman named Diana who spoke with an English accent. Because we had just established that our table neighbours were Swiss diplomats, and since she had mentioned that she was moving back to England very soon, I asked her if she too was in the diplomatic service. Not exactly, she replied, she was moving to England because her husband had just been appointed the new governor of the Bank of England.

Nice work, Doug. Or as Linwood Barclay's wife would say, "You twit."

A sad Ottawa story for all book-lovers. Before the 2012 Writers' Trust dinner I walked down Sussex Drive to the site of the old Nicholas Hoare bookshop. Before its shameless landlord — the National Capital Commission! — raised the rent and put it out of business, it used to be a fine, elegant store, so well-placed opposite the glass glory of the National Gallery and so spacious that I selected it regularly for launch parties and readings for books by important Ottawa authors like Jeffrey Simpson and Graham Fraser and Eddie Goldenberg. On my retirement Jane and I even held a farewell soiree there for our literary friends, with the help of the manager, David Dollin. I, like thousands of book-lovers, was devastated when the store closed.

By happy contrast to this Ottawa disaster on Sussex Drive there is the thriving bookstore in little Arnprior. The morning after my time swanning around the Château Laurier as an honoured guest at Politics and the Pen, I was picked up at the hotel (after admiring the lobby's Karsh photograph of Leacock in his garden in Orillia) and whisked an hour northwest to Arnprior. The whiskers were my old friends David Lewis Stein and his wife, Alison. Dave is famous as an author (whom I'm proud to have published), as an early Writers' Union chair, and as a *Toronto Star* columnist who dressed like a Damon Runyon character, a fedora always perched on his "Stop the presses!" head. He was also famous as a man who *really* knew Toronto city politics, inside out, and was the ultimate street-wise, gravel-voiced, big-city guy. And now he has retired to Arnprior, a little town of about 8,000 in the Ottawa Valley, where Alison's family has ancient links.

How are they doing? Very well indeed, to judge from my happy stay with them at the big Victorian house that stands a three-minute stroll away from the distinctive Arnprior Museum, where Alison puts in volunteer time. Another fifty paces down the main street stands

Gwen Storie's inspiring bookstore. That evening the amazing Gwen and her staff rearranged the store to accommodate forty paying customers (fifteen dollars, which included a delicious snack in the bakery next door!) and I gave my show. We sold twenty copies! If you walk down the street in Arnprior, the odds that the first person you meet on the street has a copy of my book at home are pretty good.

The more serious message here is that a good local bookstore can act as an important community centre — and I'm always glad to do whatever I can to help the Gwen Stories of this world, even avoiding puns to do it well.

The morning after the Arnprior show, Dave and Alison fed me kippers, then took me on a sentimental journey to Renfrew. This was the town, eighty kilometres northwest of Ottawa, where Robertson Davies, born in 1913, spent what W.O. Mitchell called "the litmus years," from 1919 to 1925. The town, a little larger than Arnprior, its rival to the east, had a huge influence on Davies during these formative years. As Judith Skelton Grant shows in her expert biography, Davies did not enjoy Renfrew, and he got his revenge with the picture he painted of Blairlogie in 1985's *What's Bred in the Bone*. I note in the paperback edition of my own book that R.D. wrote to his New York editor that he was finding the writing of the Blairlogie scenes "heavy and exhausting work. It has roots in my own childhood — in the emotions, not in the actualities — and it is painful to drag out of the past." Even at the age of seventy, his feelings about Renfrew were so strong that he felt that he had to write "to get it out of my system."

In the novel he says, "It thought of itself as a thriving town, and for its inhabitants the navel of the universe." (The physical metaphor could, I suppose, have been much worse.) He wrote about the town's proud ignorance, and its exclusivity where newcomers were concerned. He commented specifically on the three-layer cake of its inhabitants, with the Scots on top, above the French, then with the newer, Polish immigrants at the bottom. I got a whiff of this on our Renfrew tour.

We began with a visit to the McDougall Mill Museum, kindly opened up for us by the very knowledgeable Mr. Gilchrist. The museum itself is sturdily impressive, a thick-set stone building set beside a fast section of the Bonnechere River. Since Renfrew was

Robertson Davies (1913–1995)

at the heart of the timber trade, the museum is rich in examples of the tools involved in "hurling down the pine." There are also many photographs of the local bands that must have entertained young Robbie Davies, and posters for the O'Brien Opera House, which we know he attended. For *What's Bred in the Bone* he turned Senator O'Brien (who was in fact an important figure in the lumber trade that built London's offices and houses, *and* in the development of hockey, since he was the man behind the Renfrew Millionaires) into "Senator McRory."

We noticed that the photos of the sports teams from the pre–First World War years all featured Scottish and Irish names. By the 1950s there was a fair sprinkling of Polish names on the teams. But I didn't see any Batterinskis, like Felix, the Ottawa Valley hero of Roy MacGregor's fine 1983 hockey novel, *The Last Season*.

We tried to trace the three Davies houses in Renfrew. Of the first house Judith Skelton Grant writes that "the Davieses were dismayed to find that the house . . . arranged for them was in the Polish section of town." We found the house on Cross Avenue, and I wandered around outside, taking in the stark brick exterior. As if on cue a young man came out to check the mailbox (with a Polish name) just by the front door. I greeted him with my usual charm. "Hi there! Did you know that a famous author once lived in this house?"

"Huh?"

"Yeah, his name was Robertson Davies, a famous Canadian writer. He lived right here when he was a boy, about a hundred years ago."

If I'd told him that birds sometimes landed on his roof his shrugging reaction would have been the same: "Whauuh," followed by a determined return to the house and a loud, final slamming of the door.

We found the old site of the *Renfrew Mercury* office, where young Robbie sometimes helped his father; at the age of nine he even wrote a review of a local event, where a lady performer must have been relieved to find that she had sung "very acceptably." The newspaper office that made the Davies family prosperous is now a sporting goods store, right next door to the grand central post office on Raglan Street. We failed to find the second house, but did cross the dramatically swaying suspension bridge over the Bonnechere River that Robbie crossed every morning to get to school. And we did find the dramatic final Davies house (now a doctor's surgery) in the best part of town, marking the rise of the Davies family throughout those Renfrew years.

We didn't knock on the doctor's door. Although the friendly woman who runs the sporting goods store *had* heard of him.

For eleven years the little Ottawa Valley town of Eganville has played host to the Bonnechere Authors Festival. The moving spirit (there is always a moving spirit for these things) is a Force of Nature called Doyne Ahearn. She contacts you, tells you just how remote her festival is (about five hours from Toronto) and how they can't really afford to pay anything, but you can stay with her and Frank in their big log house and get to know the Ottawa Valley, including nearby Foymount, the highest inhabited town in Ontario.

How can you say no?

Well, I tried, just as others such as Nino Ricci before me had tried (until Doyne somehow arranged for *a police driver* to bring him from Toronto), but Doyne wore me down. Too busy for the summer of 2012? OK, we'll put you down for 2013.

So Jane and I planned an anti-clockwise sweep, first up to Peterborough, then to Marmora and the gold-rush country near Madoc, then via Bannockburn (in the summer of 2014 I was involved in organizing a 700th anniversary symposium in Toronto about this admirable battle) up to Bancroft, then sidling north and east to Cormac, near Eganville.

Our arrival at the famous log cabin coincided with the descent of amazingly thick clouds of flies, but Doyne and Frank were there to greet us. Doyne is an imposing figure, as you'd expect, but her husband, Frank, is built along the lines of a butterfly, and seemed in danger of being carried away by the swarms of insects. We were soon to learn that neither Doyne nor Frank should be considered a lightweight. They introduced us to the joys of "bug suits," and we were able to go swimming off a raft moored in the bug-free middle of a lake, Lake Doyne. The raft, by the way, was reached by means of a circulating rope ferry system, the rope pulled by Jane or me as keen, bug-suited Charons.

A fine dinner was followed by a tour of the Valley, far from the county seat of Renfrew. In Eganville we learned about "the Catholic side" of town, as it was in the old days (and as late as the 1920s Orange-Catholic hostilities were so fierce that the military came in "with cannon," we were told, to keep the opponents to their own side of the Bonnechere River that divides the town, both physically and religiously). In these saner times we toured the fine old museum, and the library, which the Authors Festival helps to maintain.

Late in the day "extreme weather" took over. Rain fell in sheets, thunder rolled, and lightning flashed. The pre-show dinner at the best restaurant in town was shaping up well, with our mouth-watering orders taken by the friendly waitress, when everything went black. The power was off.

It stayed off, and dinner was cancelled, and we groped our way out. Showtime was approaching. Since my show was due to take place in a windowless church basement, the lack of power was fatal. For safety reasons we would not be allowed in the dark basement.

With thirty minutes left before the show, it was time for plan B. I suggested that with the thunderstorm rain now gone we could bring chairs out to the parking lot and I could do the show there, in the open air. We had started to bring the chairs out, and then, *ta-da*, the lights went on . . . and, after some heart-stopping flickers, they stayed on.

And the show went on! We all had fun, and a few books were sold. Doyne told me that we attracted the very first standing ovation the festival had seen in its eleven years; I could get to like the experience, especially when the reluctant Jane joins in. And I was very pleased to receive a fine original painting, entitled "The Storyteller"! Local delicacies made up a very welcome "gift pack."

When we got back to Doyne and Frank's big log cabin, the power was off there, so we went quietly to bed. And the next day, after a lavish breakfast, we set off for the long ride through Algonquin Park, armed with Frank's fascinating book on the subject, *Algonquin Park: Through Time and Space*. What a revelation! It turned out that our modest, self-effacing host, quietly supporting his wife as she ran the literary festival in fine style with lots of local help, was a PhD in astrophysics. Even better, he had turned his telescope upside down, and observed the world from space. Specifically, he became a world leader in adapting satellite images from space into a useful source of on-the-ground information. Looking at these Algonquin Park images, you'd like to see exactly where the hardwood trees are? OK, no problem. Here's how. And so on. Amazing.

As my father's son, who grew up around sawmills, I found the Algonquin Park Logging Museum a constant delight. And then, after leaving the park, via Huntsville, Rosseau, and Foot's Bay, we were back at beloved Loon Island, the cottage on Lake Joseph owned by our good friends Hope and Phil, who live next door. After four days of swimming (*why do they put the navigation buoy we swim around farther out in the lake each year?*), canoeing, rowing the skiff, cruising the lake admiring the moon and stars, and gathering buckets (oh, all right, cups) of the world's best blueberries, it was time to head south to Barrie and Toronto, after almost 900 Ontario kilometres.

On this occasion we didn't head west to continue our tour of Ontario libraries, although later we had fun in Thornbury, and Collingwood, and even, thanks to our friends Barry Penhale and *his* Jane Gibson, on "the roof of Ontario" at Flesherton. But as usual, after Barrie we headed south down Highway 400, across the Holland Marsh.

I thought of two things while crossing the Marsh. First, the phone call I took as I was sending Betty Kennedy's 1979 book, *Hurricane Hazel*, to the printer. The man at the other end had a story that was, I said dismissively, simply too late to fit into the book . . . until he told me about being a kid in Holland Marsh when the hurricane raised the water so that *his house floated away*. In pitch darkness he and his parents and brothers and sisters spent hours squealing in terror as their house spun and whirled around, dipping and creaking, until finally it ran aground, miles away. I took his story down over the phone, and you'll find it in the book.

The second story is in the name, which has nothing to do with sturdy Dutch farmers, as most people suppose. I can't go across the Holland Marsh without thinking of how it's named after the surveyor general from 200 years ago, our old friend from the Niagara frontier, Samuel Johannes Holland. You'll recall that his son fought a duel in Montreal to defend the family honour, and died with the duelling pistol presented to his family by General Wolfe falling from his hand.

Fascinating history is all around us.

CHAPTER 10

GOOD TIMES IN THE MARITIMES

Halifax, Warden of the North . . . From HMCS *Sackville*
to Sackville . . . Three Cheers for Donald Jack . . . Acadian
Adventures in Wolfville . . . From the Blomidon Inn to
Blomidon . . . The MacLeods Are Everywhere . . . To Port
Medway, and Beyond . . . Ernest Buckler and the Spine of
Nova Scotia . . . Dancing on the Annapolis Basin Shore . . .
Only One Adjective for Grand Manan . . . Across David
Adams Richards's New Brunswick . . . Stories of PEI, and Will
of Green Gables . . . A Spring Tour of Universities . . . A Brian
Mulroney Diversion . . . Silver Donald Is Solid Gold . . .
Moncton and Northrop Frye

I once sailed into Halifax Harbour off the Atlantic Ocean on a bright sunny morning. Our Adventure Canada ship had just cruised out of the Arctic, all the way down the dramatic Labrador coast, with a side slip into some Newfoundland ports of call. As we moved west towards Halifax I was alone on deck, thinking about the millions of immigrants who first saw Canada, just like this, on their way to Pier 21, or to even earlier arrival points on this historic waterfront.

As I was thinking these serious thoughts, the sky went dark. I whirled around, baffled by this change on a calm, sunny morning. The *Queen Mary 2* had just glided to the east of us, blocking out the sun as she moved her ten-storey bulk swiftly past, to take her place as the biggest structure in the port of Halifax. The twice-yearly visit of the giant cruise ship is, in every sense, a huge event for Halifax. And I had just been an astounded witness to her smooth, silent arrival on the waterfront.

Halifax was always built around its harbour. It was, for most of its life, a British naval base with a city attached. My authors Hugh MacLennan and Charles Ritchie have both written about their native city's strange relationship with Britain, which made London seem closer than "Upper Canada." Charles Stewart Almon Ritchie, the diplomat and diarist, knew all this in his bones; in a 2014 visit to the ancient central St. Paul's Church I was pleased to discover the memorial plaque that was devoted to his Almon great-grandfather, a respected medical man in Halifax around 1800. And it was no accident that Hugh MacLennan, the author of *Barometer Rising*, chose to have his most famous author photo taken at the Citadel, looking down over the city and its harbour.

I had visited Halifax many, many times, and on my 2011 promotional book tour I gave my show at the theatre in the lower level of the Art Gallery of Nova Scotia on a Saturday night. The audience included the veteran publisher Jim Lorimer, who chuckled his way through my tales of publishing disasters. Along with his future wife,

Ree, in the centre of the audience of fifty people sat none other than John Houston, the filmmaker son of my old igloo-dwelling friend James. You can imagine what it's like to speak affectionately about an old friend, now gone, when his son is in the audience. But John knows how I feel: in the documentary he made about his father, he tricked me by asking, on camera, how I felt on hearing about his father's death — and then played the endless seconds of silence as my face grew ever bleaker, in wordless sorrow.

The next day I went down to the Halifax waterfront, admiring the historic corvette HMCS *Sackville* that's tied up alongside as a floating museum. It's a fine memorial to the Battle of the Atlantic, which was largely fought out of Halifax and St. John's. The ship always draws me to it, reminding me that these U-boat hunters were surprisingly small, and in mid-Atlantic storms they "rolled like pigs," but they won their part of the war, escorting the convoys through, and keeping Britain fed and supplied as she stood alone against Hitler.

Another reason for being on the waterfront is that it was the location for Halifax's Word on the Street Festival. I roamed around the tented areas, visiting publishers' booths and meeting old friends like Goose Lane's Suzanne Alexander and Lesley Choyce of Pottersfield Press, who now publishes Harold Horwood's classic, *Dancing on the Shore* (1987). But my main role was to be the host/interviewer for two author events. I'm always glad to help out at any festival I attend, in any useful role — swabbing the decks, trimming the sails, or acting as the host or interviewer. In this case we were right out on a pier, and so close to a large luxury cruiser that we all had to speak up above the hum of the power link that kept the boat's heart beating, and that, apparently, could not be silenced.

This meant that the interviews (first with Nova Scotia's Ami McKay, author of *The Birth House* and *The Virgin Cure*, and later with Marina Endicott from Alberta, whose most recent novels are *The Little Shadows* and *Good to a Fault*) had us arching like gospel singers at stand-up mikes at opposite sides of the stage. But they are both fine writers and impressive performers. And in both cases, our time on stage flew by, and I was able to escort them to long book-signing lineups right on schedule.

This was just as well, because I had to rush uphill from the waterfront, then, taking a last deep breath of Atlantic air, jump in my car, and drive west all the way out of the province — past Truro, then Amherst, then across the Tantramar Marsh that links Nova Scotia and New Brunswick (once famous as "the world's largest hayfield," in horse-drawn times when that resource outshone oilfields), and on into Sackville. I was to perform at Mount Allison University, at the Owens Art Gallery, that same night.

Driving into little Sackville, a university town of a little more than 5,000 people, I was reminded of the scale of my old university, St. Andrews in Scotland. There, too, there was a huge difference when the university was in session ("The fleet's in!"). In *The Canadian Encyclopedia* Dean Jobb has shrewdly described Sackville as "a town of fine old homes and tree-shaded streets, dominated by the red sandstone buildings of the university." That afternoon I encountered town and gown separation at its worst. Two young teenage girls at the town's main crossroads (perhaps the only stoplight in the little town) had no idea where the university's Owens Gallery might be. It was perhaps four minutes' walk along the very street where we talked.

In the opposite direction lay the Marshlands Inn, the grand old Victorian hotel in town, where I had stayed on my previous visit. That was when, as my first book describes, on a side trip to Shediac during Festival du Homard time, I became an Acadian, under the influence of the lobster and the fiddle music. This time I was picked up at the inn by Christl Verduyn, an old friend from her Trent University days, now on the Mount A. English faculty. She and the student newspaper had done such a great job publicizing the Sunday evening event that we had sixty-four people in the audience, with some standing, and there was a welcome clatter as the pre-show nibbles and drinks and meet-the-author session was interrupted by puffing people bringing in extra chairs.

The Owens Art Gallery is indeed the university art gallery, a separate neoclassical building with a fine sense of space. As you can imagine, it's pleasing but intimidating to perform beside the screen showing the authors that I'm talking about (and sometimes I advance the PowerPoint slides more efficiently than other times) when I'm standing alongside major works of art.

Thanks to Christl's shepherding, all went well, and nobody (town or gown) fell noisily asleep or stalked out, snorting. And my time wandering through the compact Mount Allison campus showed me why the little university has generated such affection among its alumni across the land.

Afterwards, I was taken for dinner to Joey's in downtown Sackville by my friend Chris Paul, of Sybertooth Inc. This is a gallant Sackville-based publisher that has picked up The Bandy Papers series by Donald Jack that I was proud to publish originally. Just as there are young people who think that my greatest publishing contribution was to set Roy MacGregor writing about the Screech Owls, there are also many not-so-young readers who consider The Bandy Papers series my great legacy to the world.

Bartholomew Wolfe Bandy is a (fictional) minister's son from Beamington, Ontario, who gallantly signs up to fight for King and Country in the First World War. In Flanders Fields, after leading a daring assault that results in the capture of his own colonel, he is transferred to the Royal Flying Corps, and miraculously becomes a flying ace. His "memoirs" follow his career, which leads him up and down the ranks, and in and out of bedrooms, and into very surprising positions (his capture of a Bolshevik train in Russia in 1919 is notable, as is his eventual rise to a place in Mackenzie King's Liberal Cabinet, while rum-running on the side). In due course he drifts into a role in the Second World War, with the details of the imminent D-Day landings plans of keen interest to his Gestapo interrogators, all highly inquisitive chaps. Then, in the final volume, while he is at Yalta he finds that Josef Stalin seems to bear him some sort of grudge . . .

The roll-call of titles will bring thousands of admirers to giggling attention: *Three Cheers for Me*; *That's Me in the Middle*; *It's Me Again*; *Me Bandy, You Cissie* (stunt flying in Hollywood); *Me Too*; *This One's on Me* (which brings Bandy in touch with the maharajah of the Indian state of Jhamjhar, who needs someone to head up his air force); *Me So Far*; *Hitler vs. Me*; and, finally, *Stalin vs. Me*. I can claim to have started the series, with the first two books, and to have also edited and published the last two books, but it is Chris Paul out of Sackville, New Brunswick, who now keeps the Bandy flag flying, reminding the world of P.G. Wodehouse's quote about The Bandy Papers: "I enjoyed every word. Terrifically funny."

Chris also reminds us of another side of Donald Jack's assault, through Bandy, on the officers who ran the killing machine in Flanders, and elsewhere. "These books," wrote military historian J.L. Granatstein, "are as powerful an indictment of the bloody waste of war as has ever been written by a Canadian."

That evening Chris and his writer wife, Krista, drew me useful maps of how to explore the magical Tantramar Marsh, in this part of Canada made famous by Sackville poet Sir Charles G.D. Roberts. The next morning, after wandering with my binoculars in Sackville (amazingly, the town is designed around birdwatching boardwalks), I drove to High Marsh Road, rambled across and through a covered bridge, then spotted a perched birdwatcher who confirmed that the dozens of little brown birds exploding into the air around us were indeed migrating Savannah sparrows.

It was time for me to migrate east to Wolfville, on the Bay of Fundy.

In Nova Scotia, all highways lead to Truro. Yet a Wolfville-bound traveller with time to spare and a love of the landscape can turn off the 104 fast highway system at Truro and drift west along the Fundy shore, winding through little towns like the magically named Maitland. Gifted with that middle name (my mother, you'll recall, was Jenny Maitland), I was excited to find that it's a little town graced with beautiful old traditional houses, many now being restored. It's like one big heritage village, a showcase for Victorian architecture at its varied best.

I stopped at the local store to grab a sandwich, and casually asked how the place got its name. "It's a native name," I was told. My comment that this would be news to thousands of Scottish Maitlands made little impression. Could this be part of the weird intermingling of Scottish and Native history in Nova Scotia, where some believe that Glooscap was really a Scottish explorer named Sinclair? An enquiry for another time.

I drove happily on to Wolfville, pausing to notice that the incoming Fundy tide, off to the right, was racing in so fast that I could see sandbars disappearing every ten seconds. The traditional warning about incoming tides that could drown you was that they moved "as fast as a galloping horse." It seemed appropriate.

Wolfville is a university town. Just as the ebb and flow of the Fundy tides rules the landscape, so the Acadia University year rules the town. During the academic year, when the 3,500 students transform the area, the movement of young people down from the slopes of the campus into the town is almost tidal. Driving along the main street I foolishly wondered what was causing the stop-and-go traffic. Then I realized that we were obviously between classes, and scores, even hundreds, of students were casually exerting their right to drift across the street, halting cars like mine. Not a bad traffic planning principle, especially since there are no boringly conventional stoplights in town.

It is time to celebrate the Acadia school song. It goes:

> Far above the dykes of Fundy
> And its basin blue
> Stands our glorious alma mater
> Glorious to view.
> Lift the chorus
> Speed it onward
> Sing it loud and clear
> Hail to thee,
> Acadia, hail to thee.
> Far above the busy highway
> And the sleepy town
> Raised against the arch of heaven
> Looks she proudly down.

They don't write them like that today. I'd love to hear it sung.

I'm sorry to report that nobody serenaded me when I drove up the hill to the K.C. Irving Environmental Science Centre to meet my gracious host, Andrea Schwenke Wyile. But before we went down to the basement theatre we paused to peer in at the main hall, which is arguably the most welcoming space in any Canadian university I have ever seen. Almost worth going back to the world of classes and papers just to get to sit, read, and lounge there, and to think great thoughts.

Andrea (a specialist in books for children) was able to help me with the technical setup, but the absence of security meant that we had to babysit the computer once it was ready to go. Her gallant husband, Herb Wyile (author of the well-known book on Canadian historical fiction *Speaking in the Past Tense*, not to mention *Anne of*

Tim Hortons) brought her food from home, and I was able to slip away to the Blomidon Inn to get into my "publisher's costume."

As usual, before the start of the show I was happy to greet my audience at the door, mingling with them and welcoming them to what I hoped would be a good time for all of us. This evening before the show I was delighted to meet Terry Fallis's in-laws, who live in Wolfville, and who were later pleased that I incorporated Terry with a tribute that has now been included in my expanded paperback version of *Stories About Storytellers*.

When the event started, in introducing me Andrea laid great stress on the role of Jennifer Knoch, a recent and fondly remembered Acadia graduate, and the editor of my book. I went on to repeat the tributes, so that many miles to the east Jen was blushing hotly for some reason unknown to her. The Acadia students were visibly pleased by all this, an inspiring example of good things happening to Acadia graduates just like them.

The show went well, the Q&A session was fun (and included questions from some of Jen's old teachers), and I signed a few books. Then I followed the line of least resistance down the hill and drove back through town, past the splendidly named bookstore, the Box of Delights, to the grand old Blomidon Inn. It is such a traditional Victorian mansion that when I asked for a drink they directed me to a deserted drawing room, the Rose Room. There I sat sipping my colour-coordinated cranberry juice, thinking that Wolfville is a very fine place to be.

Waking up to a fine fall day at the Blomidon Inn in Wolfville is a perfect beginning. Roaming around the inn's varied gardens is a very good way to ease into the day. But walking into the little town, then drifting down to the dykes that created the original Acadian settlement, is another level of happiness.

In *Stories About Storytellers* I talk about my fascination with the dyking system introduced by the early Acadian settlers. So you can imagine my delight in being able to walk along the top of the historic dykes that run very close to downtown Wolfville. Down among the grasses, a class of lucky young students from Acadia was being introduced to the natural wonders of the dykes, but I walked east, away from town, noticing that the fields walled off from the sea are still so rich that some of them are devoted to growing fine, demanding crops of corn. And the Fundy sands were still red, the waters of the Bay were still blue, and the great wedge of Blomidon still stretched into the bay, like a backdrop to an Alex Colville painting. (My friend Alex was still alive then, and I'm deeply sorry that I didn't take the chance to visit him, to renew our acquaintance and talk again about his father's Fife hometown, Markinch, which I knew.)

I had seen Cape Blomidon, the legendary home of Glooscap, in the distance in some Colville paintings, and in real life, but I had never been there. This was the day to fix that. I drove west, then turned right towards Blomidon and reached "the Look Off." (I wonder if locals shout warnings of "Look off!" rather than "Look out!") From that height you can see much of the Annapolis Valley laid out before you with the "sleepy town" of the Acadia school song in the middle distance, looking very fine.

I drove on to the Blomidon Park (although I was tempted to drop in on Ami McKay, who lives nearby) and climbed down the steps to walk along the silent beach. I wasn't exactly dancing on the shore, but it was a delight to get red Fundy sand on my shoes, and to dip a hand into the salt water. Then it was back to the idyllic town of Canning for a fine lunch, regretting the fact that its succulent former name, Apple Tree Landing, had been changed to honour a British prime minister with a name like an industrial process. Then it was ho, for Halifax, and my last event. Although at a roadside stand I did load up on local apples — Gravensteins (I can still taste the juicy crunch) — on my way back to the capital.

Lean, fit, young Alexander MacLeod is a well-established teacher at St. Mary's University (as well as being my friend, and a fine fiction writer with excellent bloodlines). In 2010, Dan Wells of Windsor's own Biblioasis made the literary world sit up by publishing Alexander MacLeod's first collection of short stories, *Light Lifting*. Before that, I had noticed some of Alexander's stories appearing in literary magazines (traditionally the place where new fiction writers first swim to the surface), and had liked them. So I had taken Alexander aside at one point and suggested that I'd be interested in looking at all of his stories, with a view to publishing a collection.

He was very polite in turning down that idea. He was pleased to be asked, he said, but I was "the wrong publisher." I would be seen as his father's publisher, now kindly taking on the son, so his stories would not be given the chance to stand on their own feet. He was right, of course, and I backed away. In due course, Dan (followed by impressed foreign publishers) published *Light Lifting*, and it was shortlisted for the Giller Prize. Now the literary world is waiting and watching for the next book by Alexander MacLeod.

And Alistair, a modest man who was very reluctant to talk about his own work (as I saw, yet again, when I took the French scholar Christine Evain to Windsor to interview him), would almost burst his buttons with smiling pride when asked to talk about his son's work.

When I arrived in Halifax, Alexander had kindly arranged for me to stay at the Waverley Hotel, east on Barrington Street downtown. It was a revelation! A traditionally furnished old Victorian hotel, where Oscar Wilde once stayed (with no comments about his room's wallpaper ever recorded). I warmly recommend it to all literary visitors. As I learned on a later visit, it is possible to book the Oscar Wilde Room, where he stayed in 1887, although you risk being disturbed by his ghost (who played dead the night we slept there).

As for St. Mary's, Alexander drove me to the fine old campus and established me in the room where I performed my show to about forty kindly people, including my old friend Harry Thurston, the notable writer about the natural world and now the Writers' Union chair. Harry, I'm glad to say, later wrote that he found my show "entertaining and moving," which was a pleasing combination. And, as you'd expect, it was a pleasure to play "Niel Gow's Lament" and talk about my affection for his father in front of Alexander.

The next day, after a pre-breakfast stroll down the hill to where early-bird anglers were hauling dozens ("I've got about forty in the bucket here, so far") of mackerel out of the Atlantic-facing harbour, it was time to leave that particular shore, and fly back to Toronto. But I was soon to be back in welcoming Halifax, to deliver the annual Flemming Lecture at King's College. It was a great honour, and naturally around our house it became known as "The King's Speech."

I enjoyed my time at the podium (but why do young people cluster at the farthest corners of a lecture hall, destroying any sense of community among the audience?) and enjoyed it best when I could get out beyond the podium to handle the lively Q&A session with the fifty or so bibliophiles in the audience attracted by my title, "With a Pinch of Genius: A Recipe to Produce Great Authors." Afterwards, thanks to the fine people at the King's Bookstore (working in the tradition of James Rivington, who opened Canada's first English bookstore, in Halifax in 1761), I was able to sign copies of my book, before going off to dinner with some lively friends. They included Brian Flemming himself — local lawyer, former Trudeau advisor, and for many years the proud owner of Charles Ritchie's boyhood home, The Bower, where he encouraged me to come and snoop.

I spent the night at the Lord Nelson Hotel, just along from where Hugh MacLennan's boyhood house used to stand. The hotel is celebrated in my book as the place where an alert house detective saw something fishy in Don Harron, dressed to do book promotion for me as "Valerie Rosedale," and told him sternly to move along from the lobby, where he was politely waiting for his publicist, teetering a little on his high heels.

In the summer of 2013 Jane and I flew in to Halifax then headed all the way down the South Shore beyond Bridgewater to the famous little literary festival at Port Medway. We had heard about the pleasures of the festival from previous visiting authors like Margaret Atwood and Bill Weintraub, so we were keenly excited.

The festival is the loving creation of a number of local literary types, and keen summer visitors like Philip Slayton and Cynthia Wine, whom we know as friends in Toronto. Philip Slayton is an alert-looking dark-haired man of medium height and build, but with a very level gaze through his glasses that catches your attention. The law professor-turned-Bay-Street bigwig saw law and politics and business at the highest levels, and let us all in on the secrets he had learned. His 2007 tell-all book, *Lawyers Gone Bad*, outraged the legal profession, but enthralled the rest of us. I am certain that, after his revelations of outbreaks of greed and malpractice in the profession, every bad apple has been removed from the barrel, and no further problems will ever return to vex us.

For some reason, after years of cutlass fights with legal pirates, Philip found himself drawn to Nova Scotia's South Shore, where piracy (from the LaHave River, with New England merchant ships a regular target) has a long history. In fact, in the 1980s (as Peter

Rehak's book *Undercover Agent*, published by me, happily reveals), little Lockeport down the shore was the site of what was then the largest drug-smuggling bust in Canadian history. When Philip and the accomplished Cynthia Wine (now there's a name for a fine food writer!) found the place sixteen years ago, they promptly bought a summer home there, right beside the ocean. Then, eager to spread the news about the hidden treasure tucked away here in Nova Scotia, they founded the Port Medway Readers' Festival in 2002, and the rest you know. It continues to attract locals, as well as come-from-aways based in Canada or in "the Boston states."

Not content with that remarkable piece of public service, as I write, Philip is now the head of PEN Canada, demonstrating the legal mind at work as he summarizes situations very crisply and briefly. We're lucky to have Philip in charge of this important group defending our rights to read and write in freedom, without, as one recent minister of justice, Vic Toews, scolded us, "being on the side of the child pornographers." Alarmingly, Mr. Toews has since been appointed as a judge. Standing on guard for all of us, PEN Canada's role is not just a formal one. I'm proud to be a member.

Driving straight down to Port Medway reminded us yet again that somewhere along the line, the people planning Nova Scotia's highways had made a bargain with the devil. "All right," Old Nick said, "you've got a beautiful province, with lots of attractive little roads curling slowly around the coastline. If you really want to move people fast around the province, I'll let you cut main highways straight through the bush, with nothing to see. Only when they get off the highways will drivers come across fine views, and houses, and towns, and real, live people. The highways will be people-moving tunnels, fast and ugly. OK?"

So they made the bargain. The result is fast, boring driving on many of the highways, where the view of endless trees contrasts with the instant delight of the little roads as soon as you turn off, into the land of real Nova Scotians, the people who live in idyllic places like Chester and Mahone Bay and Lunenburg, and on and on.

We drove across the LaHave River, until we could turn left off Highway 103 towards the ocean, and to downtown Port Medway. The village population now is only around 200, but the harbour recalls the days when it was such a big port for shipping timber that it boasted a customs house, for Heaven's sake, and you could take a passage from Port Medway *directly to Europe*. As instructed, we took a right turn and drifted along the shore road, Long Cove Road, looking in vain for the street number for the cottage that was to be ours. We overshot and were heading back when we stopped to talk to a man wandering along the road that was full of late-afternoon sun, and blackberries, and the drowsy sound of bees in the salt air. He was a short, lively fellow in his seventies, and he wasn't surprised to see us. In fact, he was just heading in to see Philip and Cynthia, at this place right here, and looking forward to meeting the visiting Gibsons.

He was (it turned out) the famous American writer Calvin Trillin. Or "Bud," as he became, as we mingled with Philip and Cynthia and the gang, including my old pals Marq de Villiers and Sheila Hirtle (South Africa meets South Shore). Bud kept us intrigued by his theories about the eventual onset in men of the dreaded "DTS" — Diminishing Tush Syndrome — which seems to be, to hear him tell it, altering the medical landscape. Can cosmetic implants be far behind? And behind whom?

Shrewd editors in New York had recently employed him to test the new "self-parking" car. As he told it, he had stopped the talented car next to a tight Manhattan parking spot, then barked out the magic word "Park!" Nothing happened. "Um, no, it takes a little more than that," they had explained, and he was still disappointed by the car's feeble response.

We spent a blissful night in our private cottage (the distinguished food writer Cynthia's genius as a hostess showed in a well-stocked kitchen that included — yes! — Solomon Gundy, local South Shore herring snacks for my breakfast), then went to check out the church where I was to give the show. The Old Meeting House dates from 1832, and is happily preserved by the income from the reading series. In the front entranceway we saw the photographs of visiting authors, like Wayne Johnston, Michael Crummey, Lisa Moore, and George Elliott Clarke, plus husband-and-wife teams like Graeme Gibson and Margaret Atwood, and Michael Ondaatje and Linda Spalding. While we were prowling around, our local contact, Bob Whitelaw, a casually dressed guy in his sixties, showed up by chance ("I saw the car, and thought that maybe it might be you"), and we made the technical plans for the evening show, where he would introduce me.

It's literally an old church, a meeting house with a high pulpit and a central aisle splitting the rows of pews stacked up to face each other. Instead of orating from on high, I decided to put the screen near the pulpit, and put myself right down on the floor, pacing the centre aisle. Risky, since at every moment I'd have my back to half of the audience, until (talking all the time) I made the slow climb up to the pulpit to tell my final W.O. Mitchell story. Would this work? I was very worried.

But they were a notably friendly group, pleased to have me greet them at the door ("Hey, we should ask all our authors to do this!"), and as the show went on, with me pacing the centre aisle, turning constantly, it was clear that these village people in a little Nova Scotia church beside the salt water were genuinely interested in the stories of Canada's best authors.

The slow climb up to the pulpit, when it came time to speak about W.O. Mitchell, was a revelation. Every child raised in a church-going family wonders what it must be like to be the preacher, up there in the pulpit. (In fact, my very first public-speaking event was when I was selected from the Sunday School to read the Christmas Lesson. In true Presbyterian style, Dr. Bain introduced the ten-year-old me, and then cut me down to size by adding "And I hope he speaks up!") Now, in the Old Meeting House, I was in the ancient pulpit, and all of the congregation's faces were turned up towards me. *Ah, so this is what it's like!* From this position you're allowed — no, *expected* — to tell people how to live their lives.

Later, at the volunteer fire hall across the way, while sandwiches were consumed, I got to chat with many in the congregation/audience as I signed their copies. Even better, at the end the delighted bookseller told me that I had sold more copies than any other speaker not named Gibson. Apparently, over the years of signings by all the distinguished readers, my total sales had been equalled only by my fellow clansman, Graeme Gibson. I was pleased.

The next stop was Bridgewater, with a side trip to a party at Lunenburg given by my friend Kiloran German, whose father, Tony, wrote for me the history of the Canadian Navy, *The Sea Is at Our Gates* (1990). Lunenburg is one of my favourite towns. In *Storytellers*

I recount a previous tour of the inner harbour by kayak during which I came upon the skulking *Bluenose* undergoing repairs, and gave her hull an encouraging prod with my paddle. It doesn't seem to have worked, and the bills keep mounting.

Sadly, the Houston Art Gallery, selling Inuit art, has now closed down. And our Bridgewater friend, Stephanie Tompkins, continues to scoff about how much worse the weather always is in misty Lunenburg. But, my goodness, it is a handsome little town, and it shelters one of Canada's best investigative writers, my friend Michael Harris, who gave us the true story of the death of the cod fishery in his 1998 classic, *Lament for an Ocean*. (I told him, "What happened here is a great crime. We need a fine crime writer to explain it." And Michael certainly delivered. In 2014, he delivered *Party of One*, an equally scathing look at Stephen Harper in power.)

Our visit was hosted by the Bridgewater Public Library, and they had hoped that I could give the show in the new library building. But the usual construction delays occurred, so Jeff Mercer had to scramble to find a new venue. Fortunately, St. Mark's Place, a richly converted church right on the river at Middle LaHave, proved to be a perfect location, where old friends from all over unexpectedly showed up. One had driven all the way from Cape Breton and another, fresh from Halifax, was the great Gaelic bard Lewis MacKinnon, a short, smiling fellow, shaped like a barrel of the best Scotch whisky.

Here's something that you perhaps didn't know about literary Nova Scotia — the best Gaelic poetry in the world is being written there, today. For proof just look at my friend Lewis, the only man from outside Scotland ever to win the Scottish national literary "Mod" competition there. He's a friend, and a former house guest of ours in Toronto when he won the award as "Canada's Scot of the Year" in 2013 in recognition of his international Gaelic feat. A remarkable man representing a remarkable culture.

That sunny evening in the former church they let me toll the bell, for fun (remembering Thomas Hood's pun "They went and told the sexton, and / The sexton toll'd the bell"), and I hoped that the ringing bell might attract curious locals to the converted church. We did get a great crowd, but as I gave the show I had the heretical thought that the fine, airy space in the former church was perhaps working against me. The beauty of the redecorated spacious setting tended to draw the thoughts of the audience upward, away from my very earthly show. Just possibly these old church architects knew what they were doing. In any case, all of the attracted visitors helped to swell the attendance, and to swell the Bridgewater Library's funds. No pirates made a threatening appearance up the LaHave River, so the treasure chest remained unburied.

The next day, crossing the province, we angled from Bridgewater to the Annapolis Valley, via Highway 8 (and Maitland Bridge!), passing Kejimkujik National Park to come swooping down South Mountain into the Valley near Annapolis Royal. This is Ernest Buckler territory, of course: he lived in a farmhouse in Centrelea, just outside Bridgetown. Although I never knew him, I was well aware of the importance of *The Mountain and the Valley* (1952).

I knew, too, of the unusual link between W.O Mitchell (1914–1998) and Buckler (1908–1984), his Nova Scotian counterpart and near contemporary. Bill Mitchell's 1948 novel of the West, *Who Has Seen the Wind*, followed young Brian O'Connell growing up on the edge of the prairies, becoming aware of his family and friends and the Prairie people around them. *The Mountain and the Valley* follows the boy David Canaan as he turns into an articulate young man growing up in a close rural family. He feels different from his Annapolis Valley neighbours, yet wants to write about them, "the best people in the whole world."

Bill Mitchell, another small-town kid who, like Buckler, went on to do well at university studying philosophy, seemed to sense what the Dalhousie graduate was trying to do in his writing. So in his role as fiction editor at *Maclean's* magazine he corresponded encouragingly with Buckler back on the Valley farm, taking on some of his short stories, and dispensing lots of friendly advice. His support was so strong, in fact, that the 2005 biography *Mitchell* says: "Bill continued promoting Buckler at Atlantic Monthly Press, and Buckler was 'grateful' as he wrote to a connection at Curtis Brown [literary agency] 'to that wonderful guy and expert writer, W.O. Mitchell, who keeps up a sort of unobtrusive press-agentry for me whenever he gets a chance.'" After Mitchell told the editor Dudley Cloud about Buckler's novel-in-progress, *The Mountain and the Valley*, "they made an offer for an option of $250."

Who knew that in the Annapolis Valley I would feel so close to my crackly voiced old friend, and to Weyburn and the flat, open prairie, otherwise so different in every way from the nearby mountains and enclosed valley near salt water? Is it fanciful to see Buckler's novel as the eastern equivalent of *Who Has Seen the Wind?* Maybe, but its greatness was recognized proudly close to home. It was New Brunswick's Alden Nowlan who called it simply "one of the great novels of the English language."

There are other similarities. Buckler thought that you could find the important things in life anywhere. He told Silver Donald Cameron, in *Conversations with Canadian Novelists*, that far from feeling out of the world, "I think in the Nova Scotia country, almost specifically in the country where I live, you get the universals more than you do almost anywhere else. I've found this a great sustenance. . . . You don't need to budge from here to get the whole story." Mitchell would have agreed.

Buckler may have been shy, while Mitchell was certainly not, and towards the end of his life, according to his friend Greg Cook, he spent many days alone. But like any author he also loved recounting great reactions from his readers. Like this: "When *The Mountain and the Valley* came out I used to get letters saying, 'This thing has meant a great deal to me,' and of course that is the only kind of reward that you have. I think the nicest letter — well, the most amusing one — I ever had was from somebody in Cape Breton. Talk about succinctness: he wrote me, and he said, 'I enjoyed your book very much. It was such clear print. Sincerely.'"

"Annapolis, Annapolis! Oh yes, Annapolis must be defended: to be sure, Annapolis should be defended . . . Pray, where is Annapolis?" That's the prime minister of Great Britain, the noble Duke of Newcastle, in 1758, showing his level of familiarity with London's far-flung possessions overseas in Nova Scotia, even those named after a queen.

In Annapolis Royal we roamed around the historic little town for old times' sake (how many bookstores do you know where your friends also sold furs?) before heading south past the elegant old white-painted fort named after Queen Anne. Then we drove along the shore of the basin towards Digby. We had a dinner date with Harold Horwood's family.

Harold Horwood (1923–2006)

In *Founding the Writers' Union of Canada*, Andreas Schroeder marvels at Harold Horwood, who was "a phenomenon . . . He had this voice that cut, a really sharp voice that he made no effort to de-emphasize. When Harold talked, it always sounded as if you were being accused or your death sentence was being read." In my chapter on Harold Horwood — the "neglected genius" — and in my show, I urge people to read his last book, *Dancing on the Shore*, about the natural world of the Annapolis Basin. At Upper Clements, right opposite Champlain's original fort at Port Royal (you remember "The Order of Good Cheer," and all that), Harold and his family bought the land, and by judicious planting and spreading natural fertilizers, and hard, imaginative work, transformed it into a sort of local Garden of Eden, bursting with healthy trees and shrubs and berry bushes, loud with the song of hundreds of birds, and blessed by the feet of visiting four-legged friends, while the warm waters of the basin teemed with schools of fish, and the graceful willets danced on the shore.

I was looking forward to seeing how everything had developed since Harold's death in 2006, and had been delighted to accept his widow Corky's invitation to dinner, to join her and their son Andrew. I was amused to learn that Leah (the daughter of the man I had described as "a Viking") had moved to Norway.

But as I turned down off the road at Upper Clements, the lane seemed very narrow, the evergreen trees surprisingly thick. So thick that they seemed to crowd in on the car. Were we in the right driveway? We found the house, of course, and climbed out, eager to be shown around the Eden that I remembered.

And it became clear that the last laugh belonged to Nature.

Everything in the well-planted and well-fertilized ground had grown up. The old views were blocked, the sun no longer reached this garden, the trees here had overwhelmed this fence.

Harold had written lovingly about "the great spruces that line the shore," and told us about the aspens, maples, larches, hawthorns and birches that he tended. Even better, he listed the fruits provided by his apple trees and peach trees and so on, and the summer-long parade of pin cherries, black cherries, and chokccherries. Best of all, he wrote about the serviceberries on his land. "How much better is the Newfoundland name chuckly pear! Serviceberry indeed! And how much uglier the American name, shadbush. But whatever you call them, their blooming is a high point of the year. . . . I have never seen any forest anywhere more beautiful with bloom than the Annapolis woodlands in May during the brief flowering of the chuckly pears."

Whether you call them serviceberries, or juneberries, or (my preference) saskatoonberries, if you know the sweet purple fruit with the nutty little seed, you'll understand Harold's statement, "The chuckly pears were one of the attractions that brought us to Annapolis Basin." (He even made wine out of the purple berries.) Now, on our visit in August, there is no sign of them. That was possibly just a seasonal matter. But, much worse, it was clear that everything was hopelessly overgrown, the crowded undergrowth turning brown for lack of sunlight.

Corky, well into her eighties, was still an amazingly nimble guide as we roamed the steeply sloping property with Andrew, but it was clear that it was now too big a job for the two of them to keep this rampant growth in check. And everything was quiet. We were on the lookout, and the listen-out, for the birds that used to live there in such numbers. But all was very still. And Andrew sadly confirmed that the willets no longer came to enjoy dancing on the shore — or, as Harold put it, "dancing not only on the short salt grass that is covered monthly by the tide, but dancing in air, like butterflies, or salamanders wrapped in flame."

Harry Bruce has led a wonderfully productive life writing about his Maritime roots. He has done much more, of course, as his classic 2009 book for me, *Page Fright: Foibles and Fetishes of Famous Writers*, demonstrates, as it reveals the superstitious ways writers throughout time have worked to keep the magic supply of words coming. But the 1977 book he produced, *Lifeline* (on the ferries that ply the Maritimes shores), shows that he realizes just how central these ferries are to life in this part of the world. Yarmouth, its ferry to Bar Harbour temporarily suspended, learns this, in painful daily lessons. By contrast, Digby, at the entrance to the Annapolis Basin, is a prosperous port town, thanks to the ferry right across the Bay of Fundy to Saint John.

Every Canadian should have the fun of rising early, then setting out westward through the morning mist from Digby into the open bay. Jane and I loved it, crossing the deck excitedly to see the misty land on this side ("Look, it's Digby Neck!"), then the other, recede from view. Then we'd catch exciting wildlife sightings up ahead with our binoculars. ("Is that a whale, or was that a dolphin jumping?" "Did you see that gannet dive?" "What is that crowd of gulls doing in the water? Look at all the fish!") That is, when you're not relaxing below decks, enjoying a hearty meal.

The straight-ahead passage is not nearly as exciting as the B.C. ferry ride from Victoria through Active Pass, and it becomes dramatic again only at the end as you approach the New Brunswick shore just south of Saint John. But on this trip we were tempted by thoughts of piracy, to take us straight to our destination. If Saint John stood at 12 on the clockface, we were really headed for 9 o'clock, Grand Manan. A swift takeover of the wheelhouse, and a turn hard to port, would have saved us several hours.

But they were happy hours, and even when we sailed into the big industrial port we thought of Jane's nephew, Jeff, and the work he had done as a deep-sea diver out of these big oil stations near Saint John. On the central waterfront I could see the steeple of the downtown church where I had once watched the outraged minister, hands on hips, glaring at two attractive tourists sunbathing in their bikinis on a patch of grass beside the tombstones. No caption was necessary, and his determination not to be a narrow-minded old spoilsport colliding with carefree youth was clearly putting his blood pressure at risk. I wonder how it ended.

We lost no time in driving ashore and turning south on Highway 790 towards the Maine border. But we were bound for Blacks Harbour, to catch the ferry to Grand Manan.

Why Grand Manan? In a world where most authors were sitting wistfully at home, wishing there were some way to promote their book, why were we off, both beaming, our hair blowing in the breeze, to this remote little island to give my *Stories About Storytellers* show to a surprised audience of locals? *Because* it's remote, closer to Maine than the New Brunswick coast, about as far to the south and east from the Pacific Islands of Haida Gwaii as you can get without leaving Canada. And *because* I suffer from the geographic compulsion that, for example, had me jubilantly dipping my toe off the southernmost point of land in all of Canada at Point Pelee. And *because* Jane's cousin Dyanne and her husband, Alex (the Alex Frame behind

Peter Gzowski's *Morningside*), had invited us to come and see their wonderful home on the island that they loved.

On the map the island is shipshape, looking like a sloop with ragged sails heading north and east towards Saint John. We learned that it's an ancient island, skirted more by cliffs than gentle beaches, surrounded by Fundy tides so full of whales that, to help identification, local leaflets show the tails of humpbacks, right, and sperm whales. The extraordinary location means that more than 400 types of migrating birds are affected by the predictable storms that go with the sea climate. We learned how organized the settlement of roughly 2,500 residents is when we asked for the address of Dyanne and Alex's place. "OK," we said. "We've got the number. But what street? Ahhh, there is really *just one street*, Route 776, right down the island? OK."

And that gives you a sense of this island, with the three Loyalist communities of North Head (where the ferry arrives, and where there are actual streets), Grand Harbour (where the home of early settler Moses Garrish Farmer, who came in 1784, now houses the Grand Manan Museum, ideal for public meetings with visiting authors), and Seal Cove to the south, where curious seals popping up in the water to groom their moustaches explain its name. Apart from Route 776, the main link is the clifftop walking path that runs across hundreds of private properties, and is carefully maintained by the Grand Manan Trails Association.

I was delighted to make my show — held in the museum, and introduced by Dyanne — a fundraiser for the Trails people. We raised a fair amount of money, and I got some great stories. For example, the Grand Manan folks — unlike any other audience, before or since — burst into song when I played the piano version of "Brother Can You Spare a Dime?"

And it's not as if these hardy islanders have never been anywhere else. We found that one of the Frames' friends had served in the Arctic with James Houston, and even had one of his cartoons framed on the wall at home, alongside other Inuit art, to remember those great days in the North.

But this is all very remote from world literature, right? Not quite. The famous American novelist Willa Cather spent every summer for many years on Grand Manan. And Alice Munro visited the island in 1979, and set a story there. You'll find that story, "Dulse," in the collection *The Moons of Jupiter* that I published in 1982. It's notable for a number of reasons. First, it's clearly set far from Alice Munro Country. Second, it allows Alice to deal with the subject of readers who become unbalanced admirers of a chosen author, like the extreme Willa Cather fan "Mr. Stanley" whom the narrator encounters, just as Alice did in real life on the island, as Robert Thacker records in his biography. Third (and Alice Munro scholars love this), while the original version of the story that ran in the *New Yorker* was in the first person, Alice changed it to the third person for the book. And I, of course, went along with it, since in these matters Alice's instinct was always right. And Bob Thacker (also a Willa Cather scholar) notes that "the most compelling changes between the two published versions lie in Munro's depiction of Willa Cather — this story offers a beautiful analysis of a writer's self-absorption, and of Cather's in particular. In her revisions, Munro makes her Cather more inscrutable and much more compelling."

Like a true, unbalanced admirer, on the island I sought out the hotel where Alice had stayed: "A guest house overlooking the docks, with their stacks of lobster traps, and the few scattered stores and houses that made up the village." It was closed when we dropped by, but we could still peer into the windows, revealing what looked like a perfect memorial piece, frozen in time, for Alice's visit in 1979. And the "dulse" of the title, the edible seaweed collected and dried on Grand Manan, is still a proud local specialty. I can report that it is an acquired taste.

The next day we took the ferry back to the mainland, then were almost the only car on the wide new highway north out of Maine. We whizzed past Saint John ("Is that a codfish or a salmon at the top of that old church spire?") and did not make a detour this time up the lovely Saint John river valley to Fredericton, the capital, and the centre for the University of New Brunswick. I have fond memories of the elegant elm trees down by the river, and of many capital literary stories. It was at a Fredericton bookstore that Dennis Lee once offered to sign copies of *Alligator Pie*, to be told, diplomatically, "If it were Pierre Berton or Farley Mowat, I'd say yes, but *in this case* I don't think so."

My publisher friend Bill Clarke (of Clarke Irwin) once attended a Fredericton funeral, in this case for his author Alden Nowlan. At the end of the solemn graveside service, the attendees were invited to participate in filling the grave. To Bill Clarke's amazement, the usual Ontario formal trickles of earth were replaced by spit-on-the-hands hard shovelling, with jackets shed by people like the premier, Richard Hatfield. Ah, New Brunswick!

We whizzed on northward, pausing to admire the downtown murals in Sussex, and passed Moncton, knowing that we would do it justice later. But one important part of the province that we ignored this time was the Miramichi, north of the Acadian Shore. David Adams Richards territory.

In the last forty years, Dave, born in 1950, has been the province's major novelist, ever since he burst on the scene with *The Coming of Winter* in 1974. I was proudly involved in publishing (although never in editing) later novels of his with typical gnarly titles like *Nights Below Station Street* (1988), *Evening Snow Will Bring Such Peace* (1990), and *For Those Who Hunt the Wounded Down* (1993). These are not the slick, memorable titles that publishers leap on. But what they lose in slickness they gain in authenticity, and Dave's novels (which have won almost every major Canadian prize going) are an authentic, clear-eyed look at the hardscrabble lives of the people of the Miramichi, around Chatham and Dave's home town of Newcastle.

Here's Jerry Bines, to give one example, in *For Those Who Hunt the Wounded Down*. He has been in and out of prison:

> Years ago Bines used to drive a truck into town with his two dogs in the truck and a knife in his boot, and one day when the dogs started to fight he took his shotgun and shot one.
> "Which one," someone had asked.
> "The one on the left," Bines said.

It's tough to be a novelist, "the writer fella," who stands out in the non-literary community that you're writing about. Ernest Buckler summed it up perfectly for Silver Donald Cameron: "When the first book came out I had an awful time around here, because all kinds of people were identifying themselves with this or that person in the book and there was a great clamour. Although strangely enough the

David Adams Richards (1950–)

people were identifying themselves with people who were not the people I had written about. But fact is no good novelistically."

I know that Dave faced similar local pressures. My friend Arthur Herriott, the award-winning designer, was once hired by CBC-TV to work on a screenplay by Dave entitled "Small Gifts," which was set in his traditional blue-collar world. To catch the right atmosphere Arthur flew to New Brunswick, and drove around the Miramichi area with Dave. All was well until he jumped out of the car in Chatham, pulled out his camera, and started to photograph the streets and the buildings — and the people.

"Jesus Christ, Arthur," Dave exploded, "what the hell are you doing?"

It was alarmingly clear to Dave that a stranger in his company going round snapping with a camera was going to confirm the local suspicions that "the writer fella" was writing about real people — *them* — and that this would be trouble. In the end, Arthur and Dave agreed to park the car secretly, with Dave in it, a block away from wherever Arthur produced his camera to take his design photos.

By the way, you may think that nobody before Dave had ever written well about that part of New Brunswick. Consider this. One of the greatest set pieces in Canadian literature is in *The Watch That Ends the Night*, when young Jerome Martell sees his mother murdered in a logging camp, and escapes at night in his canoe down the river. The river is clearly the Miramichi, and the place where he comes ashore and jumps aboard a train is clearly Chatham. And Hugh MacLennan has him re-entering the "real" world in Moncton.

But this time we left Moncton in our wake as we headed north to cross the Confederation Bridge to Prince Edward Island, the ninth province on our tour.

Arriving on the Island, like all sensible Anne of Green Gables fans, we headed northwest to Sunnyside, and worked our way clockwise through all the sites (and sights) until we reached North Rustico. There we checked in at the Watermark Theatre, where we found my friend, the lively Duncan McIntosh. He proudly showed us around his summer theatre, then led the way to the cottage that was to be our home for the next couple of days. We were dazed, not only by the perfect cottage (on kindly loan from a professor who supports the theatre), but by the setting. The cottage stood in the beach grass near the old lighthouse at the end of the harbour, with white egrets wading thoughtfully in the water in front of the house, while Cavendish Beach (yes, *the* Cavendish Beach!) lay just a three-minute stroll behind it.

We asked Duncan about where to eat. "Ah, you must go to Maxine's restaurant!" he said, and phoned Maxine then and there, to arrange for us to go to dinner there at 7:30. Sure enough, we had a fine dinner, and were well looked after by Maxine. At the end of the meal we chatted, and she revealed that she was coming to our show the next night. We looked forward to seeing her there.

The next day was devoted to drinking in the delights of Prince Edward Island in the August sun. Some pleasures were new, like buying the newly issued Robertson Davies Canadian stamps at the post office just down from the theatre. Some were old, like renewing my acquaintance with Shaw's Hotel, the family hotel where the Gibsons stayed when the girls were young, and the path through the sand dunes to Brackley Beach was the most exciting one they'd ever skipped along, wrapped in their beach towels. A chat with a young teenage guy working hard outside revealed that he knew a lot about the history of this famous old hotel, the oldest in Canada to be run by the same family. How come? Well, his name was Shaw, you see . . .

My show went just fine in the theatre that evening, and I was able to hail Maxine, among the last to slip in before I got started. Afterwards there was the usual friendly mingling, and some books were sold and signed. Right at the end it was just Jane and me and middle-aged Maxine, who seemed to want to tell us something. "I'm really glad that in the show you talked about Jack Hodgins and *Spit Delaney's Island*," she began, "because when I got married, I took my husband's name. But when we split up, I didn't want to keep his name, but I didn't want to go back to my unmarried name. So I didn't know what to do."

We didn't know where this was going, but nodded encouragingly.

"Then I came across *Spit Delaney's Island*, and I thought . . . Maxine . . . Delaney. Maxine . . . Delaney. So, you see, I've been Maxine Delaney ever since."

Then she said, "I haven't told many people this story, but you seemed the right people to hear it."

"Well, I know a man named Hodgins in Victoria who's going to be delighted to hear this story when I tell him," I said. And of course he was, once he got up off the floor. You can't invent stories like these. Not even the author of *The Invention of the World*.

On Prince Edward Island, I always feel right at home. I grew up in Ayrshire, a county famous for its potatoes, and as a teenager I dug my own potato patch. On the island you're never far from the salt water, and I grew up within a dozen miles of the sea, smelling the same scent on the wind, which after really big storms left our windows whitened with salt. The closest port was Irvine, the birthplace of our old friend John Galt. And the big family name in Irvine from Norman times onward was Montgomery.

Of course, on PEI any publisher-turned-author feels at home, because so much of the province's economy is based on a book. Since it first appeared in 1908 *Anne of Green Gables* has been published everywhere, and has sold many millions of copies.

The story behind the book is amazing. Lucy Maud was an Island girl who had written some newspaper material and wanted to be a writer. As her 1917 book, *The Alpine Path: The Story of My Career*, tells it,

> I had always kept a notebook in which I jotted down, as they occurred to me, ideas for plots, incidents, characters, and descriptions. In the spring of 1904 I was looking over this notebook in search of some idea for a short serial I wanted to write for a certain Sunday School paper. I found a faded entry, written many years before: "Elderly couple apply to orphan asylum for a boy. By mistake a girl is sent them." I thought this would do.

The rest is history. If Lucy Maud was ever asked, "Where do you get your ideas?" her honest answer would have been: "Oh, I jot them down in a notebook, and then, if they're really good, I ignore them for many years, until I'm ready to write my first novel."

Millions of tourists have been drawn to the novel's idyllic setting, including my bewitched daughter Meg, and many, many Japanese tourists charmed by "the red-haired girl," as my story about Will Ferguson will remind us.

Although I have never published Will Ferguson (author of *Why I Hate Canadians*, and the Giller-winning novel *419*, and other fine books that show the range of his talents), we have had a friendly acquaintanceship for some years, and I have a story about him and PEI that is too good not to be true.

Lucy Maud Montgomery (1874–1942)

After getting an arts degree, like so many young Canadians, Alberta-born Will headed off to teach English in Japan. He lived in an English-speaking bubble, so his use of Japanese was restricted to the usual tourist stuff: "Men's room?" "How much?" "What time train to Yokohama?" and so on. And everyone he met socially was keen to practise their English on him, so he stayed at a basic tourist level.

When he came back to Canada, after the usual spell of hanging out with friends, it became necessary to get a job. A newspaper ad for a job in tourism on PEI caught his eye. He met the general requirements — a BA, and a willingness to relocate to PEI (sounds great!) and an ability to write. But what caught his eye was a line about "the ability to speak Japanese" being an asset.

Will is like the rest of us, and he really wanted the job. So in his application, and the subsequent interviews, he did not, let's say, *understate* his fluency in Japanese. And he got the job!

He spent a number of happy months on PEI until the day his boss came into the office, rubbing his hands. "Great news, Will. You know how keen Japanese tourists are to come here to visit Anne of Green Gables sites. Well, next week, a whole busload of Japanese tourist agency owners are coming here, and you'll have a chance to use your Japanese language skills on them!"

It was a dreadful week for Will. He spent hours secretly combing through phrase books and dictionaries. Then the fateful day came, when the busload of smartly dressed Japanese men filed off their bus, and stood attentively before Will's boss. He welcomed them, in English, then proudly introduced "my colleague, Will Ferguson, who will address you in your own language."

Will stepped forward, and said, in Japanese: "As you can hear, I not really speak Japanese. But my boss here, he not know that. So please not to tell him."

There was a gale of laughter.

Then Will said, in Japanese, "Many thanks, nice to see you here, welcome to Prince Edward Island, and now I talk in English."

When he finished, he was warmly applauded. A number of the Japanese visitors even came up, congratulated him, and said loudly to his boss, "Very good Japanese."

When the successful visit was over, and they waved the bus away, his boss was very pleased. "That went really well, Will. But tell me, what was the joke you made early on that really got them laughing?"

"Ah," said Will, "it's kind of hard to translate."

The next time Jane and I returned to Prince Edward Island, its swim-before-breakfast sunny landscape had become chilly, bright, wintry Christmas card scenes. On our way to Charlottetown, we paused for lunch at Amherst. Now *there's* a place shot through with history, where every fine old building on the main street is associated with a Father of Confederation! Its association with the eighteenth-century British soldier is, of course, less happy.

But that day we shared a lunch table in Amherst with a friendly stranger who knew all about me and my book, and wished us well on PEI. And when we drove across the Tantramar Marsh, and turned north to the Confederation Bridge, it was hard to avoid the excitement of the approaching Island. It was a great thrill to find ourselves crossing the ice-choked Northumberland Strait.

Unlike our summer visit to North Rustico, this time we drove straight to Charlottetown, marvelling at how varied the hilly island landscape could be. In Charlottetown we stayed with Jane's cousin Norman and his wife, Heather, and went in the late afternoon to the CBC Radio station to talk about that night's show, to be held at the Art Gallery of Prince Edward Island, Confederation Centre. Yet again, the link between the CBC and local readers was demonstrated. When we showed up there, the crowds ("Hi, I heard about your show on the radio!") were extraordinary. So extraordinary that we had to delay the show for some minutes while extra stacks of chairs were brought up and distributed to such distant parts of the gallery that I had to give my show with my back turned to part of the overflow audience of 130.

My old Banff Centre friend Richard Lemm, who is now at the University of PEI, helped me organize this Maritime universities tour. That night, Richard (still a trim, active, athletic fellow) was very funny introducing me, recalling brave days in Banff when he and I were young, and W.O. was heading the writing program, where he told everyone how lucky they were to have brought a young writer named Alice Munro to grace their program because "she spins straw into gold!"

At the end of my show — full of good questions — I was able to sign the new paperback edition of my book for the first time. Then we were taken to Mavor's, in Confederation Centre, for a fine post-show meal. Right at the end, a political science professor named Don Desserud pulled me aside and told how he was once at an event in France where Jack Hodgins spoke, and was asked from the floor why as a Canadian he did not speak in French. Jack, always a nice guy, replied with a good-humoured story about how his childhood experience with other languages had left him badly scarred. When his family moved into a new house, when he was four, he found a stack of comic books. Although he had not yet learned to read, he spent so much time studying them that he, yes, learned to read them, secretly, working out that this word meant "No!" while this one meant "Crash!" and so on.

When his parents broke the news that next week he had to go to school, he was resistant. Why did he have to go to school?

"Well, to learn how to read."

Jack dropped his bombshell: "But I can read already! Just look at these!" and he brought out his stack of comics, and proceeded to read what the letters meant.

Then the parents dropped their own bombshell: "But, Jack, these comics are in Finnish. The Saarinens left them behind in the house. You've learned to read *Finnish*!"

That, Jack explained to the audience, had made him very suspicious of any language that was not English, so he, regrettably, had never learned French.

My spring 2014 Maritime tour also brought me to Dalhousie, where Karen Smith, the Special Collections librarian, arranged for us to stay in the Oscar Wilde Room at the Waverley Inn. At breakfast the next day we were mindful of Oscar's dictum that "only dull people are brilliant at breakfast," but enjoyed our chat with the Kingston-based writer Diane Schoemperlen who had been giving a talk at St. Mary's for Alexander MacLeod *at exactly the same time* as my Dalhousie show. The world of Canadian literature is small, but endlessly overlapping, as this hotel encounter shows.

At Dalhousie I gave my show in an intimate setting in the Killam Library, flanked by distinguished old walnut desks that belonged to distinguished old writers, topped by leather-bound editions of authors like Thomas Haliburton. The audience was heavy on Dalhousie students and academics, with a leavening of old publishing colleagues, old academic allies like Andy Wainwright, and good friends like Silver Donald Cameron and John Houston.

The Q&A session produced a story from John Houston about how I once eased his ailing father's embarrassment at coming to dinner in a dressing gown by appearing *in my own dressing gown*, so that we could behave like two trendsetting eighteenth-century beaux. Andy Wainwright recalled an early encounter with Alice Munro, which hit him so strongly that he wrote a poem about her. When she received it, gratefully, she told him that it was the first poem ever written about her, and, thanks to Andy, I now have a copy. And Silver Donald recalled that in the early days of the Writers' Union Alice was among the writers who proposed to raise money for the Union by producing a hilariously pornographic joint novel, with each racy chapter contributed anonymously. Don reported that the result was such a boring, steamy mish-mash of tangled bodies panting their way through totally unreadable sexual activities, that it left everyone involved much sadder and wiser.

The next day we drove to Antigonish. At Truro we remembered Alistair MacLeod's *No Great Mischief* story about Gaelic-speaking Cape Breton men being rousted out of a Truro backyard and finding that the muttered curse *"Pog mo thon"* led to fine hospitality from the Cape Breton woman of the house. Beyond Truro the usual tunnel vision of the Nova Scotia highway builder falls away, and in the bright winter weather we enjoyed the vistas of snow-clad hills and valleys all the way to Antigonish. We came into town, as usual, down past the St. F.X. campus, and past Chisholm Park, before finding our way to our usual home, the Maritime Inn, where Doug Smith, the poet and our St. F.X. faculty host, had arranged for us to stay.

Antigonish (emphasis on the "nish") is a delightful little town, with a curving main street at the bottom of the university hill. We roamed around, grinning happily, and revisiting the Lyghtesome Gallery where we heard news of my old friend Lynda Johns (the "bird lady"; eating with her might involve starlings and robins flying around the dining room and sampling your spaghetti). Then we came across the superb new public library on Main Street. I was pleased to see that there is a flourishing Gaelic section, and was able to read an English translation of lovely poems by Sorley MacLean, Alistair MacLeod's Scottish friend.

That evening my show was held in the Schwartz Centre (a spectacular new building devoted to the study of business, donated by Gerry Schwartz, the husband of Indigo's Heather Reisman, who should, in theory, know all about the business of selling books in Canada). The facilities are spectacular, and left some of the arts students who crowded into my show somewhat jealous. But we all had a good time. I exposed some young students intriguingly to authors they didn't know, like Robertson Davies — to the pleasure of my host, Doug Smith, who saw the prospect of swelling CanLit classes in the next year, which would be good. And of course I was glad to spend extra time talking about my two St. F.X. authors, Alistair MacLeod and Brian Mulroney.

I came away with a great story about Brian. It's well known that during his days as a skinny young undergraduate, where his nickname was "Bones," he was a keen debater. In his 2007 *Memoirs*, this kid from Baie Comeau bravely recalls a detail from his maiden speech: "The word I had used to describe the Liberal lust for power was 'insatiable,' which I mispronounced as 'in-sat-eye-able.'" Later, as he grew more polished, he was, in his words, "extremely active on the debating team." He even included the proud boast, "During those years our team was undefeated."

Hold that thought. Mulroney's book does *not* include the story that I heard from one of the St. F.X. audience, an older gentleman who approached us after the show. Apparently, when Brian was debating against another team (can it have been UNB?) the debate was going very badly for his side, and they seemed to be headed for defeat. Brian, a smoker, had some matches in his pocket. Surreptitiously he lit one, and quietly dropped it into a half-full wastepaper basket.

Flames! Smoke alarms! Fire extinguishers! And total disruption of the course of the debate, thanks to Brian's well-timed arson. (It opens up the prospects for a nice Anglo-Saxon amendment to the chant, "Liar, liar, pants on fire!"). And the St. F.X. debating team remained undefeated.

Among the kindly reports on the evening sent by Doug Smith's students (who, they revealed, had been forced to attend my show) was one I'm happy to quote:

My grandfather met [Alistair MacLeod] one day in some part of Cape Breton (I can't remember where). He needed a drive to work and my grandfather went out of his way to get him there. They had a long chat in the car and that was that. Years later when MacLeod was discovered my papa received a letter and two signed copies of his books, *No Great Mischief* and *Island*. MacLeod had remembered my grandfather's small act of kindness and wanted to thank him.

The letter concludes: "Both those books now reside on my shelf and last night you inspired me to crack open *Island* for the first time in years. Thank you. Last night was a pleasure." And it's a pleasure for me to recall that in January 2000, I wrote the Editor's Introduction to that book, ending with the words, "All sixteen of his lovingly crafted stories are contained here, organized chronologically, in the order in which they first appeared in print. They are accompanied by no commentary, no explanations, no critical apparatus. These are Alistair MacLeod's stories, and they speak for themselves."

From time to time here, you'll notice that I've quoted from a classic 1973 book entitled *Conversations with Canadian Novelists*. That's exactly what it is, in two volumes, thanks to a young B.C.-raised professor named Donald Cameron, who decided to take a tape recorder along when he talked with some interesting Canadians about their writing. The list of the subjects he chose is amazing. Ernest Buckler, Roch Carrier, Robertson Davies, Timothy Findley, Harold Horwood, Robert Kroetsch, Margaret Laurence, Jack Ludwig, Hugh MacLennan, and David Lewis Stein are in Volume One. Then there's George Bowering, Morley Callaghan, Dave Godfrey, W.O. Mitchell, Brian Moore, Martin Myers, Thomas Raddall, Mordecai Richler, Gabrielle Roy, and Rudy Wiebe in Volume Two.

Not a bad series of choices. The man should have been a publisher! To be fair, in a career spanning lots of roles, this self-described "author, educator" has been just about everything, and he was indeed the "Publisher and Founding ed." of *The Mysterious East* magazine.

But how did he get his name? In an amusing piece called "By Any Other Name" he has written a full explanation, including the tragic line, "*You wouldn't believe how many Donald Camerons there are in this debased North American Scotland. Hundreds, I tell you. Thousands.*"

So how is a Donald Cameron who tries to make a living as a writer going to stand out? When he moved to Cape Breton, local custom came to his rescue. His friend, the folksinger Tom Gallant, explained that in Cape Breton people with the same names were distinguished by having specific, personal details added to the names:

> Tom struck a chord on his Yamaha, gazed at me. "That hair," he said. It's my most striking feature, prematurely grey hair, set off by black eyebrows and moustache. Don't ask me how I got that colour scheme, ask God. He did it. Children stop me in the street to ask me if I'm wearing a wig. Adults chalk it up to noxious personal habits and secret vices.
> "That hair," said Tom. "That's it. Silver Donald Cameron."

That notable byline has since graced hundreds of screenplays, radio dramas, films, documentaries, reports, articles, short stories, and books, both fiction (*Dragon Lady*, 1980) and non-fiction (*The Living Beach*, 1998). He continues to use it in his ongoing, tireless crusade to spread the alarming news about our assault on the health of our planet.

We had been in touch over the years (I once ran into him by chance when he was sailing in Baddeck, Cape Breton), and I was aware of his skills as a sailor producing lively touring books like *Wind, Whales, and Whisky: A Cape Breton Voyage* (1991), and *Sniffing The Coast: An Acadian Voyage* (1993). So I phoned him to chat about possible future books. What follows is his account of our conversation. After Don, eager to write a new novel, had denied having any ideas for non-fiction books I spoke up in protest:

> "Come, come," said Gibson. "You must have something in the back of your mind."
> "Well," I allowed, "I've just put an engine in our boat, and it has occurred to me to sail her south via the Intracoastal Waterway, spend the winter in the Bahamas, and write a book about that."
> Aaargh, cried the Artistic Conscience. Dinna tell him that!
> "Sailing Away from Winter!" cried Gibson. "Great! Who's publishing this book?"
> "It's not a book," I protested. "It's just a notion. A passing fancy. A foggy fantasy."

"I want you to do this trip," Gibson declared. "I'm going to make you an offer you can't refuse."

One thing led to another, as Don's *Sailing Away from Winter* goes on to duly record. Urged by his mate (in every sense), Marjorie Simmins (now the author of her own book, *Coastal Lives*), Don found himself engaged in an exhausting search for the perfect little boat for this voyage. They had immense difficulties and complications, but eventually they found *Pumpkin*. They later changed her name to *Magnus*, as nature intended, and had her shipped to their place in D'Escousse on Isle Madame, at the southeast corner of Cape Breton.

I drove there from Halifax one snowy day, across the Canso Causeway, with no dangerous waves washing across the roadway. After a hard right turn through the snowstorm, I soon found myself on Isle Madame, enjoying the sign that pointed to sunny "Martinique." In Don's words: "I led Gibson to the boat-shop. He climbed up the ladder and boarded *Pumpkin*. He sat at the wheel and gazed through the windshield at the shop doors. 'Ahhh!' he said, smiling. It was all his fault, and he felt not a shred of remorse."

You can see why Jane and I love to stay in Halifax with Don and Marjorie at their place right at the end of the Northwest Arm, where boats not necessarily named "Pumpkin" or "Magnus" can moor behind the house, with the chance to sail off to anywhere in the world, as readers of *Sailing Away from Winter* learned when it was triumphantly launched in 2007.

Our final Maritime stop was specially arranged by Danielle LeBlanc of Moncton's Frye Festival, who took friendly advantage of our being "in the neighbourhood" to arrange a special Friday night show. We dropped our car off at the airport, and she (a former local girl who made the perfect guide) took us downtown, where we stayed in the central Hotel Beausejour, which is very, very central, and very, very bilingual. In Moncton people switch between French and English at the drop of a toque, and it seems to work well, with many marketing companies and their call centres making use of this bilingual workforce.

As eager tourists we made our way to the downtown shore of the Petitcodiac River at the publicized time to see the tidal bore come sweeping in from the advancing Bay of Fundy. We had heard brave tales of summer surfers riding the incoming wave for miles, which sounds like an exciting tourist trade to develop. But on this occasion the arrival of the bore was (I'm fighting a bad pun with every sinew) let's say "sedate," and involved the river simply floating the ice chunks a little higher and faster.

Downtown Moncton is very conscious of its link with the great scholar, with quotes from Northrop Frye to be found everywhere. Even our hotel had a Frye quote outside the front door: "Wherever illiteracy is a problem, it's as fundamental a problem as getting enough to eat or a place to sleep. The native language takes precedence over every other subject of study; nothing can compare with it in usefulness." That's from *The Educated Imagination*, 1963.

The literacy problem didn't affect the fine Monctonians who came to my show in the Aberdeen Cultural Centre, in Northrop Frye's old high school. The crowd was swelled by, of course, my lucky interview on local CBC Radio. That night, after a tactful opening sentence in French, I had fun celebrating Alice Munro's Nobel Prize.

Despite the many book-lovers in attendance and the local support for the Frye Festival, headed by the lively Dawn Arnold, it was disheartening the next day to see the lead story in the *Moncton Times Transcript*, which reported that New Brunswick, dragged down by some rural areas, suffered from the lowest literacy rates in Canada. But in a minor, local way Northrop Frye, the advocate of literacy, is doing what he can to change that. Outside the main door of the downtown Moncton Library stands a friendly, inviting bench. At one end sits a lifelike sculpture of Norrie Frye, at his most avuncular, beaming as he reads an illustrated book on his lap. (A week later I checked the same statue outside Victoria College in Toronto, daringly brushing snow off his head to confirm that some of the statue details do differ, very slightly.)

As I stood admiring the statue of the scholar revered by academics around the world, a class of eight-year-olds came out of the library after a happy visit. "Say hello to Mr. Frye!" their teacher sang out. All of the kids filed by, saying cheerfully, "Hello, Mr. Frye" as they passed his bench. "Hello, Mr. Frye."

CHAPTER 11

ROCK TALK

Gordon Pinsent vs. Kevin Spacey . . . Icebergs Are Cool
. . . Jim Lamb's Corvette Navy . . . The Bloody War of Hal
Lawrence . . . Wayne Johnston and My Very Stupid Decision
. . . A Richard Gwyn Footnote . . . Death on the Ice . . . Farley
Mowat's New-Founde-Land . . . West to Woody Point . . .
Charles Ritchie, the Axeman of Black Duck . . . Four Great
Newfoundland Characters . . . The Secret View of St. John's
. . . A Toast to Alistair MacLeod

The Shipping News (1993) by E. Annie Proulx was a very successful book that introduced life in Newfoundland to an appreciative audience around the world. In due course, Hollywood decided to make the Pulitzer Prize winner into a movie, and Kevin Spacey was selected to star in it, with a supporting cast that included the veteran Newfoundland-born actor Gordon Pinsent. Naturally, they filmed it on location on the Rock. One famous evening in 2000, the cast showed up to relax at Rocky's bar in Trinity (population: 200) and soon, as word got around, the place was so crowded that the walls were bulging out.

Kevin Spacey — a decent man, despite being a Hollywood star — quietly told the bartender not to worry, that his security people would make sure that these fans didn't get out of hand, and everything would be fine.

"Kevin, me son," said the bartender kindly, "these crowds aren't here because of you. They're here to see Gordon!"

In *Stories About Storytellers* I state flatly that "I never met a Newfoundlander I didn't like." My friends on the Rock turn thoughtful when I repeat this, treating it as a sort of challenge ("Ah, just wait till he meets grouchy old X, or that mean bastard Y — I must arrange it, then we'll see"). Or perhaps they regard it as evidence that my list of acquaintances in Newfoundland is much too short, or that I have led a timid, sheltered life. But despite their best efforts, my statement remains true.

And it's certainly true about Gordon Pinsent. We had bumped into each other occasionally over the years, when the famous actor entered the book world with a couple of novels, and a memoir, and I liked him a lot. But we became friends after he had starred in the 2006 movie *Away from Her*. As you probably know, this fine Canadian film by Sarah Polley is based on the Alice Munro story "The Bear Came Over the Mountain." Gordon stars in it alongside Julie Christie, who (with the help of a Canadian accent that would fool immigration officers) drifts off tragically into the mists of Alzheimer's. A lovely movie, about an all-too-common family tragedy, and Alice, I know, admires it very much.

After the movie came out, I was sitting beside Alice at the Giller Prize gala when I saw Gordon, agelessly resplendent in his tuxedo, sitting at a table across the room. I slipped away, and asked him if he had ever met Alice Munro. His eyes widened. No, but he would love to. So I had the pleasure of taking him over to meet Alice. He bent over her hand and these two remarkable stars, born within a year of each other, lit up the room with their obvious delight at finally meeting.

And I — standing alongside with a beam that extends to this day as I recall the memory — was able to reflect on how lucky my life had been, putting me into such a happy position, metaphorically introducing unknown writers to the world, or literally introducing Gordon Pinsent to Alice Munro.

At the end of May 2014, I went back to Newfoundland to attend the AGM of the Writers' Union of Canada, of which I am a proud honorary member. In St. John's, true to my instincts to find the edge wherever I go (Haida Gwaii, Point Pelee, Grand Manan) and because I had already, on an earlier visit, tramped down Cape Spear, the easternmost point of the continent, I instantly hiked up Signal Hill, to look out at the wide Atlantic. And there, coming smiling out of the crowd of tourists looking for an iceberg, was a solidly built, dark-haired Toronto fellow much less formally dressed than when he works in Garfield Weston's head office: none other than my friend George Goodwin. He was in town with Sheila for a family wedding. And right there on Signal Hill we recalled the work we had done, involving Gordon Pinsent as a gracious volunteer, in staging the huge fundraising in Toronto for Al Purdy's A-frame. We marvelled at how Al Purdy's influence clearly stretches right across the country, to the very edge.

Turning eastward, we marvelled, too, at the stroke of scenic luck that had left a picturesque iceberg adrift right off Signal Hill, the subject of a million snapshots. We even devised the theory that the iceberg was really an inflatable white plastic mock-up, cunningly created and towed into place at night by the Newfoundland tourism authority.

Seriously, icebergs are big business in Newfoundland. I remember one that many years ago attracted thousands to Clarke's Beach to see its remarkable shape, like the Manhattan skyline. A few years ago there was almost blood on the water in a fight over a big, dramatic iceberg that had floated close to shore. On one side were the industrial boats that were licensed to harvest the ice, taking large chunks of the spectacularly fresh water off the iceberg, to turn it into cool drinks like vodka and beer. Fluttering protectively around the diminishing chunk of ice were the opposing forces of the tour boats that ferry tourists out from St. John's to see a real live iceberg. "Hands off our iceberg!" "Icebergs are cool!"

Sadly, you can guess who won.

The most important view from Signal Hill is not out to sea, but straight down to The Narrows, the rocky gateway into the wide St. John's Harbour. The whole harbour is shaped like a hair dryer, with The Narrows as the thin handle. Between the cliffs, the passage into the harbour seems amazingly narrow, as if you could throw a baseball right across it. In the old days even a few inaccurate, rusty cannons on the heights could easily lob cannonballs down onto suicidal attacking ships, making St. John's one of the safest harbours in the world.

The British navy used it for centuries. As you stand on Signal Hill you can almost hear the snap of the sails of the ships that squeezed through here over the years, carrying men named Cook, and Bligh, and Nelson, and thousands of others. But none of the ancients were involved in a battle more desperate than the one to keep the world free from Hitler in the Second World War, the Battle of the Atlantic. In the early years of the war when Britain stood alone, it seemed that the German U-boat submarines were winning the war. They were sinking so many of the supply ships travelling in convoys across the Atlantic, carrying troops, and arms, and fuel, and food to the besieged British Isles, that Winston Churchill himself feared the worst. In the end, the U-boat war was won, thanks especially to St. John's — christened "Newfiejohn" by the Canadian sailors who made up the corvette navy.

The Corvette Navy was the title of the book that I published in 1977 by James B. Lamb. Jim was a big, cheery Toronto-born fellow who had spent the war serving in corvettes, rising to command HMCS

Minas, then HMCS *Camrose*, before going on to a career in newspapers in Moose Jaw and Orillia. Stephen Leacock's Mariposa, where the main naval story concerns the sinking of the *Mariposa Belle* in five feet of water, was an unlikely place for a Canadian naval war classic to emerge. But that is what we got from Jim Lamb, an absolute classic about what may have been Canada's greatest contribution to the war.

It was a grim, deadly business, living — constantly wet and tired and often seasick — on the cold North Atlantic, trying to keep dozens of merchant ships in line and haring off to pursue the German submarines in the wolf pack when they made their presence known by sinking yet another ship. All too often there was no time to pick up survivors struggling in the water or shivering in lifeboats. The priority was to keep on hunting the submarines. On occasion this meant dropping depth charges into waters where your own men were swimming, screaming for help . . .

Despite that deadly background, the book is full of humour. Describing the fierce Royal Navy efforts to turn the new recruits — prairie farm boys, Toronto taxi drivers, Quebec bricklayers — into quick-thinking professional seamen, Jim tells the story of the terrifying British admiral, in full, gold-braided uniform, who came aboard a Canadian corvette determined to impart a lesson:

> Coming aboard this ship, the Admiral suddenly removed his cap and flung it on the deck, shouting to the astonished quartermaster: "That's an unexploded bomb; take action, quickly now!"
>
> With surprising sang-froid, the youngster kicked the cap over the side. "Quick thinking!" commended the Admiral. Then, pointing to the slowly sinking cap, heavy with gold lace, the Admiral continued: "That's a man overboard; jump to it and save him!"
>
> The ashen-faced matelot took one look at the icy November sea, then turned and shouted: "Man overboard! Away lifeboat's crew!"
>
> The look on the Admiral's face, as he watched his expensive Gieves cap slowly disappear into the depths while a cursing, fumbling crew attempted to get a boat ready for lowering, was balm to the souls of all who saw it.

Jim also writes fondly about St. John's and its people, as the place that was "home" after each hazardous Atlantic crossing. And he writes with especial fondness about the Crow's Nest.

If any single place could be said to be the heart of the corvette navy, the Crow's Nest, officially entitled the Seagoing Officers' Club, would be it. Certainly it was home to all of us in the escort ships; a place where you could drop into at any time of day or night and be assured of a welcome, a drink, or a simple snack — the hot ersatz eggs and Spam sandwiches were always good — from the assiduous Gordon and his wife, who presided there. Dozens of enormous leather armchairs were scattered about the bare floor, and grouped about the fireplace, with its comfortable padded fender. The walls were resplendent with the crest of every escort ship in the western ocean; original works of art, most of them, and always worth a tour of inspection to see what new ones had been added since the last visit.

I can add that because HMCS *Wetaskiwin* was universally known as the "wet-ass-queen," an anonymous artist was inspired to produce an unforgettable ship's crest, which some might call a triumph of "Primitive Art."

I can report this, because *the Crow's Nest still exists*! On my 2014 visit I went to see a show by Ted Barris about his book *The Great Escape*, to be given in the old club. It's now a National Historic Site, right beside the War Memorial downtown. I went up the famous fifty-nine steps, to find the welcoming collection of armchairs, and the fireplace, that Jim Lamb wrote about. At the end of Ted's exciting show I poked around, and introduced myself to a great Crow's Nest veteran, Gary Green. When I mentioned the magic words *The Corvette Navy* and "Jim Lamb" I was welcomed with open arms. *Jim Lamb's publisher*! Gary took me around, showing me the dining room, then the collection of crests — then the ultimate prize, beside the bar, the captured U-Boat periscope, one of the very few in existence.

I crouched to peer through it, and remembered how, around 1980, I was the movie reviewer for CBC Radio's *Sunday Morning*. I had to cover *Das Boot*, the war movie about a German U-boat crew being hunted by corvettes, and sinking deeper and deeper in the attempt to hide from the depth charges until its rivets start to pop under the strain. I took Jim Lamb to the movie with me to get the response of an old U-boat hunter. He was surprisingly sympathetic to the plight of the submarine's crew. A gracious winner.

If I was a celebrity in the Crow's Nest when I mentioned that I had published Jim Lamb's book, the celebrity was compounded by my admission that, yes, I had also published Hal Lawrence's 1979 naval memoir, *A Bloody War*. That title came from the old Navy toast to "a bloody war, and a sickly season," both of which were likely to lead to losses, producing promotion opportunities for keen young officers.

Hal, who came from a Toronto military family, joined the Navy as a midshipman in 1939, and after training was excited to receive his first posting . . . which proved to be a tug in Halifax harbour. This posting was not as unimportant as it sounded. Ever since a German sub had got into the Navy's Home Fleet anchorage at Scapa Flow, torpedoing the battleship *Royal Oak*, at the cost of 833 lives, the Navy had been fussy about manning the submarine nets outside its ports. That U-boats were lurking around Canada's coasts was made painfully clear later, when HMCS *Charlottetown* was torpedoed in the St. Lawrence River, *near Quebec City*. Hal and his shipmates on the *Andree Dupree* supervised the opening and closing of the net protecting Halifax. No U-boat ever got through in the course of the war.

Hal's book is subtitled "One Man's Memories of the Canadian Navy 1939–1945," and it covers a wide variety of exciting actions. But the centre is that same Battle of the Atlantic that we know from Jim Lamb. Here's Hal Lawrence's account of winter 1941:

> The escorts of that winter's convoys rushed from emergency to emergency, from sinking to sinking, outnumbered by U-boats, with inadequate equipment, through survivors howling for help, chasing a precious ASDIC contact that might give them a kill. . . . Sleet, snow, rain, ice a foot thick on the forward superstructure; four hours on watch, two hours chipping ice, sleep and eat in between. It was a macabre and desolate winter.

Even when they were allowed to slow down and send out lifeboats to pick their men out of the water, it was not always pleasant work. Once, Hal reached out to grab one man, and his arm came off in Hal's hand.

But Hal, too, spent many happy hours in the Crow's Nest, and writes about it. Then his ship, HMCS *Oakville*, was sent south, and he became a hero. The *Oakville* found the surfaced U-boat, U-945, and Hal and Petty Officer Powell were ordered to arm themselves and board and capture her. The *Toronto Star*'s subheadline was "U-Boat Rammed Thrice by Corvette *Oakville* Then Two Leap Aboard." (Note the use of "sub-headline.")

The "leaping aboard" was not as simple as it sounds, since they came under friendly fire, and had to jump into the water, and when Hal made it back to the sub, his belt snapped and his naval shorts collapsed around his ankles. He kicked them aside, and prowled around the sub's deck naked, apart from a pistol, which secured the cooperation of the captured Germans (who were being kept below by his pistol threat, as opposed to his alarming naked state). But since Hal didn't speak German, there was a failure to communicate.

> I knelt by the hatch, "*Sprechen Sie Deutsch?*" A clamour told me they all did, "Ja, Ja."
> "No, no, I mean *Sprechen Sie Englisch?*" Silence.
> "How are you going to get them up?" Powell asked mildly.

In the end all is well, Hal escapes the sinking sub just in time, and they all head off to the nearest American base, a place named Guantanamo. In due course, Hal the hero is brought back to Canada. A special propaganda poster of his capture of the sub at gunpoint is produced (tactfully restoring his shorts), and he tours around places like Toronto and, of course, Oakville, spreading the good news of this particular Canadian triumph. On one occasion, however, the rum-loving naval hero celebrated too well, and the resulting radio broadcast, he admits, was not a success . . .

We jump forward almost forty years, to 1979. Hal has stayed on in the Navy after the war, and had a distinguished career. Following retirement in 1965 he has joined the staff of the University of Ottawa, lecturing in English. Even better, he has produced his first book, and we, Macmillan of Canada, are about to publish it. Because of our success with *The Corvette Navy*, I know that we are likely to do very well with this dramatic, well-written book, and I have invited Hal to come to our sales conference to present it.

I should explain that a sales conference is hugely important. It's the event when the entire publishing company, and especially its far-flung sales representatives, assemble in one central spot, often a Toronto hotel, and for days they learn about the new books that they will have for sale to the bookstores and libraries over the next few months. Some readers may remember that my piratical trip to Alistair MacLeod's house was prompted by a looming sales conference, where I had to speak about *No Great Mischief*, and had not yet read it.

In the case of Hal's exciting new book, *A Bloody War*, we had a heroic author (later in the war he had shelled the German-held beaches at D-Day) who was impressively well-spoken. This would send the sales force out on the road with gusto, metaphorically cheering and waving their cutlasses.

Hal was due to appear just before lunch, and I slipped out of the room to meet him and bring him in with due ceremony. The Sheraton Hotel has long corridors, and as I stood there expectantly, with Hal due in five minutes, I saw a strange sight in the distance. It was like a sort of long-range video game, where the travelling object was bounced from one wall to the other, then back again. As the bouncing continued, the approaching figure became . . . Hal, in a dark suit. As he came closer, the dark suit showed many brown, dusty marks, as if it had been in contact with the floor.

When Hal got within range of me, he stood there swaying, one hand at his brow. He repeated the words "flu . . . terrible flu." And weaved some more.

I excused myself and went back into the meeting room to announce that there was a change of plan, and Hal Lawrence would be presenting his book *after* lunch. I took him to a back table at a coffee shop out of the way and poured coffee and food into him. As the time for the afternoon session approached he was doing much better, but I was still very nervous. I helped him to dust off his dark suit, spruced him up, and led him into the conference.

After I introduced him I sat anxiously beside him. It did take him some time to warm up. Then, to my alarm, he became very warm indeed. Soon he was leaning forward, pounding his fist on the table and bellowing, "I *enjoyed* killing Germans!"

The effect on the sales force was dramatic. They loved the old sea-dog and his tales of action, and they practically carried him out of the room on their shoulders. "What a guy!" they said, and couldn't wait to get out and sell his book. It became a huge bestseller, of

Wayne Johnston (1958–)

course — although I never thought then that it would open doors for me in St. John's some day. I'm sorry that Hal is long gone, because he would have loved the Crow's Nest story, about the continuing impact of his book's name in his old haunt.

If I'm happy to accept credit for books that I *did* publish, it's only fair that I should own up to take the blame for fine books that I decided not to publish. So here goes. I was part of the editorial group that turned down Wayne Johnston's 1998 novel, *The Colony of Unrequited Dreams*.

Stupid, stupid, stupid. But publishers are in the business of making hasty, stupid decisions. Intelligent outsiders marvel at how many publishers, for example, turned down *Harry Potter* when J.K. Rowling sent the manuscript around. Insiders know that publishers are dealing with hundreds, no, thousands of manuscripts, and in the rush to cope, stupid mistakes are made. Often.

Since I have made so many in my time, I'm keen to explain that choosing this piece of writing over that one is always a subjective decision, involving judgment. It would be fine to say: "Well, we're looking for a 100,000-word book, and this one comes in at 99,500, so let's take it." No such luck. There are no such objective measures. The editorial meetings typically involve discussion by editors saying, "I've read it, and here's what I think about it" (and many readers will know how rarely book club meetings are unanimous). Meanwhile, a sales manager predicts likely sales for such a book, based on the historical record of similar books. Then there is discussion, and an editorial decision is reached.

I remember the discussion about Wayne's book. We had published him in the past, and enjoyed the process, but neither of the books had been a big success. As for the new novel, *The Colony of Unrequited Dreams* was very long (my current copy, brought out by a wiser publisher, runs to 554 pages), and thus would be expensive, both for the publisher and the book-buyer, which made it risky. And the title made it clear just what an ambitious, risky book this was . . . a first-person account by a real historical figure, not long dead, the remarkable Joey Smallwood, whom we watch as he performs the real historical deeds for which he was famed — and sometimes excoriated — as he changed the history of Newfoundland. To make things more complex the book's other main character, Sheilagh Fielding, is a totally fictitious character, whose unusual relationship with Joey spans many decades, but never involves physical love. To make room for Sheilagh, the "real" Joey's real-life wife, Clara, makes what in effect is only a walk-on appearance.

A very unusual book, in other words, and some of our experienced editorial team did not like it. I felt constrained from joining the debate too vigorously, because I feared that my judgment was impaired by the fact that I had known — and been charmed by — the real Joey. In the 1970s he had visited a number of Toronto-based publishers to whip up interest in acquiring his memoirs. You'll recall that he visited me and a colleague at Doubleday Canada and began to tell the two of us about his planned book. As his oratory flowed, he jumped out of his chair, seized his lapels, and began to pace around the small room, addressing us like an outport meeting. I was hopelessly smitten, and stayed that way — which in the Wayne Johnston debate kept me more in the role of listener.

The book's advocates at the meeting, of course, caught the sweep of Wayne's ambition, which was to tell a sardonic version of Newfoundland's long journey through history until she joined Canada in 1949. They spoke admiringly of his larger-than-life central character and of the outrageous fun Wayne has with Joey during his years as premier, when his determination to get his people to turn their backs on the sea led him to throw money at any outside industrialist who promised to set up a factory in Newfoundland (although fortunately when a condom factory was suggested, it was kept away from Conception Bay). Perhaps the most outrageous of his advisors in all this was Dr. Alfred Valdmanis, a Latvian economist who shrewdly made a point of always gravely addressing Joey as "my premier." This is *non-fiction*.

As an inspired piece of *fiction* Wayne has Sheilagh Fielding travel with Joey and the Latvian deal-maker, apparently sleeping three to a bed, as she reports in her newspaper column:

As for your premier and your director-general of economic development, dear reader, they will often lie awake, late into the night, side by side in their pyjamas, their hands behind their heads, talking, planning strategies, devising schemes. To think that the most masterful of which to date may have had their origins in pillow talk!

"We will dot Conception Bay with factories," your premier said the other night. I, too, lay there, listening, wondering if I had perhaps misjudged them.

They are a lively, fun-loving pair who betimes will while away the hours playing "pedals," a Latvian children's game in which two participants lying flat on their backs at opposite ends of a bed, with their hands behind their heads, place the soles of their bare feet together and "pedal" each other like bicycles, the object of the game being to pedal one's opponent off the bed, though my premier and the Latvian are so evenly matched that neither can budge the other and they pedal themselves into a state of mutual exhaustion, then fall asleep.

Brilliant! You can see why, when we turned the book down, it went on to win numerous prizes, to gain ecstatic reviews ("Wayne Johnston is a brilliant and accomplished writer," said E. Annie Proulx, and "As beautiful and imaginative as writing gets," said David Macfarlane, in the *Globe and Mail*), and to establish Wayne as one of Canada's best writers, a rank that has been confirmed by subsequent books such as *Baltimore's Mansion* (1999), *The Navigator of New York* (2001), and *The Son of a Certain Woman* (2013).

Raised in Newfoundland, Wayne now makes his home in Toronto, where his cheery face makes him a welcome presence in his neighbourhood. As anyone who has met him at an authors' festival will tell you, he's a great storyteller in person. Here's one story, about his return to Newfoundland as writer-in-residence at Memorial University.

He was the third writer in the post, so the professor behind the still-young program was very keen that everything should go well. Wayne soon got an excited phone call from him with the great news that *the Dean himself* had invited both of them to lunch. It was made clear to Wayne that he had to be on his best behaviour . . . the future of the program depended on the lunch going smoothly.

And so it did, at first. Because lunch was at a grand old St. John's hotel with a traditional menu, both Wayne and the professor politely ordered the cod's cheeks on the menu. They were both working their way through this delicacy, chatting politely with *the Dean himself*, when Wayne saw the professor turn red, and hunch his shoulders a little. Concerned, Wayne asked him if he was all right. He waved a hand dismissively, as if to say, "Yes, I'm fine, don't worry about me." But he got even redder, and hunched even more. "Are you choking?" Wayne asked in alarm. The professor tried to wave away the question, not wanting, at any cost, to disturb this important lunch. But as Wayne pressed the question, he finally, very sheepishly, nodded. Wayne sounded the alarm about *a man choking here*, and as if by magic, a flying squad of waiters descended on the table, and dragged the victim away, his feet trailing. All eyes followed them to the kitchen.

A short time later the professor returned. He was no longer red-faced. In fact, he was a little pale, wiping his mouth on a napkin. "My goodness," he said in wonder, "these boys know how to deal with that."

And so the man who had been willing to sacrifice his life to preserve the writer-in-residence program lived to look after it for another year. His fondness for cod's cheeks may, however, have been lost forever.

The famous journalist and historian Richard Gwyn became a Newfoundlander by marriage. His beloved wife, Sandra (author of such fine books as *The Private Capital*), was the creator of the phrase praising Newfoundland's astonishing cultural scene as "flowers on the rock." This recognized the achievements of old Newfoundlanders like the painter Maurice Cullen and the poet E.J. Pratt (who was a colleague of Northrop Frye at Toronto's Victoria University), even before the explosion of writing talent with Lisa Moore, Michael Crummey, Michael Winter, Kathleen Winter, and others, worth a whole book in themselves. Even after Sandra's death Richard kept the faith with Newfoundland, where he and Carol Bishop Gwyn still live every summer.

His superb 1971 biography of Joey is singled out for special thanks by Wayne Johnston at the end of his novel with the words "I acknowledge a special debt to D.W. Prowse's *A History of Newfoundland . . .* and to Richard Gwyn's *Smallwood: The Unlikely Revolutionary*." I happen to know that Richard is not completely happy about how extensively his book was used in the novel, although he has made no formal complaint. I followed my recent rereading of Wayne's book by rereading Richard's well-researched account, and was struck by the problems of patrolling this area. I'd urge you to take a look at both books, and see what you think.

One of the finest things about Richard Gwyn's book is that he pays full tribute to the man who introduced me to Newfoundland, my author and friend Harold Horwood. I devote a whole chapter in my *Stories About Storytellers* to the amazing Harold, whom I describe as a "Neglected Genius." He played a huge role as Joey's "left-hand man" in the campaign to join Canada, one of the so-called "Bolsheviks" around him. Then Harold was elected to represent Labrador in the Smallwood government. After he broke with Joey in 1951, Gwyn quotes him once describing Smallwood as "a mountebank . . . with an inferiority complex the size of Signal Hill." Harold's role as a "fierce critic as a columnist for the *Evening Telegram*" so infuriated Smallwood that he approached the paper to offer them the provincial printing contract — worth many, many dollars — if they would drop Harold's column. They refused.

If publishing *The Corvette Navy* opened some doors for me in St. John's, editing Cassie Brown's *Death on the Ice* has opened just about every door in Newfoundland. I've told the story of how Cassie, a young woman from the southwest of the Rock, became a reporter, a columnist, and a playwright in St. John's. At some point she became fascinated by the story of the great Newfoundland sealing disaster of 1914 (and the "Newfoundland" tag applies twice, since the seventy-eight men who died on the ice were off the sealing ship *Newfoundland*, and the disaster was the worst in the history of the island). She started to read everything she could dig up on the event — court records, memoirs, and other documents — and then interviewed the few survivors she could find.

Then, out of the blue, she sent it in to me as a potential book. I didn't get it wrong this time; I didn't turn her manuscript down. But I didn't accept it, either. I told her that it was much too short to make a book, and she would need to dig up more about the weather records, and about the ships involved, and research the living conditions aboard . . . and so on. And then we would see. Usually when an author gets a letter full of troublesome requests like that, the book never happens. The author decides that life's too short. But Cassie

Brown — silver-haired Cassie Brown with the straight-backed bearing of a queen — didn't give up. She buckled down to the challenge, so that by the end she had spent two full years researching the book, and a full year writing it.

When the revised version came in, I was ecstatic. I quickly brought Harold Horwood (a superb writer, sprung from a line of sealing skippers) to contribute to the project, and his enthusiasm for what we were creating was total: "*Death on the Ice* is the most moving story I have ever read. I am proud to have played some small part in preparing it for preparation" is how he ends his Introduction. I even hired a young fellow (hey, this was 1972) named David Blackwood to create the perfect cover, showing the lost party on the ice. The original print hangs in our house today, thanks to the generosity of David Blackwood, the young printmaker in the leather apron.

The 1972 book became a classic, known to everyone in Newfoundland, and many far beyond. The year of my last visit, 2014, marked the 100th anniversary of the disaster. In The Rooms, the combined art gallery and museum and provincial archives high on the hill above St. John's near the basilica, there was a special display devoted to the disaster. A moving short film by the NFB, "54 Hours" (named for the hours the soaked, freezing men were left stranded on the heaving icefield), written by my admirable friend Michael Crummey, a man with talents galore, played on a continuous loop. Meanwhile photos of the men on the ice, and the corpses being brought in to St. John's, flickered on the wall opposite. Downstairs, in the bookstore, copies of Cassie's book were piled up, still adorned by David Blackwood's cover. I turned to the description on the back, and recognized it. I had written it in 1972, and it was still going strong.

Once, on an Adventure Canada Cruise down the Labrador coast, I had the eerie experience of talking about this tragedy, soon after we had sailed over the sealing grounds off the northwestern tip of Newfoundland. This meant that we had just sailed over the bones of the drowned men from the *Newfoundland* who had dropped off the ice and were listed as "died and never found": Henry Jordan, David Locke, Michael Murray, Art Mouland, "Uncle Ezra" Melendy, Henry Dowden, James Howell, Philip Holloway.

Say the names.

If you're interested in pursuing this further, it's possible for a visitor to walk a few blocks to see where this tragedy hit St. John's. Just south of the War Memorial on Duckworth Street (beside the steps to the Crow's Nest, and near the larger-than-life statues to the Newfoundland dog, and its rival, the Labrador dog) you're looking at the pier where 10,000 horrified people gathered to see the *Bellaventure* returning the stacked corpses of the frozen sealers. Just west of there, on Water Street, you'll find the King George V Institute (the foundation stone, apparently, was laid by the king in Buckingham Palace by means of "an electrical current," on the day of his coronation in 1910). The institute served as a hospital for the frostbitten sealers who survived. Its swimming pool was used to thaw out the seventy bodies of those men and boys who did not.

It was such a hammer blow to Newfoundland that the outbreak of the First World War later that year seemed almost an anticlimax. Indeed, the story of *Death on the Ice* is so central to Newfoundland that in his novel about Joey Smallwood's life, Wayne Johnston has devoted many powerful pages to Joey's memories of sailing as a journalist on the *Newfoundland* that fateful year, and watching helplessly from the ship, because "Captain Kean was adamant that if I set foot on the ice, I would no longer have the use of his telegrapher." In Johnston's telling, Joey Smallwood's horror at what he sees onboard ship, out of the porthole, and from the deck of the returning ship as the corpses are unloaded in St. John's, apparently led him to take up the Socialist cause.

It's a powerful story, and the scenes of the frozen men on the ice are unforgettable. It's also fine fiction. Let me stress that: Joey Smallwood was born on Christmas Eve, 1900. When the Newfoundland disaster occurred in spring 1914, he was thirteen years old.

There can be no quibbling about the symbolic importance of the event to all Newfoundlanders. Farley Mowat quotes one old man saying, "It seems to me as something broke in the heart of our old island that spring of 1914 and never rightly healed again in after times."

Turning to Farley Mowat, Harold Horwood, as so often, is my point of entry. When he still lived near St. John's, at Beachy Cove, Harold would have his good friend and fellow naturalist Farley stay with him. The visitor so loved the caressing sea breezes that he would stroll the beach in a pair of stout boots — and nothing else. This scandalized the local fishermen. There were complaints. Farley strode on. This, after all, is the man who once declared that to sell more books he would happily do handstands in his kilt in any town square in Canada. Compared to that (and of course he wore his kilt dangerously untrammelled) why should he care about a few prudish Newfoundland fishermen — normally a contradiction in terms — averting their eyes in shock.

When Farley's long and creative life came to an end in May 2014, I was asked by a number of radio and TV programs to speak about his amazing career. Such interviews are always hurried and unprepared and, in my case, often inexpert. I feel that I did not do Farley justice, and would like to do better now.

Mind you, in his ninety-three years Farley led so many lives, and produced so many books of so many sorts, that he deserves a whole book. In fact he already has one, a fine biography entitled simply *Farley: The Life of Farley Mowat* (2002), by James King. It is an informative, balanced look at a fascinating character, and I found much there that surprised me. For example, who knew that Farley's father, Angus, a prominent librarian, was also, in effect, a bigamist who set up a rival household with another woman and enlisted his son in a conspiracy of silence against his mother?

There are so many Farleys — son, naturalist, soldier, sailor, possibly tinker (but with no recorded tailoring or candlestick-making), Northerner, husband, historian, environmentalist, biographer, children's book author, father, controversialist, nationalist, enthusiastic celebrant, friend, and many more — that it is hard to write about the whole life of the whole man. So I plan to see him through the prism of Newfoundland.

His 1989 book, *The New Founde Land*, which I was proud to publish at McClelland & Stewart, speaks in the Introduction of his determination one day to produce "a magnum opus about the Rock and its people. One day I was bemoaning my failure to Newfoundlander and fellow writer Harold Horwood. He brought me up short.

"'Farley,' he snapped in his waspish way. 'Don't be so bloody dense! You've already written your "Great Book" about us, but

Farley Mowat (1921–2014)

you've been flinging the pieces of it about like so much confetti. All you need to do is gather the bits together. Why don't you just get on with it?'"

And so he did.

The book is an updated collection of his best writing about the province down through the decades. It begins magnificently:

> Newfoundland is of the sea. A mighty granite stopper thrust into the bell-mouth of the Gulf of St. Lawrence, it turns its back upon the American continent, barricading itself behind the three-hundred-mile-long rampart that forms its western coast. Its other coasts all face the open ocean, and are so slashed and convoluted with bays, inlets, runs, and fiords that they present more than five thousand miles of shoreline to the sweep of the Atlantic. Everywhere the hidden reefs and rocks (called, with dreadful explicitness, "sunkers") wait to rip the bellies of unwary vessels. Nevertheless, these coasts are a seaman's world, for the harbours and havens they offer are numberless.

Then he's off to "the high, rolling plateaux of the interior, darkly wooded to the north but bone-bare to the south," and it's clear that this superb writer really knows Newfoundland. There are splendid pieces from his books like *Westviking* (1965), about the early Norse explorers. Then he deals with the Outport Way, which brings him into conflict with Joey Smallwood and his policies. "Newfoundlanders were directed to reject the sea which had nurtured them for five centuries. Fishing and fishermen, ships and seamen, were deemed obsolete. Progress, so the new policy dictated, demanded the elimination of most of the thirteen hundred outport communities that encircled the island, and the transformation of their people into industrial workers." (There was a time, James King reminds us, when Farley made friendly overtures to Joey, and they went so well that Joey suggested that Farley might write his biography. These warm approaches, which even involved Farley being flown to a dinner in a government helicopter, outraged Harold Horwood, who wrote to Farley: "Watch Joey! Watch the fucker! He has designs on you, and you're not beyond the power of flattery any more than the rest of us.")

In the end, Farley's opinion of Joey and his ruthless clearing of the outports was not charmed out of him, and came through loud and clear. Just listen. The setting here is a "snug kitchen of a fisherman's home in the outport of Francois."

The father speaks to the writer from away. "It's been fine you came to visit. I hopes you found some yarns to write, and you'll make a good voyage out of it. But still and all, I'm wondering could you do one thing for we? Could you, do you think, say how it was with we? We wouldn't want it thought, you understand, that we never tried the hardest as us could to make a go of things. I'd like for everyone to know we never would have left the places we was reared, but . . . we . . . was . . . drove!"

In the silence that follows, he repeats, "Aye, Jesus, Jesus God, but we was drove!"

On another occasion Farley tells of going out after cod in a fishing skiff with some local men.

> One of our number, a young man just entering his twenties, was working alongside the skiff from a pitching dory. He was having a hard time holding his position because of a big swell running in from seaward. An unexpected heave on the twine threw him off balance and his right arm slipped between the dory and the skiff just as they rolled together. The crack of breaking bones was clearly audible. He sat back heavily on the thwart of his dory and held his arm up for inspection. It was streaming with blood. A wrist-watch, just purchased and much treasured, had been completely crushed and driven into the flesh.

In this emergency, the skiff's master prepares to drop the net and go to rescue the injured man. "Don't ye be so foolish!" the young man shouts, and proceeds, with one hand and his teeth, to hold his position with his oar until they take him on board. For twenty minutes he grins encouragement while they haul in every last cod.

Farley went along with him to the doctor, "who set the bones and took sixteen stitches to close the wound." As they leave the office the young man apologizes to Farley. "Skipper, I hopes I never spiled yer marnin!"

"No, he had not 'spiled' my morning. And how was I to find words to tell him what kind of a man I knew him to be?"

Books drawn from in this selection include *This Rock within the Sea* (1968), *Wake of the Great Sealers* (1973), *Sea of Slaughter* (1984), *Grey Seas Under* (1958, which will have you grasping the arms of your chair as Atlantic waves batter your walls), and *The Boat Who Wouldn't Float* (1969). A word about that last book, which Farley's biographer calls "magnificently exaggerated." The joint purchase he and Jack McClelland made, on Harold Horwood's advice, of a little Newfoundland bummer, makes for a very dangerous book. First, Harold's Newfoundland pride was offended by the idea that he would ever actively recommend a bad boat. Second, Farley not only involved his friend and publisher Jack in the venture, he also wrote about him, *and made him a figure of fun!* This, I must explain, is not only dangerous conduct for any author, it is, in my opinion, simply reprehensible.

That said, the really significant addition to the crew as they sink their way around Newfoundland is not the co-owner, Jack McClelland, but a daring young woman named Claire Wheeler. Before long she and Farley (long estranged from his first wife, Fran Thornhill) were living together in Burgeo, on the south coast of Newfoundland. In time, they drove all the way to Mexico with the faithful Harold Horwood, so that Farley's divorce could be followed by a wedding. To this outsider's eye, Farley and Claire were a happy couple right to the end of his life. They both were lucky.

Things were not always easy. As Farley's 1972 book, *A Whale for the Killing*, reveals, his environmental instincts conflicted with the instincts of too many of his Burgeo neighbours for their stay to be prolonged, and Claire and he left Newfoundland in 1967, to return to Ontario.

His legacy as an author was immense. Forty-five books, in sixty countries, with about fifteen million readers across the world is Ken McGoogan's estimate. Certainly millions of readers knew Farley Mowat's books, whether from happy times as kids spent shivering over *The Curse of the Viking Grave* (1966), or as intrigued adults learning about Siberia in *Sibir* (1970), or laughing over Farley the wolf-watcher being watched by wolves in *Never Cry Wolf* (1963, inexpertly translated into Russian as *Wolves, Please Don't Cry* — although it caused Russia to change its laws on the culling of wolves).

It's interesting to learn that his librarian father, Angus, liked to place exciting non-fiction books among the fiction titles on his shelves, to ensnare fiction-loving readers into giving them a try. In the same spirit, I think, Farley employed many of the eye-catching tricks of fiction to liven up his non-fiction books.

In fact, his old friend Silver Donald Cameron has suggested that perhaps we should acknowledge Farley as the father of "creative non-fiction," a style of book that is increasingly popular (leaving Myrna Kostash as perhaps the mother). Ken McGoogan, in *How the Scots Invented Canada*, writes perceptively about that, citing Farley's *People of the Deer* (1951), a bombshell about the mistreatment of the Ihalmiut people in the North: "Years before the 'New Journalism' became fashionable, he created his real-life narrative by using techniques more associated with fiction — creating scenes, for example. The spectacular success of the resulting book — critically, commercially, and in effecting political change — launched Mowat on a singular career as a writer-activist."

Certainly, we can acknowledge Farley as one of the world's first environmental writers, a man who was aware that our ongoing battle against Nature would in the end defeat us. No one who reads *Sea of Slaughter* can be in any doubt about that.

In his personal life, Farley was such a pugnacious fellow that he seemed to be constantly feuding with someone. He and W.O. Mitchell feuded for decades about just how helpful Bill had been to him as the fiction editor of *Maclean's* magazine, a quarrel you'll find summarized in the Mitchell biographies *W.O.* and *Mitchell*. There were people in Port Hope, Farley's final berth, who were not on speaking terms with him, and vice versa. He even had a brief feud of sorts with me, I think, though the details are long forgotten. I'm glad to be reminded by James King's book that after Farley chose, late in his life, to leave McClelland & Stewart, I didn't abandon him: King writes that "in subsequent years, Gibson has approached Farley and Claire several times to ask them to come back to McClelland & Stewart." I was always glad to see him, and for a small man, he certainly knew how to fill a room. Once, when Avie Bennett and I took him to lunch in Port Hope, I noted how well the restaurant staff were treating him. "Ah, yes," he said. "The last time I was in here I was with Sigourney Weaver" (who starred in the movie made from his book *Virunga*). We all will miss him.

For a Canadian author, being invited to attend the Writers at Woody Point event in August is the equivalent of winning a major international prize. It has been running for more than ten years now, and has attracted a galaxy of literary stars "from away," like Michael Ondaatje, Richard Ford, Alexander McCall Smith, Linda Spalding, Elizabeth Hay, and Will Ferguson — bolstered by the major talents from Newfoundland such as Lisa Moore, Michael Crummey, Michael Winter, and others, who could fill this chapter many times over.

It all started with Stephen Brunt, the well-known Toronto-based sportswriter and broadcaster. Steve has written a number of fine books, including one for me that took the reader behind the scenes in the NHL. Unfortunately, the terms allowed the NHL to "approve" — that is censor — the TV show and the accompanying book. This meant that I spent an unforgettable time negotiating with my friend Nancy Lee, the head of CBC Sports, over how many swear words could be quoted ("OK, we'll drop these three 'shits' if we can keep this one 'bastard'") without tarnishing the NHL's valuable image. The role of publisher contains many surprises, and Steve was sympathetic to my dilemma as I fought to retain his accurate reporting.

Far from the NHL, and its coaches who exclaim "Oh, my goodness!" in moments of stress, Steve had the idea that outsiders would love to discover Woody Point, his idyllic summer home. The tiny community of about 700 lies halfway up the long west coast of Newfoundland, surrounded by Gros Morne National Park — a little like an East Coast Banff, without the fudge shops. The sort of sweeping views of fiords and mountains that you get in those clever ads from the Newfoundland Tourism folks lie all around the little town, and the open waters of the Gulf are just around the corner, as Jane and I found when we borrowed kayaks from our friends Peter and Robert early one morning.

Gros Morne, of course, is a World Heritage Site. Its high, orange Tablelands (amazingly, derived from the ocean floor thrust upward, as tectonic plates collided) were what proved that the revolutionary continental drift theories of Toronto's John Tuzo Wilson and Newfoundland's own "Hank" Williams were true.

A key moment in the history of the Woody Point writers' festival was when Stephen Brunt's local crew (including his wife of undetermined ethnic heritage, Jeanie MacFarlane) persuaded the marvellous Shelagh Rogers, of CBC fame, to get involved. Now she is the voice of the festival, introducing all of the main events at the grand old Heritage Theatre. She even conducts live onstage interviews for her CBC Radio show, *The Next Chapter*. Her talk with Greg Malone, actor, comedian, and author of *Don't Tell the Newfoundlanders*, made astonishing listening for anyone who, like me, believed that Newfoundland joined Canada gratefully, after an honest vote.

The writers' events run morning, noon, and night. My own show *began* at 11 at night, followed by some more music, by Pamela Morgan and Sandy Johnston. (Later, Shelagh announced Pamela as "Pamela Anderson," which led to many jokes busting out all over.) Often the first readings were at 9:30 in the morning, and the nature walks and other events through the day kept us hopping, and sometimes missing appealing readings that clashed with our chosen event. Saturday morning started with a church hall fundraising breakfast for the local firemen, and the Saturday and Sunday evenings ended with a big dance at the local Legion.

We were staying within earshot of all this, at a central B&B named "Aunt Jane's." How could we resist? Will Ferguson was there, too, and others came and went.

The usual unbelievable coincidences occurred. After my show a woman from the faraway Cypress Hills district in Saskatchewan shyly informed me that when she was growing up she knew my cowboy author, R.D. Symons. She was even able to tell me what happened to his son, Gerry, ranching on another frontier in Colombia in the 1970s, under siege by Native people who attacked the ranch with flaming arrows. The news was not good.

And when we had dinner with the multi-talented Des Walsh and his lady, Ruth, he told me that he had known Harold Horwood well, even attending the rebel school called Animal Farm that Harold established, in the teeth of fierce St. John's police pressure. The police were deeply suspicious of long-haired kids who were likely to smoke dope and use words like "pigs," but regular raids never produced any culprits. Like all schoolboys, he could even do a fine imitation of his teacher, Harold, throwing back his long-haired head, before speaking in what Farley accurately called his "waspish" way.

On one occasion at the Legion bar in Woody Point I ran into a sturdy barrel of a man who had enjoyed my show. His name, he said, was Young. I was off right away, talking about my father's mother, Jessie Young, before he cut short this promising exploration. No, he told me, his family were pirates, and they had *stolen* the respectable name of Young.

A key part of understanding the lure of Woody Point is realizing that you are part of the community. People who elsewhere might be strangers come up to you on the street and chat. Fishermen and carpenters (I'll try not to be too biblical) reveal that they were at your show, and enjoyed it, but have a question about Brian Mulroney. Going out for dinner produces comments and questions from the staff, and paying your bill involves a long conversation. Village life! That's what I grew up with in Scotland, so I loved every minute of it.

I had been to Woody Point once before, coming in by sea. This was on an Adventure Canada Cruise, where I was a member of the staff, and Alistair MacLeod was the main onboard attraction for the 100 or so guests. We started in Ungava Bay, sailed north around Cape Chidley, then ploughed all the way south down the Labrador coast, stopping ashore in the Torngat Mountains, and at remote settlements like Hopedale. Just north of Newfoundland was where I gave my talk, above the graves of the *Death on the Ice* victims. Then we passed Red Bay (the old Basque whaling station) to starboard, and sailed down the Strait of Belle Isle and docked at Woody Point.

The next day we went around Port aux Basques, en route to La Poile (accessible only by sea) but not before we had passed Stephenville, and Black Duck, the scene of Charles Ritchie's adventures pioneering in Newfoundland. *Charles Ritchie?* The legendary Canadian diplomat and diarist, our ambassador to LBJ's Washington and Edward Heath's London, the ultimate reedy cocktail-party aesthete . . . a Newfoundland pioneer?

The proof is to be found in the book of diaries that I coaxed out of him after *The Siren Years* (1974), his first book of diaries, had won the Governor General's Award. *An Appetite for Life: The Education of a Young Diarist* (1977) takes us through his time as a languid young man in Halifax, loafing around in the Bower, and then his adventures among the upper-class twits at Oxford in the time of Evelyn Waugh's

Brideshead Revisited. In between, however, lies a spell at Black Duck, Newfoundland, where his mother believes that a spell of manual labour, working for some English friends, the du Plat Taylors, will make a man of him. Charles, I should explain, was always built along the lines of a stick, and was physically skilled only in Halifax parlour pursuits such as handling a cigarette holder with elegance.

The diary entries are predictable. "The men are from around here and are half French. I talked a lot with them. They are very entertaining company, but the work went rather slowly." Soon the diaries are full of mentions of the lack of plumbing, and the abundance of flies (he even coins the word "flyey"), and before long we find:

> Spent the morning shovelling manure and then cut down trees, dragging up roots, etc. I am getting a bit handier with an axe but it rather worries me that I don't believe Colonel du Plat Taylor thinks I am as useful about the place as he had hoped. Probably he expected me to be a Canadian woodsman, and that I am not. He never says anything critical about my work but looks at the results silently and sighs, which makes me nervous.

In due course the du Plat Taylors ("They should have lived at the time the Empire was being founded. Mrs du Plat Taylor could run an empire single-handed.") recall that they have other friends coming to help, and Charles ("not a Canadian woodsman") has to leave early. But he is impressed with having got to know "the Newfoundlanders themselves. They live as they did in the eighteenth century, and have not met with democracy, compulsory education, or the motor-car. This gives the people in the fishing villages a character of their own."

I enjoyed publishing the inimitable politician John C. Crosbie, and we stay in touch. During my last visit, he told me a new story about the days when he was promoting his 1997 political memoir, *No Holds Barred.* Apparently he showed up at a major signing event where every entrance was plastered with posters announcing that he would be signing his new book. Unfortunately, the title of the book was given as *No Holes Barred*, which John thought altered the meaning in an unexpected direction.

Although he has now retired from his post as Lieutenant Governor

("Now I have to lick me own stamps," he lamented to me on the phone), John remains incorrigible. The main headline in the *Telegram* the day I left began with the words "CROSBIE RANTS . . ."

Rex Murphy is another interesting case. He clearly is one of those people who has glided into prominence on good looks alone, and the world of television is predictably full of them. So I was suspicious that Rex was just a pretty face, although his defenders tried to persuade me that his Rhodes Scholarship surely meant something. In the end, impressed by what I might call the rigorous courtesy of his hosting of *Cross-Country Check-Up* ("And how would you go about ensuring all of these voluntary confessions that would free up our courts, sir?" — a made-up example), I arranged to publish a selection of his most opinionated pieces. The resulting collection was highly satisfactory, but when it came time for him to promote the book, Rex was missing in action. His generalized enthusiasm for the promotional task always foundered on specifics, and we had to disappoint dozens of hosts keen to have Rex come along on a particular date that proved impossible.

I notice that Rex has appeared in public to promote subsequent books. And I note with gratitude the fine, eloquent appreciation he wrote after Alistair MacLeod's death.

Donna Morrissey is a very successful novelist, and a bright, lively figure, and our paths crossed at the Elephant Mountain Festival in B.C. She has many fine stories to tell, especially this one, which explains that anyone from outside Newfoundland is "from away." As she tells it, she was part of a group of excited teenage girls visiting Toronto for the first time. There was a problem with a camera. So they took it into a store. The man in the store examined it gravely, then announced that he would have to send it away to be fixed. Confusion!

"But," protested one of the girls, gesturing at the shop around them, "this *is* away!"

I never met Ray Guy, but I admired him immensely. He was the Newfoundland writer who pushed many boundaries. He opposed Joey Smallwood in print when that took courage. More frivolously, he brought out a collection based on the sturdy habit in Newfoundland of calling sea urchins "whore's eggs." The title *You Might Know Them as Sea Urchins, Ma'am* was published by Clyde Rose in 1975. Clyde, now retired from Breakwater Books, makes his home at Woody

Point, and took us for a spin in his boat around the nearby waters of Bonne Bay — although the promised bald eagles failed to show up on time. And we missed the sea urchins.

Ray Guy's lifetime achievement was to smuggle into print (in a mainstream magazine like *Weekend* or *The Canadian*) the most mischievous bilingual joke of all time. Noticing the English possibilities of the French word for a seal, "un phoque," Ray produced a fake heraldic description for a seal placed horizontally on an ice-field, as in the Newfoundland coat of arms, as being in a "flying" or "volant" position. This piece of heraldry, Ray solemnly assured his readers, led to the adoption of the official Newfoundland motto: "Je ne donne pas un phoque volant."

Finally, we move all the way east to St. John's. For me, there were two great moments in my visit there in May 2014. The first was when, thanks to my connection with the fine folk who run sailing cruises with Adventure Canada, I was able to go across the harbour to the secret side opposite downtown. There's nothing there on the south side apart from security gates and rocks and birches and spruce trees and green fuel pipes slaloming down the steep hill from the giant white fuel tanks. As the *Sea Adventurer* fuelled up, I helped carry things aboard, pausing to survey the lounge where Alistair MacLeod and I had performed. Meanwhile, across the harbour lay the most glorious view of St. John's, from the ships along the waterfront all the way up to the twin towers of the basilica. It was an unmatched view, like seeing Quebec City from across the river, and I was among the very few visitors privileged to have it.

Yet for me, forever, the central event of the Writers' Union AGM in St. John's in May 2014 was the formal banquet, when I was asked to deliver a toast to Alistair MacLeod. I followed eloquent tributes to Heather Robertson (by Erna Paris), and to Farley Mowat (by Silver Donald Cameron).

Here is what I said — and it's wonderfully appropriate that Alistair, who famously used to write a last line for his story midway through, then write towards it, has given me this target. It strikes me as a perfect ending for a book about Canadian writers and writing: a toast to Alistair MacLeod.

Mavis Gallant . . . Heather Robertson . . . Farley Mowat . . . Alistair MacLeod. It has been a hard campaign, and we have had our losses. After Alistair's death, John Vaillant wrote to me from B.C. saying that as a writer he felt like a sailor alone at sea who was finding all of his guiding lighthouses winking out, one by one.

At the age of seventy-seven Alistair MacLeod died as the sun rose on Easter Sunday. This was in the Windsor hospital where he had lain since a hard stroke had felled him in January — something the MacLeod family had carefully kept private.

As an old friend (and Alistair and I last appeared together in public in November at the Harbourfront Tribute to Alice Munro — you could always count on Alistair's generous help at such events) I was in constant touch with Alistair and Anita, so I knew about his stroke. In fact, at the end of February Jane and I were able to visit him in the hospital. Although the stroke had paralyzed his right side — knocking out the right hand that had held the pen that set his stories aloft, and making speech very difficult for him — he had prepared to greet me with a joke. Had we, he wanted to know, "been dancing at Scotsville recently?"

This was a reference to a summer visit to Cape Breton where Alistair and Anita had taken us square dancing in the Scotsville Fire Hall, and we had seen them happily whirling among their friends and neighbours, clearly part of the community. Yet as Alistair's fame spread around the world (for instance, thanks to Japanese translations of his books) his Cape Breton neighbours had found themselves directing Japanese pilgrims to Alistair's house, where he and his admirers from afar, sharing no common language but their humanity, would solemnly exchange silent, smiling bows.

Most of Alistair's stories — and most of *No Great Mischief*, his only novel — were set in Cape Breton. But many of you here tonight will recall that the title story in his first collection, *The Lost Salt Gift of Blood*, is set right here in St. John's. It's a powerful story about a father, and a son who will never know him. I made the mistake of reading it on the train down to Windsor for the first visitation, on the day after his death, and I'm sure some passengers are still talking about the man with the beard who spent so much time in tears.

I heard that there were many tears at his funeral in Broad Cove, Cape Breton. In fact his cousin Kevin, a pallbearer, told me that he wept so copiously that a Cape Breton neighbour was highly impressed. "Kevin," she said, "when I die, I want you at my funeral."

Laughter and tears.

As you know, Alistair's greatest pride was for his family, Anita and their six children, and the grandchildren he used to scandalize by saying, "See you later . . . crocodile!"

And this, of course, was the beloved writer whose death was mourned across Canada and around the world. The *New York Times*, for example, devoted half a page to a fine obituary — which unfortunately targeted a villainous publisher who travelled to Windsor to seize the manuscript of *No Great Mischief*. (And I should tell you that Heather Robertson was part of that story. That fateful day I met her at the Toronto airport and told her that I was off to Windsor to grab Alistair's manuscript. Heather was torn: her natural instinct was to defend a writer against a bullying publisher — but what if the publisher was acting for the common good? Tough call. A year later, Heather was part of the jury that unanimously awarded the Trillium Prize to *No Great Mischief*.)

And Alistair, as some of you may know, went on to describe my benef-icent visit as "a home invasion." That is, when he was not employing what, after last night, we might call "The Vanderhaeghe Variation," where he claimed that for months he had tried in vain to get Doug Gibson to read his novel.

And now he's gone. And no authors' festival will ever be quite the same, because to be with Alistair was to be in touch with greatness disguised by modest, friendly decency. As I told the Canadian Press, he was a great writer, and a great man.

And yet . . . he's not really gone. Because as everyone in this room realizes — and as Heather and Farley certainly realized — writers have found a way to cheat death, to allow you to meet them long after their death. The work lives on. And what also lives on is the impact of lines like the unforgettable final words of *No Great Mischief*: "All of us are better when we're loved."

So many discoveries. A proud love-child. A careful suicide. An admired writer killed, in effect, by a jealous sister. A PEI woman who changed her name because of *Spit Delaney's Island*. A future prime minister who used arson to win a student debate. Stories about wolves, bears, hockey players, and bush pilots. A little bird hitching a ride on a salmon's back. A moment of inspired grace from David Johnston, when he was the principal at McGill. And Jane Austen appearing out of a crowd in Queen Charlotte City.

In *Stories About Storytellers*, my first book, shrewd readers spotted that a theme was how much I enjoyed travelling around Canada, getting to know the country and its people. Can you imagine how much joy it brought me to be able to promote that book by taking my show about it on the road, travelling to all ten provinces?

Memories crowd in. The sound of a solitary sandpiper as we walked across the open prairie with Trevor Herriot, and the silence inside W.O. Mitchell's boyhood home in Weyburn. The taste of the lobster supper in PEI, the dulse on Grand Manan, the wild saskatoons in Nelson, and the raspberries I gathered in Jasper with a bear around the bend on the trail. The shock of being plunged into shadow as the *Queen Mary 2* glided past us into Halifax harbour. The feel of my last hug with Don Starkell in Winnipeg.

Or performing my show on a barstool in Toronto's hip Ossington district, or on the stage of Quebec City's ancient Morrin Centre, or in Moose Jaw's grand old theatre, or fighting the sound of snow-making machines offstage at Collingwood's Blue Mountain, a local hazard — not to mention striding unzipped around the Improv Theatre stage in Vancouver, or properly clad among great paintings in the Windsor Art Gallery, or in the Sunshine Coast's giant log auditorium, near Gibson's, where later I posed with my arm around the oilskin-clad central statue of George Gibson.

So many stories, as you've seen. What they have in common is the Canadian book world. My wonderful tour was always created by book festivals, or bookstores, or libraries, or universities, or schools, or book clubs, or other authors, who were often our generous hosts. I hope that you've enjoyed meeting some of our finest authors, and being reminded of their books, and tempted by them. Books supply a special sort of passport in this country, and I'm proud to be a part of that world.

A suggestion for everyone, if you've enjoyed this book. Canada is a country with a remarkable history and spectacular geography. Get out there and explore it.

So many people right across Canada helped me with this book that I'm certain the list that follows will be incomplete. My apologies. You know who you are, and how you helped, and that I'm grateful.

Province by province, I was helped and encouraged by hosts, guides, advance readers, and friends, including authors quoted here who may not have been aware of the help they were giving. Special thanks go to my volunteer readers and advisers, Silver Donald Cameron, Andreas Schroeder, Don Nichol, Trevor Herriot, Gordon Sinclair, Mark Abley, Guy Vanderhaeghe, Hal Wake, and above all, Jack Hodgins. All remaining errors are my own.

"The Story Begins": Dorothy Colby and the Sleeping Giant gang, Miriam Toews, Richard Scrimger, Paul Inksetter and Penny, R.H. Thompson, Molly Thom, Bill Houston, Charles Gordon and Nancy (the Business Manager), Gordon Sinclair, the late George Swinton and Don Starkell, and Jake McDonald, who took me to see the bush planes heading north from Selkirk.

"Hogtown Heroes": Stuart Woods, Antanas Sileika, Judith Skelton Grant, Jennifer Surridge, Peter Paterson, Matie Molinaro, William Toye, Don Gillies, Martin O'Malley, Jack McLeod, W.J. Keith, Cathleen Morrison, Bruce Cockburn, Jonathan Manthorpe, James Bartleman, John Gordon, Ruth Panofsky, my hip surgeon Dr. Earl Bogoch, Rev. Doctor Malcolm Sinclair, Mike Spence and the Arts and Letters Club, Bob Missen, Janet Inksetter, George Fetherling, Ben McNally, Aaron Milrad, Mark McLean, Betty Kennedy, Doug Knights (another of Jane's cousins!), Peter Kent, Anna Porter, Margaret Atwood, the memory of Larry Gaynor, Helen Walsh, and Alistair Chan and the other *Literary Review of Canada* people.

"Saskatchewan Pioneers": The Robertsons from Arelee, Ron Graham, Frans Donker, David Carpenter, Nik Burton, Stuart

Houston, Bill Waiser, Sherrill Miller, Gail Bowen, Maggie Siggins, Guy Vanderhaeghe, Ken Dryden, Harold Johnson, John Vaillant, Jalal Barzani, Bob Currie, Trevor Herriot (and the white-faced ibis), Bob Luterbach, Kam and Megan at the Weyburn Library, and Jamieson at W.O.'s boyhood home, and Joanne Bannatyne-Cugnet.

"Alberta and the Mountains": David Cheoros, Jean Crozier, Sharon and Steve Bodnarchuk, Scot Young, C. Anne Robertson and the Fairview family, Pauline Gedge, Bella Pomer, Fred Stenson, Noah Richler, Peter and Heather Brenneman, Sherrell Steele, Myrna Kostash, Erna Paris, Peter Oliva, Aritha van Herk, Anne Greene, Ken McGoogan, Stephen Smith, Sid Marty, Brian Brennan, Roddy Doyle, D.M. Thomas, Lynn Krause and the Elephant Mountain organizers in Nelson, Anne DeGrace, Gail Bowen, and the Mosaic Books people in Kelowna.

"The Coasts of B.C.": Hal Wake, Alma Lee, Bill Richardson, Anne Giardini, the late Carol Shields, Jim Douglas, Scott McIntyre, Howard White, Jean Baird, Paul Whitney, Jim Munro, Robert Wiersema, Ralph Hancox, Alan Twigg, Jane Davidson, Sally Quinn, Jack and Dianne Hodgins, Andreas Schroeder and Sharon Brown, Graeme and Ann Young, Angie Abdou, Caroline Adderson, Maude Barlow, Pauline Holdstock, Derek Lundy and Richard Wagamese, Debbie Frketich and her Denman gang, Stewart Giddings, Del Phillips, John and Marion Dillon, Peter Karsten, Richard and Nancy Self, Noel Wotten, Susan Musgrave, Jane Austen, and Angus Wilson.

"Alice Munro Country": Alice Munro, Lena Jordebo and Sven-Ake Visen from Sweden, Elizabeth Waterston, John and Monica Ladell, David Worsley and Mandy Brouse, Martin Dowding, Ross Procter in Wingham, Rob Bundy in Clinton, and Mary Swan and Mary Brown in Bayfield.

"Hugh MacLennan's Country": Bill Weintraub, Dick Irvin, the shrewd folk at Paragraphe Books, David Wilson, Mary Friesen, Charles Foran, Andrew Westoll, Lynn Verge, Simon Dardick, Mark Abley, Patricia Claxton, Desmond Morton, Ted Phillips, Gregory McCormick, in Quebec City Elizabeth Perreault, Peter Dubé, Neil

Bissoondath, Peter O'Donohue in the Eastern Townships, Pat and Norman Webster, Ruth McKinven, Alison Pick, Michael Ogilvie, Graham Fraser and Barbara Uteck, Linda Morra, and Michael Goldbloom.

"In the Middle of Canada": Lawrence Hill, Anita MacLeod and the family, Dan Wells, Alana Wilcox, Paul and Sheila Martin, Nino Ricci, our Sarnia hosts Sue Brighton and Chris Curran, Paul Wells, Susan Chamberlain and her staff at The Book Keeper, Peter Edwards, Peter Stokes, Barry Penhale and The Other Jane Gibson, Sheila Lui and her London Library colleagues, Mary Lake and Robert Collins, Anne Dyer-Witherford and Nick, Doug Minett and the folks at The Bookshelf in Guelph, Jonathan Webb, Dorothy Scott, Tim Struthers, Stephen Henighan, Elizabeth Ewan, Graeme Morton, Daniel MacLeod, Tom King, Richard B. Wright, and William Thomas.

"The On-to-Ottawa Trek": Linwood Barclay and Neetha, Ian Elliot, Richard Bachmann, Bryan Prince, Andrew Pyper, Terry Fallis, Shelley MacBeth, Jonathan Vance, Lewis MacLeod, Stephanie Forrester and the Lakefield Festival people, Orm and Barb Mitchell, Norman Jewison, Kathleen Winter, Lauren B. Davis and Ron, Linda Spalding, Jane Urquhart, the rowdy ghost of Al Purdy, Carolyn Smart, John McGreevy, Charles Wilkins, Steve Heighton, Phil Hall, Christopher Moore, David Baker and Birthe Jorgenson, Mary Lou Fallis, Molly Stroyman, Flora MacDonald, Sean Wilson, Amanda Hopkins and Mary Osborne, Jeffrey Simpson, Eddie Goldenberg, Charles Gordon, Amy Castle, Diana Carney, David Dollin, our Ottawa Valley hosts Dave Stein and Alison, Gwen Storie, Doyne and Frank Ahearn, Roy MacGregor, Araby Lockhart in Thornbury, and Hope Thompson and Phil Haines next door.

"Good Times in the Maritimes": Silver Donald Cameron and Marjorie Simmins (who gave us a Halifax base), Graham Pilsworth and Jamie Pratt (ditto), John Houston and Ree Brennin, Jim Lorimer, Suzanne Alexander, Lesley Choyce, Ami McKay, Christl Verduyn, Chris Paul and Krista in Sackville, Dawn Arnold and Danielle LeBlanc in Moncton, Andrea Schwenke Wyile, Herb Wyile, the late Alex Colville, Alexander MacLeod, Harry Thurston, Brian Flemming, Harry Bruce, Philip Slayton, Cynthia Wine, Calvin Trillin, Marq de Villiers, Sheila Hirtle, Bob Whitelaw, Kiloran German, Stephanie Tompkins (our perennial Bridgewater hostess), Lewis MacKinnon, Corky and Andrew Horwood, Dyanne and Alex Frame, Arthur Herriott, Will Ferguson, Duncan McIntosh, Wade MacLauchlan, Karen Smith, Doug Smith (and his St. F.X. students, and especially the elderly audience member who remembered Brian Mulroney's inflammatory debating style), Richard Lemm, Don Desserud (cousin alert!), Norman Finlayson and Heather, and, of course, Maxine Delaney.

"Rock Talk": Don Nichol, Richard Gwyn, Michael Enright, Gary Green, Bill Evans, Cedar Bradley Swann, and Bill Williams of Adventure Canada, Gordon Pinsent, Michael Crummey, John C. Crosbie, Claire Mowat, Steve Brunt and Jeanie MacFarlane, Shelagh Rogers, Gary Noel, Des Walsh, Rex Murphy, Donna Morrissey, George Goodwin, and many kindly ghosts.

For this very Canadian book I've been encouraged by the interest shown by friends in Scotland, especially my sister-in-law Amanda, and Kate and Robert and Richard, and by Keith Christie and Cynthia (a B.C. girl!), and Janet and Walter Reid. In Mexico (*Hola!*) Jane and I were pleased by the enthusiasm of Doug and Janet Clark, and by Alison Wearing and Jarmo (who once showed us a tree adorned by five different types of oriole).

At home, more general thanks go to all the friends and neighbours ("How's the book going?") who were encouraging, and to supportive friends like Bill Harnum and Kathy Lowinger, Brian and Nancy Anthony, Michael and Jennifer Barrett, Bob and Sally Lewis, Avie Bennett, Diana Massiah, Marc Coté, and dozens of old publishing colleagues astonished by the spectacle of a publisher dog walking on two legs.

As with *Stories About Storytellers*, I am working gratefully once again with my friends at ECW Press. As always, I was expertly treated by my suitably demanding editor, Jen Knoch, who ushered the book through to completion. In this she was assisted by the keen-eyed copy editor, Nathan Whitlock, who is learning to love puns; proofreader Steph VanderMeulen; and the ECW team, led by Jack David and his distinguished successor, David Caron, including Rachel Ironstone and the production group and Erin Creasey and the sales gang. Once again I was pleased to have Sarah Dunn handle the publicity for this new book by a shy and retiring author.

As with the previous book, I'm delighted that I persuaded the brilliant Anthony Jenkins to enrich my work by providing his superb portraits of some of the major authors featured here. He really is a national asset, and I hope that this book will help to spread his fame.

Above all, I thank my family . . . Meg and Lauren and Lindsay and Alistair, and Katie and Cindy, for their support and understanding while I was touring and writing.

As for Jane, "my lovely and talented assistant," techie, travel planner, fellow traveller, driver, dresser, gentle critic, and fond companion, words fail. But it's all been such fun, we've got to keep on doing this.

Onward!
DOUGLAS GIBSON
Toronto, Christmas Eve, 2014

Douglas Gibson (1943–)

In 2007 the *Globe and Mail* called Douglas Gibson a "publishing icon." Earlier the British wit Frank Muir noted that he wrote "alarmingly well for a publisher."

In his first book, *Stories About Storytellers* (2011), he tells the story of his career as a Scottish immigrant who came to Canada in 1967, armed with degrees from St. Andrews and Yale, and a determination to do "something interesting."

His career as an editor — and as a publisher who kept on editing — took him in 1968 to Doubleday Canada, then in 1974 to Macmillan of Canada, where he became the publisher in 1979. He established the first editorial imprint in Canada at McClelland & Stewart in 1986, and was the publisher at M&S (in those days "The Canadian Publisher") from 1988 until 2004, when he moved back to concentrate on his imprint, Douglas Gibson Books. He "retired" in 2008 at 65.

He has won many awards over the years, and he is the first publisher to be made an honorary member of the Writers' Union of Canada. He lives in Toronto with his wife, Jane, when he is not travelling the country with his one-man stage show, *Stories About Storytellers*. His website is douglasgibsonbooks.com.

Editor for the press: Jennifer Knoch
Cover design: David Gee
Text design: Tania Craan
Illustrations: Anthony Jenkins

Library and Archives Canada
Cataloguing in Publication

Gibson, Douglas, author
Across Canada by story : a coast-to-coast literary
adventure / written by Douglas Gibson.

Issued in print and electronic formats.
ISBN 978-1-77041-253-8 (pbk).
ISBN 978-1-77090-778-2 (pdf).
ISBN 978-1-77090-779-9 (epub)

1. Gibson, Douglas. 2. Authors, Canadian—
Anecdotes. 3. Authors and publishers—Canada.
4. Publishers and publishing—Canada—Biography.
I. Title.

Z483.G53A3 2015   070.92   C2015-902806-X
C2015-902807-8

Printing: Friesens 5 4 3 2 1

The publication of *Across Canada by Story* has been generously supported by the Canada Council for
the Arts which last year invested $153 million to bring the arts to Canadians throughout the country, and by
the Government of Canada through the Canada Book Fund. *Nous remercions le Conseil des arts du Canada de son
soutien. L'an dernier, le Conseil a investi 153 millions de dollars pour mettre de l'art dans la vie des Canadiennes et des
Canadiens de tout le pays. Ce livre est financé en partie par le gouvernement du Canada.* We also acknowledge the
Ontario Arts Council (OAC), an agency of the Government of Ontario, which last year funded 1,709
individual artists and 1,078 organizations in 204 communities across Ontario, for a total of $52.1 million,
and the contribution of the Government of Ontario through the Ontario Book Publishing Tax Credit
and the Ontario Media Development Corporation.

PRINTED AND BOUND IN CANADA